NO PLACE *for* SOVEREIGNTY

What's Wrong with Freewill Theism

R. K. McGregor Wright

foreword by Alan Myatt

InterVarsity Press
Downers Grove, Illinois

*This book is dedicated to
my wife, Julia Ann Castle,
whose love and criticism
and continuous encouragement
during twenty-five years of marriage
have made her the best possible
companion in our ministry together.*

© *1996 by R. K. McGregor Wright*

All rights reserved. No part of this book may be reproduced in any form without written permission from Inter Varsity Press, P.O. Box 1400, Downers Grove, Illinois 60515.

Inter Varsity Press® is the book-publishing division of Inter Varsity Christian Fellowship®, a student movement active on campus at hundreds of universities, colleges and schools of nursing in the United States of America, and a member movement of the International Fellowship of Evangelical Students. For information about local and regional activities, write Public Relations Dept., Inter Varsity Christian Fellowship, 6400 Schroeder Rd., P.O. Box 7895, Madison, WI 53707-7895.

All Scripture quotations, unless otherwise indicated, are taken from the HOLY BIBLE, NEW INTERNATIONAL VERSION®. NIV®. Copyright © *1973, 1978, 1984 by International Bible Society. Used by permission of Zondervan Publishing House. All rights reserved.*

ISBN 0-8308-1881-2

Printed in the United States of America ♾

Library of Congress Cataloging-in-Publication Data

Wright, R. K. McGregor (Robert K. McGregor), 1940-
  No place for sovereignty: what's wrong with freewill theism/
R. K. McGregor Wright.
    p.   cm.
  Includes bibliographical references.
  ISBN 0-8308-1881-2 (pbk.: alk. paper)
  1. Providence and government of God.   2. Calvinism.   3. Free will and determinism—Religious aspects—Christianity.   4. Arminianism.
I. Title.
BT135.W75   1996
234'.9—dc20
                                                                                    96-2810
                                                                                    CIP

| 18 | 17 | 16 | 15 | 14 | 13 | 12 | 11 | 10 | 9 | 8 | 7 | 6 | 5 | 4 | 3 | 2 | 1 |
| 11 | 10 | 09 | 08 | 07 | 06 | 05 | 04 | 03 | 02 | 01 | 00 | 99 | 98 | 97 | 96 |

Foreword from the Mission Front

On the first voyage of the USS *Enterprise-D* in the twenty-fourth century, Captain Picard and his crew meet an omnipotent being, a part of the "Q continuum." Q puts the Captain and his crew on trial for the crimes of humanity. As an avid "trekkie," I was delighted that Picard managed to buy humanity more time. Subsequently, I grew quite fond of Q's arbitrary wit and the inventive dilemmas he created for the *Enterprise*. What a great concept for a sci-fi show—an immortal being of infinite power who is yet a fellow resident of the space-time universe, the realm of being, in which all creatures participate and live. Assuming that all that exists is the spatial and temporal reality of the *Star Trek* universe, Q is the closest thing to a personal God that one could ask for in such a worldview.

Could it be that perhaps the writers of *Star Trek* were not too far off the mark? Aside from the arbitrary and capricious behavior of Q, could it be that God is simply another—albeit much more powerful, good and loving—being who exists in time as one among the rest of us? Some evangelical theologians have suggested this possibility, proposing that the classical view of God's omniscience as including knowledge of all future events be jettisoned. God, accordingly, is neither beyond time nor immutable. The notion of such a God is said to be limiting to human freedom. Instead, we are encouraged to adopt a view—not unlike that of process thought—that represents God as growing, changing and contingent. Is not this type of God, in essence, a being similar to our friend Q?

Regardless of whether one agrees with my judgment that the concept of a time-bound God is remarkably like the Q of *Star Trek* fame, evangelicals are clearly being asked to accept an idea of God very different from the God of traditional orthodox theology. Were this an isolated incident, it would not be so alarming. That it is being echoed by a growing chorus of evangelical thinkers is quite another matter. Ideas that would have immediately been considered heretical fifty years ago are now promoted without so much as the batting of an eye. It seems, as we enter the third millennium, that much of evangelicalism has lost its bearings.

Contemporary evangelicalism is often characterized by a cliché-ridden superficiality that focuses more on pragmatism and what feels good than on the systematic application of biblical doctrine to the issues of life. The recent "Toronto blessing" phenomenon is a good case in point. Beyond such an obvious example, today many churches, denominations and missions agencies are as likely to base important ministry and administrative decisions on purely pragmatic considerations as they are to consult God's Word. It seems that the drive to be relevant and practical must be carried through, even if it means abandoning biblically based traditions.

Various writers have recently pointed out the current state of apathy, confusion and often outright antagonism that exists in the popular evangelical mind when it comes to the subject of theology. They have demonstrated that the lack of a theological mind is responsible for a great deal of the confused and spiritually unhealthy behavior that involves so much of modern Christianity in worldly (how outdated the term now sounds) compromise. However, they have not always diagnosed the roots of this compromise. A prescription for its effective eradication is often lacking. In this volume, Bob Wright has provided a penetrating assessment of the nature of the challenge that confronts us, as well as some timely counsel concerning how it might be met.

To the average reader these may seem to be grandiose claims. Isn't this, after all, just another book about the age-old debate between Calvinism and Arminianism? Hasn't that subject, like the proverbial dead horse, already been beaten past the point of any positive gain? What relevance could it possibly have to the practical problems faced by the average Christian? These seem to be natural questions, but the fact that they are likely to be raised is another indication of the pragmatic mindset of evangelicalism. Conditioned more by the thirty-second sound bite than the two-thousand-year-old discourse of Christian orthodoxy, the modern evangelical wants practical solutions in a theological vacuum. But just as nature, Christianity abhors a vacuum. It turns out that underneath the atheological mindset there is a definite theological foundation: the defense of the notion of human autonomy.

Human freedom, considered as subject to God's eternal and sovereign plan, is an important aspect of human nature. As responsible creatures, we are able to participate in and to help realize that plan through our uncoerced choices. This in no way implies that human choices are somehow free from causality in the flow of history or from the finality of God's eternal plan by which he "works all things according to the counsel of His will" (Eph 1:11 NKJV). Human freedom, biblically defined, is quite different from the Arminian doctrine of human autonomy. *Autonomy* implies that the will is subject neither to more ultimate causes in history nor to the eternal counsel of God. Ultimately, it implies a limited God.

The seriousness of this question has been brought home to me during fifteen years of ministry to the cults. I have found at least one common denominator among all of those I studied—the belief in human autonomy. From the Jehovah's Witnesses to the Mormons and a host of other modern cults, war has been declared against any form of Calvinism. If Dr. Wright is correct, then this is no accident.

The message of Bob Wright's book is that a God limited by human autonomy is not capable of meeting the needs of a lost world. Theologically he shows that autonomy is both unbiblical and irrational. He argues that history has shown that the dogma of human autonomy gradually eats away at the foundations of orthodoxy until eventually it collapses entirely. The idea of God is radically modified or discarded altogether as the hope for salvation is transferred to humanity's determination and ingenuity rather than God's sovereign grace. In the church, the doctrine of autonomy encourages a dependence on humanly created methods for the propagation of the gospel, rather than the providence of God. The gospel must be made palatable to the sinner, whose personal autonomy, after all, must be respected even by God. The result is that marketing techniques and pragmatic solutions, rather than scriptural principles, inform our evangelistic strategies. Hence, the impotence of evangelicalism before a pagan culture that is itself built on the dogma of autonomy.

This book is both challenging and controversial. I commend it to all who are interested in the redemption of postmodern culture and the restoration of a vital evangelical witness. This will come only when the great doctrines of the Reformation are once again given their due among those who claim its heritage. That is the plea of this book. May it be well heeded!

Alan Myatt
Professor of Systematic Theology
Baptist Seminary of South Brazil
Rio de Janeiro
June 1996

Acknowledgments

I am first of all grateful to Sandra Wilson and to long-time friend Patrick Knapp, who both made the first contacts with my publisher and kept them interested in the book.

Alan Myatt (now a missionary in Brazil), Keith Albright, Frank Geis, Tony Falette, Julia Castle, our pastor Davis Cooper, and four kind readers who remain anonymous at the publisher's request all read the manuscript and offered many valuable suggestions, saving me from all sorts of blunders. Any errors that remain are my own entirely.

Historical and philosophical books of this kind are possible only after many years and much reading, during which one absorbs numerous ideas and whole patterns of thought from dozens of previous authors. I sincerely hope that people like John Owen, Francis Turretin, Gordon Clark, David Steele, Curtis Thomas and Cornelius Van Til, who have obviously influenced me, will all look indulgently from heaven or from their busy pastorates and find my work both the sincere compliment and the real complement to their own efforts that I intend it to be.

Introduction

Evangelical scholars have noticed with alarm the steady decline in the cohesion and intellectual integrity of much that passes for *evangelical theology. David Wells of Gordon-Conwell Theological Seminary documents the changes that have taken place in the latter half of the twentieth century in his *No Place for Truth* (1993). James Davison Hunter has also examined the decline in doctrinal precision among the present generation of evangelical seminarians in *Evangelicalism: The Coming Generation*. Mark Noll, in *The Scandal of the Evangelical Mind* (1994), follows earlier critics as widely diverse as Harry Blamires and *Gordon Clark in warning evangelicals that too often they have not done their homework where non-Christian thinking is concerned. Alister McGrath has been more optimistic, but his *Evangelicalism and the Future of Christianity* (1995) contains some unnerving criticism nevertheless.

In earlier days evangelicals looked to the gospel and its theological explication for the answers to humanity's problems. In our own day many evangelical publications simply reflect the doctrinal vacuity around them, showing

---

*A variety of technical terms and names of people that may be unfamiliar to readers have been included in a glossary near the end of this book. At their introduction into the text they have been preceded by an asterisk.

little or no concern for the theological basis of claims often made from secular disciplines or experience alone. This shift of attitude from serious acknowledgment of the centrality of doctrine for the evangelical testimony to impatience with any theological basis for anything has resulted not only in the distortion of salvation and spirituality, where evangelicals have always differed, but now also in the modification of the basic attributes of God to accommodate the assumption of human autonomy. The God of some modern evangelicals is very different from the God of reformational evangelical thought of forty years ago.

Today's evangelicals do not look so much to the Bible, to the reformation principle of *sola Scriptura,* for clues about how to present the gospel to the world of unbelief. They look instead to the smorgasbord of secular psychologies, philosophies and spiritualities to find contact points. And their gospel is no longer the theologically articulated gospel of forty years ago. Today it is a syncretistic combination of secular methodologies and superficial biblical language aimed at "felt needs" rather than hellbound sinners. Can we really imagine the apostle Paul insisting that the gospel be made "user-friendly"? Paul taught that the power of the gospel is located in the preaching of God's Word, not in its ability to absorb intellectual pop culture.

This book examines modern evangelical *Arminianism, a basic form of this syncretism, by challenging its essential assumption, the *freewill theory, and by analyzing both its effect on the consistency of the Christian's mind and the resultant method of defending the gospel.

Presuppositions Determine Results

Provided that we obey the rules of logic, our presuppositions control all of our thinking, much like the rules in the game of chess. The International Rules define what counts as a valid chess move and determine what counts as a possibility on the board. Any move not described in the Rules is an invalid move; it is simply not possible by definition. Likewise, our assumptions about the world as a whole and our place in it determine everything we think and do, and prevent us from considering alternatives incompatible with them. These assumptions form the underlying structure of our *worldview and determine how we interpret our experience and what the "facts" are allowed to mean. It goes without saying that once the controlling importance of presuppositions is realized, a person controlled by unconsciously held presuppositions must be recognized as a slave to the unknown. This is one reason the Greek philosopher *Socrates said "Know thyself" and concluded that the unexamined life is not worth living. By the standards of Christianity he was wrong on both counts, but Socrates believed that the autonomous human consciousness is its own sufficient reference point, so the key to ultimate truth is to be found "within." As Christians informed by God's Word, we realize that the world cannot interpret itself. True knowledge of the self involves first hearing God speak in Scripture. Christians have also concluded that the value of a person's life does not depend on the ability to examine oneself in terms of some philosophy, but on the place that person has in God's plan. Nevertheless, self-examination is just as difficult now as it ever was, and we all have areas of our life that we do not examine very closely. Presuppositions still determine our destinations, despite a good deal of inconsistency on the way.

This book challenges today's evangelicals to reexamine their priorities in an important area of Christian thought, and to face squarely the implications of that prioritization for the relationship between the doctrines of *systematic theology and the practice of apologetics. The doctrinal area I refer to is the much-contested subject of God's sovereignty in our salvation, over against the popular theory of free will, which is a development of the Greek assumption of the autonomy of human consciousness. Areas that are more technical will be left to the reader to follow up at leisure with the help of further reading suggested at the end of each chapter.

We will first take a brief look at the issue as it has taken shape in history. The principles of grace dominant in the Reformation will be contrasted with those of evangelical Arminianism. Then we will try to elucidate the issue by developing some definitions. Finally, we will turn to the implications of free-will thinking for the practice of apologetics in our own day. In the chapters on the biblical evidence, care will be taken to show how different the emphasis and methods of the Bible are from current popular evangelical syncretism.

The unfamiliar term *apostate autonomism* has been chosen to indicate the unity of fallen thought—from the original debacle in Eden to the syncretistic irrationalisms of our own day. *Apostate* indicates that a previous historic position has been abandoned, first in Eden and again after the Reformation. *Autonomism* is the theory that the human consciousness can interpret its experience of the world without any reference to a higher source of meaning outside of the world (except those principles that might be brought in at human convenience). A reader of an earlier draft of this book noted that B. B. Warfield referred to autonomism as "will-worship." Indeed, the absolutization of the will by autonomism amounts to worship in one sense.

The Problem Is Syncretism

By "syncretism" we mean the perennial tendency of believers in every age to combine the unique blessings of scriptural revelation with the vagaries of whatever currents of thought are happening to capture the popular imagination. As *Tertullian so succinctly put it, "What has Athens to do with Jerusalem?" This question is no easier to answer today than it was then, but each generation is culturally obligated to give its own answer. Tertullian was contrasting Christianity with Stoicism in this famous query, yet he was himself strongly influenced by that philosophy, which had loomed large in his own education as a Roman lawyer. Although a theory may be unclear in the popular mind, a definite answer is always being given in practice, for the question cannot be avoided and underlies everything else the Christian does (i.e., evangelism, philosophy, etc.). I am convinced that *everything* the believer does eventually has implications for the whole of the culture we live in and that therefore Christianity must necessarily be seen as a comprehensive worldview affecting civilization as a whole.

While teaching apologetics, women's ministry and systematic theology at the Emmanuel Bible Institute in Turnu-Severin, Romania, during the spring quarter of 1993, my wife and I decided to prepare a teaching manual on our worldview apologetics program. At the heart of this method of defending the gospel lies our conviction that evangelicals must take the Reformation doctrine of *sola Scriptura,* often called the "sufficiency of Scripture," more seriously than they have in the past. In particular, they must be more willing to accept the Bible's own critique of how the unbeliever thinks. Consequently, evangelicals must be less ready to combine the gospel with secular philosophies in their effort to be heard by the world.

This study is therefore intended to be preliminary to a much fuller presentation of our own Reformational worldview apologetic method, tentatively titled *Two Worldviews in Conflict: The Divine and the Demonic Constructions of Reality*. An idea of its program in outline may be found in chapter four.

1

An Ancient & Continuing Controversy

*T*he history of religious and philosophical thinking shows that there are just a handful of fundamental topics that are of perennial interest. The same questions seem to pop up in every generation and capture the attention of certain thinkers in every culture. These topics include the relation of the unity of the world to the diversity of our individual experience, how we can be certain of the knowledge we have, whether or not there is a God, the nature of the "stuff" the world is made of and how we must navigate ethical issues. All the great civilizations have asked these types of questions, and most have given definite answers to them.

These questions underlie the essential manner in which all peoples interact with God's creation. We cannot function as human beings nor develop a civilization without answering these typical questions, and so all the religions and philosophies of the past have chosen from the relatively small number of logically possible answers, and they have based their worldviews on those answers. Where these questions are concerned, religion and philosophy are essentially the same.

One of the enduring questions concerns the relation of our sense of being free in our decisions to the fact of causation in the world around us. Is our will really free from causes and influences, or are all our actions predetermined in some way? Is it freedom or fate? Christians recognize this problem as being about the relation of the human will to God's sovereignty, or of human freedom to *predestination. Philosophers often couch it in terms of *autonomy* versus *determinism.* However we arrange the dilemma, a fundamental issue arises: In what sense can the will be called *free?*

For most thinkers, three categories of answers to this question come to mind immediately. Either (1) we have free will, and so God does not have complete control over our decisions, or (2) God's predestination includes everything, including all our choices, or (3) perhaps some compromise is possible in which both free will and divine sovereignty are somehow involved. The first response is historically labeled *Arminianism,* while the second is called *Calvinism,* because of the influential figures associated with them. The third answer points to a variety of compromising positions preferred by many modern evangelicals, including many who think of themselves as Calvinists.

In this all too brief chapter, we will look at the history of this controversy among Christians, beginning with the Christian literature after the close of the New Testament era. Historical surveys of this sort are often frustrating to historians, but some attempt must be made so the nonspecialist can view the topic in proper context.

The Apostolic Fathers

The earliest Christian literature outside the books of the New Testament is often called the writings of the apostolic fathers. They are called *apostolic* because the authors supposedly knew the apostles personally, or at least were disciples of men who knew the apostles. Whether this was really so in any individual case or not, these documents were produced very early, most of them between A.D. 90 and 150. Yet the ideas later associated with John Calvin and Jacobus Arminius already appear quite clearly in this literature.

First Clement makes quite "Calvinistic" statements in 8:5, 27:5, 32:4, 36:6, 38:3, 46:8 and 59:2. Elsewhere *Clement repeatedly calls Christians "the elect," and in the last of these references he states that "the Creator of all things will keep intact the precise number of his elect in all the world." In 32:4 he refers to "we [Christians] too, [who] by his will have been called in Christ Jesus."

Second Clement was probably written by someone other than Clement, and is usually dated around A.D. 130. Furthermore, the author was no great theologian and was mainly concerned with practical issues. However, in 1:6-8 he evinces a high view of God's sovereignty in our salvation. He says that when "our minds were blinded," "our sight was restored by his will, . . . for he called us from nothingness, and willed us into being from nothingness." In 8:2 he says that "we are clay in the hands of the craftsman."

On the other hand, in paragraph 72 of the *Similitudes of Hermas* we discover a rather "Arminian" account of the relationship between salvation and God's foresight of saving faith: "[The Lord] gave the Spirit to those who were worthy of repentance . . . to those whose hearts he saw would be pure, and who would serve him with all their heart. But to those whose deceit and evil he saw, and who would repent in hypocrisy, he did not give repentance, lest they again blaspheme his name." This seems to be an attempt to reconcile the Calvinistic idea that repentance and faith are given sovereignly by God with the Arminian notion that God's *election is based on his foresight of faith in the believer. Yet in this very same book (in paragraph 77) he seems to give a common Calvinistic interpretation of 2 Peter 3:9: "But being patient, the Lord wants those who were called through his Son to be saved."

In 1738 the great Baptist theologian *John Gill published the fourth part of his detailed refutation of the Arminianism of *Daniel Whitby. The four parts are together called *The Cause of God and Truth,* and they have been reprinted many times. Gill added the last part in order to show that the controversy over free will and predestination did not originate in the days of Pelagius and *Augustine, let alone in the mind of John Calvin. He demonstrates that strong Calvinistic sentiments were expressed in literally dozens of early church writers from the apostolic fathers to Jerome, who was a contemporary of Augustine. He provides quotations by at least forty-five separate theologians from the three centuries before Augustine. He shows that St. Augustine did not create the controversy surrounding the subjects of election and predestination, but rather merely summarized and systematized the common opinions of the church in the centuries immediately preceding him. Readers examining Gill's collection of sources will be startled to see just how common these views were in the earliest age of the church.

Part one of Gill's book consists of a careful analysis of some sixty verses used by the Arminians of his own day. He demonstrates that none of these verses teach Arminianism, and that most are simply irrelevant to the issues involved—they only seem to have any bearing at all because the interpreters presuppose an Arminian form of free will. It is this freewill theory that is challenged in the present book.

Pelagianism

*Pelagius seems to have been an Irish or Welsh monk who appeared in Rome around A.D. 400 to refute the doctrines of Augustine, the great teaching bishop of Hippo. This town is insignificant today, but at that time it was a bustling seaport about a hundred miles west of Carthage in what is now the town of Annaba in Algeria. Pelagius was a sincere moralist who became fearful that Augustine's prayer to God to "give what You command, and command what You will" would lead to immorality and laxity, for it implied that even the regenerate cannot obey God unless continually enabled by gifts of divine *grace. His own view of human nature was based on a theory of the Fall that essentially denied original sin, so that the will was quite free from Adam's influence. Consequently, sinners could obey the law of God perfectly, if only they would make the effort.

Pelagius's views were energetically refuted by Augustine in a series of studies now referred to as the anti-Pelagian writings. Pelagianism was eventually condemned as a heresy at the Councils of Carthage (418), Ephesus (431) and Orange II (529). From then to the Reformation, the Western church was mainly Augustinian in its understanding of free grace.

The importance of Pelagian ideas lay originally in the stimulus they gave to theologians like Augustine to clarify the biblical doctrines of grace and predestination. In particular, Augustine himself saw inconsistencies in his earlier book *Freewill,* and decided to write a much more "Calvinistic" clarification called *Grace and Freewill.* In *Retractiones,* his final work of clarification and correction, he defends even the earlier work from the Pelagian claim that he had left room for a free will in sinners after the Fall. The great bishop had been dead for a whole century when the second Council of Orange finally vindicated his condemnation of Pelagianism in 529.

Pelagianism would eventually infect much of popular Catholicism, and the *semi-Pelagian theories of Pelagius's disciple John *Cassian would become the dominant theology of salvation in the Eastern church. For our present purposes, it is enough to note that Augustine saw clearly, as few did before him, that the essence of the Pelagian error was its view that the will, even in fallen men, was essentially free from the corruption of sin and had the ability in itself to choose and perform good works.

Gottschalk

In the ninth century, archbishop Hincmar of Rheims wrote a book against "double predestination" in order to defend his condemnation (and cruel treatment) of the monk *Gottschalk for this teaching, an opinion now regarded as commonplace among Calvinists. Gottschalk had been condemned at a council in 848, but was defended by other scholars, such as Prudentius of Troyes, Walafrid Strabo, Servatus Lupus, Ratramnus and others. Such men represented the consistently Augustinian strain of medieval thinking on these issues.

In an attempt to refute Gottschalk, John Scotus Erigena also was invited to answer him and did so in *Concerning Divine Predestination.* Erigena not only was semi-Pelagian, but was also controlled by a *chain-of-being *ontology under the influence of the syncretistic "pseudo-Dionysius." This influential writer had tried to Christianize the pagan philosophy of Plotinus (later called Neoplatonism), which defended free will for the "wise" while insisting that those without wisdom are controlled by fate.

Hincmar's treatment of Gottschalk is a classic example of what hatred can accomplish when supported by the power to persecute. He stripped the helpless monk of his priesthood, had him imprisoned for life in a monastery and repeatedly tortured him with floggings in an attempt to force him to abandon his views. It is amazing that poor Gottschalk endured twelve years of this treatment before he died insane, still convinced that an omniscient God cannot logically choose some for salvation without at the same time choosing to reject others, even though they are no more sinful. This, of course, is the doctrine of reprobation taught today by all consistent Calvinists and found in chapter III of the *Westminster Confession. Gottschalk seems to have been among the first to see that Augustine's views required some kind of "double" predestination. Needless to say, Hincmar's own book, *The Predestination of God and Free Will,* emphasized free will while trying to reconcile it with predestination. By the high Middle Ages, a largely Augustinian doctrine of predestination was part of the theology of many great thinkers, including *Thomas Aquinas. The Dominicans were mainly Augustinian, while the Franciscans were largely semi-Pelagian. This was the state of affairs down to the Reformation. While free will was popularly spoken of as if it were an obvious truth, medieval theologians knew it was not that simple, and always sought to modify it in terms of God's sovereignty.

Augustinianism

In summarizing the best of the early church's theology, St. Augustine's thought became the foundation for the great "medieval synthesis" of nature and grace, and so of church and state. The great bishop of Hippo had two types of theology combined in an uneasy compromise in his influential vision of Christianity as the city of God unfolding in history. Augustine's view of individual salvation was based on the sovereign grace of a predestining God, and came to a systematic form in the controversy against Pelagianism. On the other hand, his view of the church was based on the notion that grace flowed to believers through the sacraments as administered by the unified body of bishops, a consolidation of his conclusions arising out of the controversy with the Donatists. This sacramentalism made salvation depend in practice on the willingness and ability of the individual to obey the church. Thus, in practice, the church became the final locus of authority rather than the Scriptures.

In his four "states" of human development, Augustine provided later theologians with an interesting framework for the traditional discussion of human ability. Before the Fall, Adam was *posse non peccare* (able not to sin). At the same time he was also *posse peccare* (able to sin), because in fact he did sin, and did so voluntarily. Now committed to sin, his descendants are *non posse non peccare* (unable not to sin). This is the bondage of the will that *Martin Luther defended against the humanism of *Erasmus. Renewed in Christ, believers are again like Adam—both able to sin and able not to sin, and which of these will prevail at any instant depends on one's level of sanctification and on the means of grace. In the state of glory, we will be better off than Adam, for we will be *non posse peccare* (not able to sin). A more recent devotional discussion of this topic can be found in Thomas Boston's *Human Nature in Its Four-fold State* (1720; reprinted Evansville, 1957).

The main difficulty with this famous presentation is that it does not explain clearly how believers differ from Adam, or how Adam came to sin in the first place. The usual Augustinian view of this is that Adam had free will, and that this is restored to us in Christ. However, we are still left with the issue of what causes the will to go one way rather than the other.

It has been often observed that the struggle of the Reformation started not with Luther's *Ninety-five Theses,* but with the battle between Augustine's soteriology (his doctrine of salvation) and ecclesiology (his doctrine of the church). Throughout the thousand years from the fifth century to the sixteenth, salvation by grace through faith sat unhappily in the same pews with salvation secured by human effort through sacramentalism. We must also remember that indulgences were viewed as minor sacramentals. In the critique of Catholicism developed by *Wycliffe, Luther and Calvin, sacramentalism was broken off from the doctrine of salvation, and even more so by Calvin than Luther. The Reformation may therefore be viewed as the victory of Augustine's doctrine of grace over his doctrine of the church's role in salvation. The two parts finally broke apart because their presuppositions were incompatible. In Calvin and *Zwingli, sacramentalism is eliminated entirely, replaced by the efficacy of the preached Word, and while Calvin's attempt to create a mediating view is still poorly understood today, most evangelicals are essentially Zwinglian in their understanding of the sacraments.

The point to be noticed here is that sacramentalism normally depends on free will, while a consistent doctrine of grace does not. Augustine allowed the medieval church to treat believers as if they were ultimately dependent on a freewill appropriation of grace in the sacraments, while at the same time insisting with Calvin that the will can only function properly when sovereignly enlivened by God's grace. For the Reformers, the Catholic abuse of the sacramental concept was the last straw that broke the back of the medieval synthesis of nature's free will with grace's sovereignty. Thomas Kuhn's model of a sudden "paradigm shift" in thinking brought about by the increasing accumulation of evidence against an accepted teaching is applicable here. During the Middle Ages, the pressure against the nature-grace synthesis in Augustine had been slowly building up until Luther attacked indulgences. Then the issue quickly shifted to the real problem, which was the church's traditionalism versus the supreme authority of the Bible. Luther was to signal this problem first in his defense of justification by faith alone, and then in his refutation of Erasmus.

Humanism

Humanism is used throughout this book to refer to the philosophy of human moral and intellectual competence apart from a supernatural revelation. Its usage coming out of the Renaissance, however, was not theological at all, but referred to the revival of ancient learning, including the study of the Bible in its original languages. In this sense, all the Reformers were humanists. But the revival of interest in ancient philosophy also meant the revival of the influence of *Platonic and Aristotelian theories of truth and reality, and reintroduced pagan theories of human nature. Syncretistic solutions soon appeared in the efforts of Christian apologists to grapple with the intellectual challenge of great philosophical minds from the past. One of the great themes of ancient thought had been the battle between human choices and "fate," an important unification principle common in the pagan worldview. Because so much Renaissance thought assumed classical formulations of, and solutions to, the problem of unity and diversity, it was commonly assumed that to deny free will meant the acceptance of Greek concepts of fate and necessity. Thinkers often fell back on freewill theories to escape *fatalism. As a result of the subject matter of much Renaissance humanism, the term *humanism* came to include philosophical tendencies that sought to free all university learning from the control of scholastic theology. This "secular" use of the term meant that humanism was increasingly thought of as the enlightened alternative to Christianity. It is this usage that dominates today. In fact, the term *secular humanism* crystallizes this development in the modern mind.

It would be relevant here to distinguish also the many stages of the Renaissance itself and to trace how the theme of "man versus fate" was treated at each stage in the main geographical areas of the Renaissance. It would be possible also to show how this theme contributed to the secularization of the sciences through its effect on the predestination-freewill debate. However, time and space forbid. We must be satisfied for now to observe that it was the educational changes generated by the Renaissance that set the stage for the Reformation, and that what Peter Gay calls "the rise of modern paganism" began initially as the rebirth of ancient pagan philosophy. The Reformation hindered this process, but not for long.

The Reformation

The Reformers were Augustinian to a man; indeed, Martin Luther started his career as an Augustinian monk. John Wycliffe (and his disciple *Jan Hus), Ulrich Zwingli, Martin Luther and John Calvin all denied free will in any sense that could be accepted by an Arminian, regarding it as clearly incompatible with free grace. We will here take Luther as a typical case.

By the *Diet of Worms in 1521, Erasmus of Rotterdam was in a most unenviable position with regard to the German Reformation. Long recognized as a Reformer himself, he was being accused by many of "laying the eggs that Luther hatched." He had wanted to reform the life of the church without changing its theology much. He was primarily a moralist rather than an analytical theologian, so his attempt to distance himself from Luther's far more radical and doctrinally oriented reforms took the shape of the moralistic *Diatribe on the Freedom of the Will* (1524). He knew that Luther rejected free will as it was understood by the great humanistic educational tradition of which he was a conspicuous and shining example. He held the typically liberal humanist conviction that arguments about doctrine were of little value, while the exaltation of natural human abilities dignified human nature. Accordingly, he encouraged human efforts such as education, which he regarded as the real key to reforming the clergy. The *Diatribe* caused the desired disassociation from the Lutheran movement and defined Erasmus as a doctrinal humanist for all time. From then on, Erasmus retreated further into the Catholic Church, continuing to plead for an inward reformation through education, while the new Protestantism took shape through Luther's prolific publications. The more moderate elements of the Catholic Counter-Reformation may be regarded as a fruit of "Erasmianism." But never again would Roman Catholicism question the humanistic view of free will as Luther had done.

Erasmus defined free will in the exact way the Arminians would a century later—as the power of contrary choice. That is, human nature is not so spiritually enfeebled by the Fall that it is incapable of making a righteous decision of faith without supernatural aid: people are always ultimately free to choose between contrary alternatives. Grace only makes the right choice possible by assisting and supplementing our natural abilities, while the will is always free to determine the final destiny of the individual. Luther naturally saw this as a return to some kind of Pelagianism, and he said so in *The Bondage of the Will* (1525).

The final paragraphs of his answer to Erasmus show how serious Luther thought this subject to be. While pleading with the great humanist to give up his subtleties and to simply accept the gospel of grace, Luther noted that "you alone have attacked the real issue, the essence of the matter in dispute," that is, between Luther and Catholic traditionalism, for "you and you alone have seen the question on which everything hinges, and have aimed at the vital spot; for which I sincerely thank you, since I am only too glad to give as much attention to this subject as time and leisure permit." Luther saw that the denial of free will was implied in the doctrines of free grace and of justification by faith alone. When Luther was thought to be dying, an attempt was made to get him to tell his publishers which of his many writings should be preserved first. He answered that there were only two books worth saving, his *Children's Catechism* and *The Bondage of the Will,* and they could burn the rest for all he cared. Martin Luther was in agreement with the other Reformers in their conviction that the denial of the freewill theory was at the heart of the Reformation doctrine of free grace.

During the Scholastic period, a distinction had been made between *metaphysical* autonomy and *moral* autonomy. The first was denied in the interests of the Christian view of God as Creator, thus appearing to preserve divine sovereignty. The second was variously equated with the autonomy of the intellect, or of the will, and was intended to preserve free moral agency despite the Fall. The end result of these artificial distinctions was to continue the philosophical tradition of *faculty psychology,* which separated the will from the intellect in order to preserve the Renaissance ideal of autonomous human freedom. This in turn was the soil from which the modern *Enlightenment theory of freedom grew. Depending on the needs of the moment, one could allow that perhaps the will was "influenced" by the Fall, while insisting that the intellect was not, or that the mind was so influenced, while the will was not. Either way, a measure of purely human autonomy, either of the will or of the intellect, was preserved over against the control of the Creator, for this was at the heart of the Renaissance notion of human dignity. Renaissance thinkers wanted to interpret the world by themselves, without the interference of theology; divine revelation could be tacked on afterward if one felt religiously inclined.

Ancient pagan writers had often contrasted human dignity with the powers of fate, and the Renaissance celebrated the importance of human abilities over against natural limitations. By the time of Erasmus, the battle between fate and human dignity had been reinterpreted in terms of predestination versus free will. After the Reformation, the autonomy of the intellect evolved quickly into the frank *rationalism of the seventeenth and eighteenth centuries. This eventually evolved further into the more consistently anti-Christian Enlightenment. Peter Gay, probably the greatest authority on the Enlightenment in America today, has therefore called the first volume of his work on this subject *The Rise of Modern Paganism* (1966), and the second *The Science of Freedom* (1969). In the Enlightenment's secularizing scheme, *freedom* means autonomy from a God who, through the influence of the old Scholastic theology, is thought of as controlling thought and limiting its possibilities. The humanists realized that any dependence on a supernatural explanation meant that the autonomy of both the intellect and the will was being curtailed by an external authority (that is, God), whether that authority was understood through the grid of Scholastic thought or not.

Arminianism

After the Reformers were gone, the main fruits of their labor were preserved in the newly Protestant state churches of Europe. The Thirty-nine Articles of the Church of England were largely Lutheran, while the state church of Holland was strongly Calvinistic, having the Belgic Confession as its main doctrinal standard. But the Reformation had also emphasized the right of private judgment, which was viewed as being independent of church tradition. The priesthood of all believers involved the responsibility of all to know the Bible for themselves. In the mind of the rationalists, however, this led to an increasing confidence in the efficacy of human reason over the authority of revelation. The increasing recognition of the new scientific studies that threatened the old respect for *Aristotle and Ptolemy also led to toleration of a wider range of theological opinions. If Aristotle and Ptolemy were wrong about the relation of the earth to the heavens, why could they not also be questioned where they had influenced theology? Toleration was an exhilarating idea, and naturally appealed most of all to those who wanted change.

In the Netherlands, a theological party was growing that called for more freedom in theology and questioned much in the generally accepted Calvinism of the Dutch state church. Modern Christians must remember that the entire process of the Reformation took place in the context of state churches, with secular powers supporting the Reformers and protecting their gains. Reformers therefore always sought ways to get politics on their side, and nobody but a handful of persecuted Baptists in the background thought of separating the church from the state. Effective reform required state support, and toleration of divergent views was automatically looked upon with suspicion by those in power. Accordingly, when the followers of Arminius tried to change the Calvinism of the state church in Holland, they formed a political party to do it. This is why the politics of their exclusion after 1619 was so acrimonious.

Jacob van Harmanzoon latinized his name as Jacobus Arminius. His followers were first called *Remonstrants, and then Arminians. Arminius was first a pastor, then later became a professor at the University of Leyden, having studied in Geneva under Theodore Beza, Calvin's somewhat Aristotelian successor. He had come to question the Calvinistic view of salvation while studying the books of the great English Calvinist preacher William Perkins. He saw clearly that the freewill theory was not compatible with the heart of Calvinist orthodoxy and slowly began his drift away from Calvinism.

By the time Arminius died in 1609, his disciples had formed a strong movement to liberalize the state church of Holland, and in 1610 they published the *Remonstrance,* a complaint against Calvinism and a plea for a broader comprehension of views in the Dutch churches. After the orthodox Calvinists failed to prevent the growth of Arminian theology, the problem came to a head at the *Synod of Dort (1618-19). This council rejected the five central contentions of the Arminians and affirmed the famous Five Points of Calvinism. The third and fourth of these "heads of doctrine" included a denial of the Arminian theory of free will, under the rubric of a strong statement about the corruption of human nature in the Fall. They contended that the human will is necessarily also fallen, along with the intellect, and is neither willing nor capable of willing to savingly believe, just as the fallen mind is incapable of understanding spiritual truth. Neither the will nor the intellect can be thought of as autonomously competent in spiritual things, although both could accomplish much for human survival in worldly matters. In their view, a fallen human nature is able to rise above itself to exercise saving faith only when comprehensively regenerated by God.

Arminius, like so many modern evangelicals, thought of himself as being squarely within the field of Reformation orthodoxy. He even continued to believe in the eternal security of the saints, although this last feature of Calvinism was abandoned by his followers among the Remonstrants a few years after his death, as they sought to develop a more consistent theology of universal grace. Arminius and his followers also originally tried to offset the complaints of their critics that they did not take the Fall seriously enough by making strong statements about the spiritual inability of the will to free itself from the influences of sin. Unfortunately this attempt to do justice to the influence of the Fall was heavily qualified by equally strong pleas for the freedom of the will. Eventually it was made irrelevant by their version of prevenient grace. This originally Augustinian term was expanded into their vision of a universal grace that was thought to enable all who hear the gospel to accept it if only they will.

English Arminianism

While the Dutch were settling their doctrinal disputes by excluding the Arminians from their now fully Calvinistic state church, Arminian views were becoming increasingly popular among the more liberal clergy in England. By the 1630s, the Arminian archbishop of Canterbury *William Laud was persecuting the rising Puritan movement and trying to exclude Puritans first from lectureships while he was the bishop of London, and then from livings throughout England after he became primate of all England. It is largely forgotten today that it was mostly because Charles I sided with Archbishop Laud against the Calvinistic Puritans that so many English pastors left for more hospitable parts of Europe, and from there some came on to the New World. The first Pilgrims who journeyed on the Mayflower came to the North American continent to escape persecution by the statist Arminians in England. This persecution was an important factor in the gathering of the Puritan movement in support of Parliament, and against the arbitrary arrogance of the absolutism of Charles I. Charles believed in the "divine right" of the king to rule above the law of the land and did not hesitate to break promises when it suited him. The result was the English Civil War, which was only settled with the execution of Charles for treason in 1649. Oliver Cromwell, who then governed England until 1658, was a strong supporter of full freedom of conscience. Thus, both doctrinal and practical Puritanism flourished during the Commonwealth. Only with the restoration of the monarchy and of episcopal Anglicanism in 1660 was Puritanism to begin its long historic decline.

During the period of high Puritan thought in the 1600s, *John Owen was a conspicuous apologist who wrote against Arminianism. His first book was called *A Display of Arminianism* (1642) because he wanted people to know what the Arminians of the 1630s were really teaching. He also "displayed" the differences between Arminian writers and the Bible in contrasting columns for easy comparison at the end of each chapter. It was his plan to write five books, one on each of the five points of Dort, but he only completed two of them: *The Death of Death in the Death of Christ* (1647), which was soon recognized as the definitive defense of particular redemption, and a large work titled *The Perseverance of the Saints* (1654), which refuted the Arminian view that even the truly regenerate can lose their salvation. Owen's attitude toward free will may be gathered from the title page of the *Display,* where he refers to "the old pelagian idol freewill."

Enlightenment Rationalism

The 1600s saw the rise of not only Puritan theology and modern science, but also of Socinianism, a form of theological rationalism, along with such rationalist philosophies as Cambridge Platonism. Many writers sought to combine Christianity with a rationalist methodology. The results were fascinating in the first generation and disastrous in the next. As the disciples supplanted their masters, the process of trying to gain greater consistency and to weed out problems led to rationalistic thought moving further and further from Augustinian orthodoxy into Arminianism, then to Arianism, and finally into the Deism of the Enlightenment in the next century. This historical sequence can be followed in Holland, in England and (finally about a century later) in America too. This process is heavily documented by Arminian and secular historians alike.

During the 1700s, Calvinistic orthodoxy declined rapidly in England, having no support from the universities or the worldly English state church. It was slowly supplanted by Arianism and Arminian rationalism. The names of Cudworth, Falkland, Hales, More, Taylor, Tillotson, Chillingworth, Stillingfleet, Burnet, Pearson and Whitby represent the mainstream of Arminianism and the philosophies it courted. Puritan theology flourished longer in the New World, but was also already on the decline in America by 1750. Here it was threatened first by the rationalists on one side, and then by romanticism and the transcendentalists on the other, as well as by Arminianism and Unitarianism in the seminaries. Many churches drifted into Arminianism, and then into Arianism (and thus into Unitarianism). As in England, apart from some orthodox Presbyterians, the main stronghold of Calvinism was increasingly found among the nonconformists, such as the Baptists and later the more conservative Presbyterians from Scotland.

Many features of Arminianism in its original form have been forgotten by modern evangelicals, including the part the movement played in the shift away from Reformation thought in the American universities and the drift into Unitarianism among the Congregationalists. The close interfertilization of liberal ideas from the Socinian movement had some good side effects, including a general rise in toleration among Christians, but it also led to the Arianizing of many Arminian clergy. In Holland, the remnants of the Remonstrant churches survive today mostly among the Unitarians.

One internal development of the original Arminianism must be noted here. The Arminian theologians soon realized that free will was not only incompatible with the omnipotence of divine sovereignty, but also with God's omniscience. Quite reasonably, they pointed out that if the decisions of an essentially free will are not controlled by God's decree, neither can they be known by God in advance. God must not only limit his power so as to give the autonomous will room to act, but he must also be ignorant of much in the future, since most of the future states of human affairs are decided by the human will. An added reason for this was the observation that if a future event is known to God, it is either known certainly or not. But to know certainly that an event will happen means that it could not happen otherwise. In other words, God's omniscience eliminates a free will in the sense the Arminians understood it. The more consistent Arminians chose to save their basic presupposition by denying a doctrine that had been at the heart of the view of God as Creator, accepted by Christian orthodoxy for 1500 years. Thus, they followed the Socinians and rejected the omniscience of God. Illustrative documentation of this point can be found in Owen's *Display*. Those Arminians less concerned with consistency simply held free will and omniscience in tension and appealed to "mystery."

This shift in theological perspective did more to ensure the further disintegration of orthodoxy in the hands of the Arminians, for it opened them up to other anti-Christian arguments already in use among the Socinians. This process is now being repeated among today's evangelical Arminians. We will take a closer look at this in chapters ten and eleven.

Wesleyanism and the Great Awakening

*John Wesley seems to have learned his Arminianism originally from his parents, although it was strongly reinforced while he was a member of the Holy Club, where the teachings of Arminian moralist William Law were studied. After his friend *George Whitefield began to itinerate with the gospel, preaching often in the open air from 1739 onward, Wesley copied him and also organized numerous societies for the growth of their converts. These "methodist" societies were eventually forced out of the Anglican Church and became the Methodist denomination. Before this happened, however, Wesley, contrary to the pleadings of his friend, waited for Whitefield to leave for the colonies and then published a rather acerbic sermon against the evangelistic preaching of the doctrine of election. Since everyone saw this untimely document as an attack on Whitefield, it had to be answered. Whitefield therefore published *A Letter to the Rev. Mr. John Wesley in Answer to His Sermon Entitled "Free Grace"* (1740). This caused a sad breach with Whitefield. The Welsh Methodists stayed Calvinistic, while the English became uniformly Arminian. Some in the awakening tried to stay above this controversy, such as Selina Countess of Huntington, who supported the movement with her fortune, but most were forced to take sides.

Eventually Wesley handed over the task of defending Arminianism to John Fletcher, a capable and gentlemanly fellow Anglican, whose writings show a kind spirit, but no real understanding of Calvinistic thought. His main concern was to prevent people from deriving a practical antinomianism from such doctrines as free grace and the security and *perseverance of the saints. He seems unaware of the vast Puritan literature on sanctification. He was strongly challenged by such writers as *Augustus Toplady, who was shocked that an Anglican could defend Arminianism in the face of the Thirty-nine Articles that he had, after all, sworn in his ordination vows to uphold in their entirety. The confession's Calvinistic nature in denying free will (Article 10) and affirming election (Article 17) was unmistakable to Toplady, who was one of the most clear-headed Calvinistic preachers of the 1700s. But finally Arminianism had gained a permanent place in the burgeoning evangelical movement. It was no longer just the politically oriented theology of the upper classes, but was now defended by the most important evangelistic movement of the age. It was Methodism that gave Arminianism its evangelical respectability.

Finney Invents Revivalism

As the Great Awakening in the American colonies began to decline in fervor, a former lawyer named *Charles Grandison Finney was led first into Christianity, and then into an evangelistic career. He was essentially a Pelagian with regard to human nature, but embraced Arminianism in matters of salvation. He became convinced that revival was not a miracle, but the natural result of the application of the appropriate means—the only question was how to identify and apply those means. Finney decided that the prime task of the evangelist was to induce the free will to give in to the blandishments of the gospel. In his view, preaching should therefore aim at convincing the intellect into agreement and moving the emotions to support that reasoning. Then the will would necessarily follow with a voluntary act of saving faith, of which all were capable because of God's universal prevenient grace.

Accordingly, Finney introduced such techniques as altar calls, where potential converts came to the front and were encouraged through prayer and further exhortation to give themselves to Christ. These "new measures" were at first controversial, but eventually the advantages of being able to quickly identify converts and visibly identify the results of evangelism overcame all objections. The old method of simply preaching the gospel and trusting God for the results gradually gave way to the expectation of visible effects that could be counted immediately. ("Sixty seeking sinners came forward to the mourners' bench last night.") Evangelism came to mean numbers turning to Christ and little else. A revival became synonymous with an evangelistic campaign; thus, the time and place of a revival could be announced in advance as a form of advertisement. The original revival had been replaced by revivalism. When *Jonathan Edwards spoke and wrote about revival, he meant something sovereignly given by God. When Finney promoted a revival, he was explaining how to induce the free will to respond to the invitation of the gospel. The new revivalism by technique provided and encouraged a less doctrinal atmosphere in which Arminian views flourished. Many revivalist "camp meetings" were organized outside the programs of the regular churches, and quickly developed an atmosphere free from the restrictions of such Calvinistic creeds as the Westminster or Savoy Confessions.

Finney's new measures were tremendously influential. Even down to our own day, whole denominations are enmeshed in the established traditionalism of revivalist preaching methods. Its present fruits were indicated by a survey of the 350,000 baptized in Southern Baptist churches in 1993: the Home Missions Board reports that more than half cannot be found now by the churches that reported the baptisms. Only nine percent of the adults responding to the survey said they joined the church for spiritual reasons.

Charles Haddon Spurgeon

*Spurgeon was the greatest English preacher of the last century and the leader of the few prominent Calvinistic Baptists in the Baptist Union. His publications exposed the heresy and liberalism of the Union, and also documented what came to be called the Downgrade among English Baptists. The leadership of the Baptist Union was becoming more liberal, and they consistently rejected Spurgeon's plea that they introduce two simple doctrinal standards for members: belief in the Trinity and the infallibility of Scripture. They opted instead for a comprehension of not only Arminians and Calvinists (which Spurgeon had never opposed), but of the growing liberal-modernist movement also, which went so far as to deny the Trinity. Eventually, the Union hounded Spurgeon out of the denomination. Once again Arminianism had divided the evangelical movement and prepared the ground for Socinian errors and a more rationalistic approach to the Bible's authority. Its pleas for a "balanced view" had the effect of giving unorthodox views unprecedented legitimacy.

Spurgeon's preaching was highly evangelistic, yet he never wavered in affirming all five points of Dort. His attitude toward the freewill theory is expressed in his sermon "Free Will a Slave." Frequently reprinted as a tract, the sermon clearly expounded in popular language the Reformation doctrine of the bondage of the will to the sin nature. He never invited anyone to "come forward" in a gospel meeting, but over four thousand joined the Metropolitan Tabernacle while he was pastor there.

Spurgeon was often called "the last of the Puritans" even in his own lifetime, a title more recently transferred to *Dr. Martyn Lloyd-Jones. Like Lloyd-Jones, Spurgeon had no real successor, and his ministry ended an epoch in evangelical history. Unlike Spurgeon's day, however, the present century has seen a widespread revival of interest in Calvinistic doctrine and preaching on both sides of the Atlantic. Nevertheless, the intimate connection between consistent Calvinism and the rejection of popular freewill theory is no better understood among evangelicals today than in recent decades.

Modern liberals have clearly understood the humanistic nature of Arminian thought. At the start of the modernist era in 1908, *Frederic Platt noted in a nine-page article on Arminianism in Hastings's *Encyclopaedia of Religion* *and Ethics* (1908) that "Arminianism was the medium by which the humanistic spirit of the Renaissance was translated into the theological and exegetical sphere" (vol. 1, p. 816). One can only pray that modern evangelicals will come to see the truth of this penetrating observation.

Evangelicalism

Evangelicalism as we understand it today is the fusion of several important movements of revival and consolidation. Rooted in the doctrinal Reformation, it began with the return to an evangelistic presentation of the gospel in the Awakenings under Whitefield and Wesley, quickly spreading from England to America. In America it combined with the rise of interest in the Second Coming and spread through the evangelization of the frontier lands. In Britain the evangelical movement was originally more concerned with the social implications of the gospel than with apologetics, but the threat of evolutionism and the influence of the rationalistic higher criticism led many evangelical thinkers after the 1860s to develop a defensive stance toward secularizing influences in education. Thus, evangelical apologetics turned largely to the defense of the infallibility of the Bible. The earlier battle between Calvinists and Arminians in the late 1700s seemed less important to the evangelicals, who were now battling the documentary hypothesis, organic evolution, widespread impatience with dogmatic theology, and liberals who were threatening to relegate the Bible to "myth."

From the 1880s on, theological liberalism turned away from an interest in the supernatural conversion of individual souls and sought instead to develop a program of communal salvation through humanitarian progress, which came to be called the Social Gospel. Until the turn of the century, evangelicalism had always laid a heavy emphasis on the social implications of the gospel. In the 1800s, literally hundreds of societies for social improvement had been started and funded by evangelicals. Yet by the 1920s, the evangelical movement turned inward on itself to become fundamentalist. It has only begun to recover its sense of social and cultural responsibility since the late sixties of our present century—largely a result of the revival of interest in Calvinistic theology. Contributing factors include the increased number of publishers (such as the Banner of Truth Trust in Britain) who have been willing to reprint the rich Puritan material of the past, the spreading influence of students of Calvinistic preachers and scholars like Martyn Lloyd-Jones and J. I. Packer, and the catalyzing effect of the prophetic testimony of *Francis Schaeffer of L'Abri, Switzerland. In recent decades, evangelicalism has freed itself more and more from the constrictions of the fundamentalist era and has begun to recover the biblical vision of Christianity as a comprehensive worldview. This historical task, however, is still only half done, and the process of full reformation struggles on.

The evangelical scene continues to be as theologically fragmented as ever. It has always included both Arminians and Calvinists, but in the past this controversy was limited to questions about how personal salvation worked out. Christians have always argued about whether the truly regenerate can lose their salvation or not. Until recently, it was also clearly understood that the controversy concerning how holiness is produced in the believer is related to the debate about God's sovereignty and the fluctuations of the human will.

Now, with the rise of the view of Christianity as a worldview rather than as just a religion, an entirely new dimension to this old controversy has opened up. The increasing feeling that a Christian should take seriously the disciplines of philosophy, the arts, politics and culture has resulted in the need to also understand the relationship of these areas to their theological foundations. With this revived interest in apologetics, apologists seemed to suddenly come out of every type of evangelical background: John Warwick Montgomery (Lutheran), Gordon Clark and Francis Schaeffer (Presbyterian), *Clark Pinnock (Baptist), *Cornelius Van Til (Presbyterian, with a Dutch Reformed background) and John Stott and J. I. Packer (Anglican). The question became, then, What is the underlying relationship of apologetics to systematic theology? Does apologetic theory have some dependence on whether one is a Calvinist or an Arminian?

A Personal Pilgrimage

My own experience has been typical of those who have wanted coherent answers to the confusion in today's evangelicalism. I was raised in a nontheological denomination in South Australia, and had to look elsewhere for such answers. I was influenced early by dispensationalism, but at London Bible

College in 1965-66 I encountered serious Calvinists for the first time and was also interested in the challenge of apologetics by meeting Francis Schaeffer. After spending time at L'Abri in the summer of 1969, it became clear to me that Schaeffer's ability to challenge the thinkers of the secular world was not based on things he had learned from traditional or classical apologetics, but from the Dutch school of apologetics, which included scholars such as Cornelius Van Til and *Herman Dooyeweerd. The historic analysis of philosophy and culture used by Schaeffer came mainly from his mentor in art history, *Hans Rookmaaker, who in turn learned his method mostly from Dooyeweerd and Vollenhoven at the Free University of Amsterdam. Schaeffer studied under Van Til in Philadelphia before going to Europe as a Presbyterian missionary. In the past, these thinkers had been mostly ignored outside their own Dutch tradition. Now it was widely realized that there were important insights in their stream of thought, and the attempt to understand Schaeffer in depth demanded that they be heard.

I pursued the relationship between systematic theology and apologetics at Trinity Evangelical Divinity School, and there met Clark Pinnock, who had made a name for himself as a defender of inerrancy and a Schaefferian apologist. As one of my thesis advisors, Pinnock was very uneasy with the issue I had decided to write on and was not happy with my conviction that apologetics had to be based on a consistent Calvinism. Through suggested readings on the topic of *common grace, he encouraged me to consider the Arminian alternative view of grace found in such works as *The Bible Doctrine of Salvation* (1941), written by Charles Ryder Smith, an English Methodist.

This material only confirmed my suspicion that Arminian writers had no understanding of the questions I was struggling with and showed no willingness to interact seriously with Calvinist exegesis. In fact, they wrote as if they were in a historical vacuum. Apart from a passing nod toward Calvin or a reference to Augustine, they wrote as if no Calvinist had ever dealt with these issues in detail before. They made no attempt, for example, to answer the meticulous demonstration by John Gill that the Arminian exegesis of key passages (such as 2 Pet 3:9 and 2 Tim 2:4-6) is fallacious. I did not see then, and do not see now, why Gill should be treated with contempt simply because he is so detailed and writes in the labored and finicky style so common to the

1700s. Pinnock made derogatory remarks about Gill, but showed no concern to answer Gill's painstaking treatment of Matthew 23:37, which I raised as an example of a solid Calvinist response to careless Arminian exegesis. I was not aware at the time that Pinnock was already in a determined retreat from his earlier Calvinist convictions, which appears to be largely a result of his encounter with Reformed apologetics and the question of how dependent it is on specific Calvinist doctrines.

Clark Pinnock was always very kind and helpful to me, and others have also found him to be so. He is considerate and patient, thoughtful and irenic. He deeply desires to make the gospel of God's grace understandable to otherwise lost souls, and his continuing concern with apologetics reveals this clearly. He has been chosen here to illustrate the recent shifts in evangelical theology precisely because of his many books, which document his own doctrinal pilgrimage. He is well known and respected in evangelical circles. Influential and representative evangelical presses publish his books, although he makes it very clear, as in *A Wideness in God's Mercy* (1992), that he is at war with much that he sees on the evangelical scene. His theological views seem to progress further away from orthodoxy every time he publishes, which I have watched with increasing alarm, especially because he was involved in my own formal education. His development is therefore of particular interest, as he often voices a desire for further published interaction. Clark Pinnock is irenic, but he is not averse to controversy. In fact, he encourages constructive debate. In one sense, this book begins the task of responding to his invitation to dialogue by focusing on a central issue in the debate: how to make the gospel of grace more of a challenge to its cultured despisers.

By the time I met Pinnock at Trinity, a comparison of Van Til's critique of the presupposition of metaphysical autonomy with Gordon Clark's refutation of the freewill theory had already made clear to me that the heart of the apologetic theory behind Francis Schaeffer's intellectual challenge also involved a critique of the confused ideas of free will that permeate evangelical thought. No hope of real intellectual consistency could be maintained while avoiding this question. This perennial controversy could no longer be thought of as a distant and trivial battle between Wesley and Toplady. I came to see it as the hidden problem behind the confusion of much evangelical thought, touching upon all the theological issues in debate on the current evangelical scene, from inerrancy to eternal security. Nothing could be settled until it was faced. Apologetic consistency really *does* depend on settling issues in systematic theology, and finally on deciding between Arminianism and Calvinism.

Why People Believe in the Freewill Theory

The motivation to believe in free will is very strong indeed and is based on certain attitudes and arguments that must be met and answered by anyone claiming to be a Calvinist. There are five main reasons people give for sticking with free will, and they will all be answered in turn in this book.

Arminians usually argue as follows:

1. *If we have no free will, we are not responsible for our actions.* I will argue in the next chapter that there is no rational connection between the idea of free will and the concept of responsibility, and that the Arminian form of free will actually makes any concept of human responsibility impossible. The Bible bases human responsibility firmly on other considerations.

2. *It is essential to the image of God.* The point is often made that if we do not have free will, we are "just puppets or robots." I will argue in chapter three that there are no grounds for thinking that free will is part of the divine image, and that the comparison with robots is based on false reasoning.

3. *The denial of free will undermines both human effort and morality.* If we have no free will, why does God command righteousness? Or why does he command evangelism if the elect will be saved inevitably? Arminians seem to think that the meaning of all human ability and action depends on our having a free will in their sense. I will show in chapter five that the freewill theory destroys any hope of relating human action to God's sovereignty and makes human action purely a chance affair.

4. *The Bible teaches free will.* If this were true, the question would be settled for the Spirit-taught believer. But is it true? Which verses teach free will? I will argue in chapter nine that there are no verses in the Bible that teach or require an Arminian view of free will—it turns out to be just an assumption brought to the text in more or less naive innocence of its real implications. An unexamined presupposition will control everything in the long run.

5. *Free will gets God off the hook in the problem of evil.* It is often thought

that if we have free will, God cannot be blamed for the existence or continuation of evils in the world. In chapter ten I will show that the assumption of free will is of no help in solving the problem of evil, and only makes it worse.

Systematic theology is so called because of the conviction that God's revelation in the Bible cannot contradict itself because his own knowledge is interdependent and cannot contradict itself (2 Tim 2:13). This means that all the truths of revelation must be part of one coherent description of reality. An error in the foundational truths will progressively affect other areas and eventually require a change in our view not only of salvation, but also of God. We will see at the end of this study that this is exactly what has happened to the evangelical theologian and apologist Clark Pinnock as he has drifted further and further from the Reformational foundations of the evangelical tradition.

The Arminian form of the freewill theory is hidden behind every important issue in evangelical apologetics today. However unpopular and threatening this type of probing may be, evangelical freewillism cannot be allowed to remain unquestioned. Too much is at stake.

In the next chapter we will seek to provide a definition of "free will" that will reflect fairly what the Arminian understands it to mean. We will then proceed to demonstrate that this view is not compatible with either Scripture or reason.

Further Reading

For the views of the original Arminians, John Owen's *Display of Arminianism* (reprint London: Banner of Truth Trust, 1967) is suitable.

For today's Arminianism, see Clark Pinnock, ed., *The Grace of God, the Will of Man* (Grand Rapids, Mich.: Zondervan, 1989).

For the influence of Arminianism and its Wesleyan form, see Frederic Platt's article "Arminianism" in *Encyclopaedia of Religion and Ethics,* ed. James A. Hastings (Edinburgh: T & T Clark, 1908-1926), 1:807. Unfortunately, the article "Free Will" in volume 6 is confusing and offers no proof, but "Pelagianism and Semi-Pelagianism" (9:703) is clear and helpful.

For Calvinism among the Baptists in America, consult Thomas J. Nettles,

By His Grace and for His Glory (Grand Rapids, Mich.: Baker, 1986).

For a brief study and critique of revivalist evangelism, see Iain Murray, *The Invitation System* (London: Banner of Truth Trust, 1967), as well as the thorough study by the same author and publisher called *Revivals and Revivalism* (1992).

For Spurgeon's views, see Iain Murray, *The Forgotten Spurgeon* (London: Banner of Truth Trust, 1966).

D. W. Bebbington has documented both revivals of interest in Calvinistic doctrine as well as declensions from it in his valuable *Evangelicalism in Modern Britain* (London: Unwin Hyman, 1989). This thorough survey covers the English scene (very different in many important ways from the American experience) from the 1730s to the 1980s.

Michael Watts has at last completed volume two of his superb study of *The Dissenters* (Oxford: Oxford University Press, 1995). Both the first volume (1978) and the second contain valuable material on the decline of dissenting churches in England due to the influence of Arianism and the repudiation of Calvinist theology.

2

The Incoherence
of the Freewill
Theory

It has often been remarked that if philosophers and theologians bothered to define their terms at the beginning of an argument, most of their debates would be unnecessary. It is certainly true that we need to have a clear understanding of what people believe and what is meant by the terms they use before we have any right to disagree. It is also true that if the meaning of a word changes in the course of a debate or during the presentation of an argument, then the debate is suddenly about something different, and the validity of the argument is destroyed. We therefore have a right to request not only that key terms be clearly defined from the outset, but also that new meanings not be smuggled in halfway through the discourse. As Protestants, we naturally expect that the main ideas of our theology be demonstrably derived from the Bible. Purely human assumptions that can be changed at random cannot be the stuff of a consistently Christian worldview.

Definitions

By the term *free will* I mean the belief that the human will has an inherent power to choose with equal ease between alternatives. This is commonly called "the power of contrary choice" or "the liberty of indifference." This belief does not claim that there are no influences that might affect the will, but it does insist that normally the will can overcome these factors and choose in spite of them. Ultimately, the will is free from any necessary causation. In other words, it is autonomous from outside determination. This view is sometimes called *libertarian* to distinguish it from a theory called *determinism,* which posits that the will is determined in its choices by external or internal causes. A third approach thought to be possible by some is called *compatibilism,* which holds that the freedom of the will coexists with all events being determined by previous states of affairs. A well-known attempt to defend it is found in *New Essays in Philosophical Theology* (1955), edited by *Antony Flew and Alasdair MacIntyre.

By *determinism* then, we shall mean the view that claims that no finite events can happen purely by chance, but that all events are causally determined in their nature and action by previous states of affairs—that there are no uncaused events in the world. The opposite of determinism is *indeterminism,* which holds that at least some events are not caused by previous conditions, and free acts of the will are held to be among them.

When Arminians say that the will is "free," they mean free from previous determining causation. We shall see further on that Calvinists also often use the term *free will,* but they do not mean that acts of the will are uncaused, much less that they are random or chance events. Arminians are anxious to exclude God in particular from being the cause of human choice in order to defend God from the accusation that he is "the author of sin." This problem will be dealt with more fully in chapter ten.

When Arminians speak of "the will," they are referring to an independent and self-determining power by which we are enabled to make autonomous choices. When Calvinists refer to "the will," this term simply means the function of willing or choosing, not an independent part of our soul's anatomy. When a choice is made, this act of the will is always the act of a person who is either regenerate or unregenerate. That is, all acts of the will are expressions of a *character,* whether good or bad. Jesus refers to this in Matthew 7:15-20 when he warns that "every good tree bears good fruit, but a bad tree bears bad fruit" (v. 17), and that it "cannot" *(ou dynatai)* be otherwise. He lays out the consequence of this in his famous utterance about character: "You will know them by their fruits" (v. 20 NASB). In Matthew 12:33 he emphasizes this again by saying, "The tree is known by its fruit."

In other words, good people habitually make good choices and bad people habitually make bad choices. While good people may occasionally make bad choices, or bad people good choices, we recognize that these odd choices are "out of character," and that they cannot be consistently maintained. The entire body of Western legislation and *ethics depends on the universal recognition that actions are the responsible outflow of a person's character.

By the term *autonomy* I mean the quality of the will or intellect that enables it to function either for or against any particular course of action, thereby exhibiting an innate ability. The term originally meant "able to make its own laws" and indicated independence of external or higher constraints. *Metaphysical autonomy* is therefore freedom from external ontological control. *Epistemological autonomy* means the capacity to understand and interpret experience with oneself as the starting point—the autonomous consciousness does not need any previous interpretation to make the world intelligible to the mind. *Ethical* or *moral autonomy* is the ability to make moral judgments from an interior sense of right and wrong, which thereby implies an ability to supply one's own standards. Finally, *teleological autonomy* is the ability to determine one's own destiny by one's own choices and to set one's own goals.

It should be apparent from these descriptions that autonomy just means free will in the commonly accepted sense of that term. Someone once said that the only people who have trouble defining free will are the philosophers. Any normal person knows exactly what it is. It simply means that "I can run my own life by my own choices without outside interference, thank you."

The Arminian Circle of Assumptions
It is important to notice that whenever most evangelicals see the word *will* or *choice,* they simply assume that free will is implied. This basic assumption is so pervasive that no attempt is ever made to "prove" free will. Should a person challenge the assumption, the conversation goes something like this (after the

initial shock passes that anyone would dare to question that we have a free will).

Arminian: Well, we must have a free will to be responsible human beings.

Calvinist: But what do you mean by "responsible"?

A: Responsibility means we make real choices.

C: What do you mean by a "real" choice? Isn't a choice real if it actually occurs at all?

A: Responsibility means that we act individually as complete human beings, in our own integrity.

C: You seem to assume that free will is a part of our humanness.

A: Well, it is. Free will is part of the image of God, and that's what makes us human.

C: So we have free will because we act in our own integrity.

A: Yes, and because we are responsible for our actions.

C: But a moment ago you based responsibility on free will. Now you are basing free will on responsibility.

A: Well, it's like a chicken-and-egg situation, and it's not too easy to decide which comes first.

C: But in the case of the chicken we know which came first: God created the first chicken.

A: Well, God created us with free will.

C: But how do you know that? Is it in the Bible?

A: But if we don't have free will we can't be held responsible for our actions.

And so forth . . .

So the discussion consists of a series of circular repetitions of ideas thought to be somehow connected, but no logical derivations are actually drawn out. This kind of conversation is extremely common in evangelical seminaries and is the reason people get so frustrated with the topic. So much is assumed without reflection that any kind of proof is impossible. In fact, one never seems to encounter an effort to *prove* free will, and occasionally the claim will be made by those defending it that it cannot be proved. But if it cannot be proved, it must be assumed, or treated as self-evident. In particular, it must be recognized as coming from outside the Bible. If it *is* regarded as self-evident, the privileged assumption will control the entire process of interpretation. This phenomenon will be given further attention when the interpretations of particular verses in Scripture are examined in chapter nine. Of course, although an assumption may not be found in the Bible, it may still be true on other grounds, but the fact that it cannot be discovered there ought to give us pause. It may turn out to be an essential element of a worldview incompatible with Christianity. In fact, we shall see in chapter four that it can be traced to the Fall.

In What Sense Is the Will "Free"?

Arminians want the will to be free from outside interference. They often say that, in particular, God never overrides our free will. This freedom from external causes is supposed to safeguard our integrity and secure responsibility. But what would it mean for the will to be free from causation? Often this problem is skirted by saying that the will is "self-caused." This does not mean that the will creates itself, but that its motions to choose one course of action over another are self-motivated or spontaneous. The will is self-moved in response to what the mind knows and can cause itself to act in response to influences or equally to resist them. The will is free to follow or resist whatever option the mind presents.

The most serious problem here is that this sort of spontaneity is indistinguishable from a chance event. We need only ask, "What causes the will to choose one way rather than another?" If it is *not* caused, it is purely random. If it *is* caused to act, then it is not free from causation. It makes no difference to this argument whether the cause is internal to the personality or impinges from the outside; however, since the Arminians are offering free will as a category of explanation of how human beings work, they are obliged to decide what they mean by "free." If they admit that the actions of the will are caused, they have slipped into some kind of determinism, while if they will not admit the will to be caused, they have a much worse dilemma, which we will now outline in three parts.

First, chance events cannot be the stuff of character. When we say that people have a "good character," we mean that they are morally predictable—that they can be relied upon to do what is right, even under strong influence to do what is wrong. A person who acts at random, whose moral decisions cannot be distinguished from merely chance events, not only has a "bad character," being unreliable, but in fact may not have a discernible character at all. A totally random personality would be indistinguishable from a disintegrated or insane personality. In other words, if the will is merely spontaneous in its actions, no character could form at all.

Second, unless the actions of the will are tied directly to the character, how can we be held answerable for our actions? How can a person be held responsible for chance events? If acts of the will are not caused in such a way as to be actually manifestations of the character, how can they be *my* actions any more than the result of tossing a coin? The simple fact is that we cannot be held responsible for a chance event, simply because we exert no causal influence. I can be held responsible for tossing a coin, since I caused it to be tossed, but I cannot be held responsible for how it comes down. In other words, the very idea of responsibility depends on causation. Therefore the freewill theory destroys responsibility rather than supporting it. The following imaginary case is pertinent.

*Lord Bertrand Russell spent his whole life as an atheist from the age of 14 to his death in 1970 at age 98. He often debated and wrote against Christianity. Suppose he arrives at the final judgment with the following argument: "Now, I realize I was wrong about there not being any God, but I don't quite see how you can send me to hell. After all, you created me with a free will and never made any effort to prevent me from acting in accordance with its dictates. This free will has always been autonomous from any previous causation and from your control in particular. Although I have often thought that perhaps it would be better if my free will acted according to my intellect, sometimes it does, and sometimes it doesn't. In fact, it doesn't seem to act according to any pattern at all. Because it is an uncaused cause of my actions, it seems totally random, and therefore unpredictable. I have had no real control of it at all, since you created it autonomous. I am simply not responsible for chance events that I cannot control or predict. How can you send me to hell for actions arising from a free will which, because it is free, is also not under my control?" We will leave the answer for the Arminian to figure out.

Third, the question must be pressed as to how a purely spontaneous ("self-moved") will could ever *begin* to act at all? If the will is "neutral" at first and not predetermined to act one way rather than another, what causes it to act at all? If it starts out neutral, how does it ever get off dead center? If it is said that the will is "induced" or "led" or "drawn" or "influenced" to act, we must insist that these are merely words for different types of causation. We are forced again to face the problem of what it really means for the will to be free from causation. Either it acts purely by chance, or it seems that it does not act at all. This, of course, completely obliterates the possibility of growth in holiness, which was a special concern of the later Arminians.

There are other problems associated with what "influences" really amount to. Are moral suasion and reasoned argument causes of the will's action or direction? Some Arminian evangelists follow Finney in believing that the will can and should be moved to faith in Christ by the use of reasoned arguments and moral examples. Therefore they quite reasonably make use of evidences and other apologetic arguments to convince the sinner to believe, finding moral and often emotional stories to move the will to faith. The free will is then apparently still able to make a free choice between belief and unbelief.

But if the will acts *because* it is convinced by reason and moved by emotion or moral example, how does this really differ from being caused to act by an outside manipulation? If it be objected that it still acts freely when presented with the evidences (i.e., the persuasions were not causal), why are the evidences and reasons needed at all? It would be better to leave the autonomous will to decide by itself, wholly uninfluenced by argument. In fact, it would appear that even so much as listening to an argument is a definite threat to our autonomy, to our moral neutrality. If I am swayed or pushed by an argument, deciding to go with the flow, the push becomes a cause of my direction—I was caused to choose by the argument. The fact that I cooperated makes no difference to the fact of causation.

The Bible makes it clear in many passages that the will is not morally neutral. In Romans 14:23, Paul concludes his explanation of why we must always act according to our conscience by asserting that "everything that does not come from faith is sin." For Paul, all human moral motions either flow out of the principle of faith or, by default, out of the flesh—mere acts of the sin nature. Therefore, there can be no morally neutral actions, including acts of the will. In Hebrews 11:6, we are similarly told that "without faith it is impossible to please God," but this seems again to imply that all human acts are either motivated by faith or they are not. Jesus says in John's gospel that anyone who does not believe is "condemned already" and that if a person continues to reject Christ, "God's wrath *remains* [continually] on him" (3:18, 36, emphasis mine). This does not sound like the sinner's situation is neutral until he or she decides for Christ, but that it is already settled—everyone is either justified or is presently under condemnation. How can there be any morally neutral territory in a universe created by a righteous God? More attention will be given this topic in chapter six ("Depravity and Election").

Omniscience and Certainty

Another question that may be raised concerns the Arminians' *certainty* that they have a free will. How could they know such a thing? They usually insist that it is so obvious that only a perverse mind could think otherwise. But reasonably intelligent and godly people have in fact been led to deny free will, so perhaps it is not so obvious to them. Obviousness may be mere self-deception. Claiming that people who do not accept the freewill theory are morally defective human beings is merely abuse, not reasoned argument. A reasoned argument requires correct presuppositions, a series of connected syllogisms or connected implications that do not violate the laws of logic, and at least one conclusion that is warranted by the premises. To a rational mind, such a conclusion is the stuff of real progress in the search for truth.

The Calvinist readily agrees that it is indeed obvious that we make real choices and that therefore the will exists as a capacity for decision-making. But this is a far cry from accepting the popular freewill theory about *how* the will behaves. Why can't the will be "free" in a sense that the Arminian (or any other freewiller or libertarian) has never thought of? There are several ways we might think of the will as free. The will may be said to be free to perform some choices, but not others. Most Calvinists agree with Martin Luther that we are free to do many things "in the world." These would include eating or fasting, choosing coffee rather than tea for breakfast, or taking a course in French history rather than Russian. However, when it comes to spiritual things, we are much more limited, having no spiritual ability to even understand what God wants, let alone the power to do it. Meanwhile, the issue that separates the Calvinist from both the Pelagian and the Arminian is not whether we make real choices or not, or whether the will is real or not, but whether it is free in the sense demanded by the Arminian.

Again, the will may be free in the sense that it is not constrained by natural forces from the outside to go one way rather than another, but it may still be able to act in harmony with other elements of the personality such as the intellect or some internal habituation, such as the effects of alcoholism. It may act quite freely in giving expression to the inner character. That is, the will may be free in that it freely expresses our nature without being autonomous or acting without a previous cause. This is the sense in which the Westminster Confession speaks of free will in its ninth chapter: "God hath endued the will of man with that natural liberty, that it is neither forced nor by any absolute necessity of nature determined to good or evil." There is nothing in this inconsistent with Calvinism, and it is hardly likely that the Westminster divines wanted to express Arminianism! The confession simply states that the will has a freedom or liberty of its own nature and that it is not forced to act nor determined by an "absolute necessity" in the materialist sense of "nature" so popular in the 1600s.

The rest of the ninth chapter points out that the will in a fallen nature is not free to perform spiritual good, speaking of a "natural bondage under sin" that only regeneration can free us from. The natural fallen will cannot even prepare itself for regeneration, let alone convert itself. It is apparent that Calvinists believe that the will (1) is free only in the sense that it is free to express the person's character, (2) must be regenerated before it is free for obedience to God and (3) is never forced to act against its own nature. To my knowledge, no Calvinist writer thinks the will can be forced mechanically to act against its own nature.

This question therefore arises: Since the assertion of free will is a claim that *no* outside causes are controlling the will's choices, how can anyone know for sure that this is so? The actions of the will are motions of the soul, and these in turn are involved with the working of the brain. The brain is an electro-chemical machine of wonderful complexity, but it can be affected by many physical things, from a simple concussion to stimuli from electrical currents.

It can be affected by the growth of a tumor or by chemicals in the blood, such as LSD. How do we know that it is not also affected by cosmic radiation? Millions of tiny particles from distant stars and galaxies pass through our bodies all the time. We have no idea what effects they may have on the atoms and molecules in our bodies with which they collide. How can a person who believes in free will be certain his brain is not being modified at any instant by a subatomic particle, causing his otherwise "neutral" will to turn this way rather than that? One would need to have exhaustive knowledge of the situation in order to be sure there were *no causes whatever* operating on the human will. Thus, belief in free will seems to require omniscience.

Inconsistent Calvinism

*William G. T. Shedd wrote an extremely valuable *Systematic Theology* in 1888, a masterful exposition of classical Calvinism, with a detailed analysis of how he thought free will works (vol. 2, chap. 3). In an earlier chapter titled "Man's Primitive State," he repeatedly uses such terms as *self-determination, self-motion, volition, inclination* and many others, leaving the reader with a sense that Shedd was one of the most subtle minds ever to write on this question. He emphasizes at length that the concept of an undetermined will is a self-contradiction (pp. 109ff.). He goes to great lengths to explain how the will must have its roots in moral causation in order to produce character.

So far, so good. But there is an antecedent problem. In the first volume Shedd goes to great lengths to explain the difference between predestination and fate: "To predestinate voluntary action is to make it certain. . . . To make certain is not the same as to compel, or necessitate. . . . An event in the material world is made certain by physical force; this is compulsory. An event in the moral world is made certain by spiritual operation; this is voluntary and free" (p. 413).

At first one might think that Shedd is merely distinguishing between two types of causation, but this is not so. In the third and supplementary volume he returns to the subject, focusing on Anselm. He says that Anselm makes a distinction between an "antecedent necessity" and a "subsequent necessity," which he claims will help us understand "the self-motion and responsibility of the enslaved will." He quotes from Anselm: "There is an antecedent necessity *which is the cause of a thing,* and there is also a subsequent necessity arising from the thing itself" (p. 162, emphasis mine). Thus Anselm defines "antecedent necessity" as being equivalent to *causation.* After more examples, Shedd continues: "Applying this distinction to the fall of mankind in Adam: *There was no 'antecedent' necessity that this fall of mankind should occur. It was left to the self-determination of the human will that it should occur"* (p. 163, my emphasis).

In other words, in his anxiety to preserve some kind of self-determination for the will, Shedd finally admits that the actions of the will are *uncaused.* This not only conflicts with his rejection of an undetermined will, but it also closes the gap between his view of the will and the one he calls Pelagian, referring to "the Pelagian idea of freedom as . . . indetermination" (p. 334). But indetermination is simply lack of causation. Shedd's position seems finally to be self-contradictory.

Shedd is typical of many Calvinists who hold a high view of God's sovereignty but cannot seem to relinquish an account of free will that is ultimately indistinguishable from Arminian indeterminism. They may try to cover their tracks with words like *mystery, paradox* or *antinomy,* but it remains just a contradiction after all.

A More Recent Case

Francis Schaeffer was a serious Calvinist and meant to uphold the Westminster Confession in its entirety. But at L'Abri, when I noticed that some L'Abri workers actually defended views of free will indistinguishable from Arminianism, I pursued the question with Schaeffer himself. I asked him how he could place so strong an emphasis on challenging the natural person's "autonomy" while at the same time defending a version of "free will" that looked much like Arminianism. He said that he wanted to maintain a clear testimony against the "determinism" emphasized in the psychology and sociology courses on the secular campus. He said, "These kids come to L'Abri from a heavy background in secular views of man that make them feel like just animals or machines. I don't want them to confuse the Christian view of God's sovereignty with this kind of thing."

This was the same strategic error that the early church and the medieval theologians made: thinking that the answer to pagan fatalism is the equally pagan freewillism. The answer to rationalist determinism is not irrationalist indeterminism, but the sovereignty and personal plan of the God of the Bible. It was a great puzzle to me at the time that this man whom God had used so signally to force the evangelical world to face its intellectual responsibilities (and who had derived much of his own views from Cornelius Van Til) seemed willing, when faced with secular determinists, to offer a non-Christian alternative to a non-Christian dilemma.

Schaeffer often used the term "semantic mysticism" to describe the way liberals use orthodox terms one moment, creating a feeling of orthodoxy, then use different terms drawn from secular theories in the next breath, thus evacuating the original terms of their real meaning. I asked him whether his denial of autonomy and subsequent insistence on free will was not an example of semantic mysticism. Since his entire apologetic method depended on challenging the unregenerate person's metaphysical autonomy, why then give it back under the term "free will"? He thought about it a bit, then said that he would give it some more thought and that I should come back in a week.

Two weeks later I caught him coming out of the chapel one Sunday and asked if he had an answer. His response was that he felt that I did not understand what he meant by "autonomy" and suggested that I read his first two books again. But his view of autonomy was perfectly clear to me—it was identical to that of Cornelius Van Til. The problem was that Schaeffer did not want to challenge people to be consistent Calvinists by speaking against the freewill theory. I did not pursue the matter with him again.

What Is "Responsibility"?
I must have fifty books in my library referring to the supposed relation between free will and responsibility, but only one of them makes any effort to question whether any logical connection exists between these two ideas. In the last chapter of his book *Religion, Reason and Revelation,* Gordon Clark points out that no one has ever demonstrated that the concept of responsibility is in any way dependent on a prior state of free will. These two terms appear often in the same context, and it is often stated that "if we don't have free will we cannot be responsible for our actions," but no one bothers to prove it.

A typical scholarly expression of this statement is made by D. A. Carson in his doctoral thesis, published as *Divine Sovereignty and Human Responsibility* (1981), an excellent study of how the literature of the Hellenistic period treats the problem. Carson concludes with an explanation of the Johannine description of both divine sovereignty and human responsibility for sin, pointing out that no attempt is made by John to produce any speculative explanation of how they work together, unlike the Hellenistic literature in which the subject is treated. Carson is duly impressed by how these two topics can coexist side by side throughout John's Gospel without any philosophic reconciliation. It does not seem to occur to Carson, however, that John himself may have noticed no tension or conflict because in fact there was none.

A clue as to why Carson is under the impression that God's sovereignty cannot be reconciled with human responsibility can be found in the section titled "The Boundaries of Free Will." The very first sentence reads, "Responsibility is certainly linked to 'free will' in some fashion" (p. 206). But once again, despite the ensuing discussion of various types of inconsistent Calvinism, Carson nowhere shows that his opening assumption is correct. He simply joins the long queue of inconsistent Calvinists who assume that free will "in some fashion" undergirds the reality of responsibility. But in *what* fashion?

I will simply repeat here Gordon Clark's challenge to the Arminians to write out a proof that responsibility is in any way dependent on, or can be derived from, their concept of free will. Of course, they may define free will in any way that will meet their theological needs, but Christians should get their premises from the Bible. Carson acknowledges Clark's book *Biblical Predestination* (1969) but does not mention *Religion, Reason and Revelation,* in which the subject of his own final chapter titled "The Formulation of the Tension" is discussed in detail. It is simply assumed that there is a tension.

It would have been helpful if Carson had explained *why* Hellenistic literature is so bedeviled by speculative attempts to reconcile the concept of responsibility with God's sovereignty, and then had explored why the Bible does not treat the two as being in tension or conflict at all. But perhaps he simply decided not to include these further issues in the scope of the study. (It should also be considered that they may only seem to be in conflict because non-

Christian thought imposes false and contradictory presuppositions on the topic as the condition for the discussion. That is, the natural mind presupposes that the Christian view is impossible before it begins its "objective" consideration of the subject.) However, Carson's thesis does make available to the reader an excellent analysis of how the (mostly Jewish) literature of the Hellenistic era handles this important dilemma of unbelief. It should be read by every Christian interested in the history of the freewill debate.

The fact remains however, that not only is there no demonstrable connection between free will and responsibility, but also that the Arminian idea of a liberty of indifference is totally destructive of any sense of responsibility at all. It may be difficult for some to understand the relationship between human responsibility and God's sovereignty—they are perfectly honest in saying that they "don't see how we can be held responsible if we don't have free will." But the point for the Bible-believing Christian is that nowhere in the Bible is responsibility linked with free will; it never uses free will as an explanatory category, not even once.

Biblical Responsibility

Perhaps a Calvinistic account of the meaning of responsibility will help clarify the issue. We must begin with a definition: responsibility is simply a synonym for "answerability," and means that we are answerable to God as the judge of our actions. That is, if God calls any of our actions into question, we are morally obligated to respond to him. We are "response-able" to God. While the Bible does not use the abstract term *responsibility* itself, the fact of our eventually being called into judgment is frequently found throughout Scripture. The Bible bases responsibility on four things.

First, we are responsible to God because he is the Creator and we are the *creatures.* God is at liberty to call any element of his creation into question at any time—it is simply his prerogative as sovereign Lord. The clay is subject to the Potter simply because he is the Potter. In other words, our responsibility is based in our *ontology,* or being, as creatures. This is the message of Job, when God answers him out of the whirlwind (38:1-4), and of Isaiah, which contains a long polemic against those who forget the Creator in order to worship the creature (40—57). Paul summarizes the results of such moral irresponsibility in Romans 1. He borrows the image of the Potter and the clay from Isaiah (29:16; 45:9; 64:8) and Jeremiah (18:1-6) in Romans 9:21. We will all finally stand before the judgment seat of God (Rom 14:10). Ultimately, "every knee will bow" (Is 45:23).

Second, we are responsible to God because he is the moral reference point for right and wrong, and not we ourselves. This is what is entailed by our recognizing God as holy. Our responsibility to God is an *ethical* necessity, because of our need of a standard outside of ourselves. Job realized that just as God is sovereign over his creation, he is also righteous over against Job's own sinfulness (40:1-5; 42:1-6). Truly, Job had done nothing to deserve the treatment he received from God. In fact, he was more righteous than his "comforters," and his understanding of the situation was more theologically correct than the speculative explanations they offered for his suffering (1:22; 42:7). But God himself is both his own and our moral standard, as Elihu showed in chapter 34. Therefore, Job had to submit to all that God did, whether he understood the reason for it or not. Job himself never even finds out what the reader of the book knows—that Job is actually a pawn in a much larger game, in the primeval contest between God and Satan (1:6-12; 2:1-7). God is not obliged to tell us everything. Rather, what little knowledge we do have is an act of mercy.

Third, we are answerable to God for the *knowledge* we have. All sinners sin against (more or less) light and truth. No one is wholly without the light of conscience, and we will be judged according to the light we have (Rom 2:12-16). Those who have less knowledge will be judged less severely than those with more light to sin against. Daniel warns Belshazzar that the king knew of God's former dealings with his father Nebuchadnezzar: "But you his son, O Belshazzar, have not humbled yourself, though you knew all this" (5:22). In Luke, the ignorant servant who disobeyed is punished less severely than the servant who knew what his master wanted and still failed to do it (12:42-48). So there are degrees of responsibility in this sense. We may call this our *epistemological* responsibility. We are responsible for what we know—it might even be said that there is a stewardship of truth for which we will answer finally to God.

Fourth, because the purpose of the creation is the glory of God (Is 43:7;

Col 1:16; Rev 4:11), we are responsible as stewards of God's blessings to fulfill the end or purpose of God in creating us in the world. God loves his creation and eventually will "destroy those who destroy the earth" (Rev 11:18, NASB). We may refer to this as our *teleological* responsibility, because it relates to our task as servants in the design of creation, which is to bring glory to God.

It seems, then, that far from basing human responsibility on some theory of a free will innate to human nature, the Bible bases it on the implications of the distinction between Creator and creature, and relates them to the four classical areas of ontology, ethics, *epistemology and *teleology. In other words, throughout the Bible, responsibility is a reflection of our relation to God as Creator, as the origin of moral meaning, as our reference point for revealed truth and as the one who gives ultimate purpose and direction to his creation. And if indeed God is the ultimate reference point for meaning in the four areas of being, knowing, ethics and purpose, where could the creature stand to mount a rational criticism of anything God might do? This is the philosophic point underlying Paul's challenge in Romans 9:20: "Who are you, O man, who answers back to God?" (NASB). There is simply no absolute starting point available to a finite being in a finite universe. For a creature, all points are relative. Only by listening first to God's revelation can a finite being have any fixed reference point at all. This topic will be raised again in chapter eleven, where we will look at the question of the location of ultimacy.

Theological Incoherencies

Consider the doctrine of creation, which all evangelical Arminians presumably believe. If a free will exists at all, it is necessarily a created aspect of our human nature. But if it is created, it must have a complex set of qualities that are collectively its nature. That is, in order to exist as a temporal entity, it must consist of a set of properties that distinguish it from other things. If it has no such characteristics, it has no discernible nature—it would not exist. If it does have such properties, they determine its nature and thus its behavior, which would mean that it is not random at all. But if the will acts according to its own previously existing properties, its actions are to some degree being caused. This is no help to the Arminian.

This problem cannot be avoided by merely insisting that God created the will with the property of freedom, since this term still needs to be defined in such a way as to avoid Bertrand Russell's plea (see p. 48). If the further claim is offered that God simply limited himself by not interfering with the will, how can the Arminian distinguish this from the conclusion that God created beings that act according to chance "blips" in their brains, which they can control even less than he?

Again, just as God's omniscience is undermined by freewillism, so is the classical doctrine of providence. If God has to continuously make adjustments in his hopes for the future by modifying his plans to fit the multiple permutations and random fluctuations of millions of human freewill decisions every second of the day, how can I have any confidence that any prayer of mine (or promise of God, for that matter) will be fulfilled? It is really no wonder that some modern freewillers have been sucked into the Heraclitean flux of process theology. They can be expected to choose the ontology that best suits their relativistic ethic and its accompanying epistemology. Freewillism leads eventually to process theology. In fact, it almost seems to require it.

Again, if it is really true that "God never overrides the free will," how can the Christian honestly pray for anyone's salvation? God could only answer this prayer by violating the independence of the will, by exercising an undue influence on the unregenerate soul. For God to answer this particular prayer would also be unjust by the Arminian's standards, because it would make God a respecter of persons, since this person we are praying for is no more deserving of salvation than any other unregenerate sinner. The Calvinist can simply answer this dilemma with a verse from the Psalms: "Blessed are those you choose and bring near to live in your courts!" (65:4). Furthermore, Jesus said that no one is able to come to God except those whom the Father draws to himself (Jn 6:44-45; cf. Jer 31:3 and Hos 11:4). Calvinists are eternally grateful that God mercifully "overrode" their sinfully rebellious will by regenerating it along with the rest of their personality, turning it toward himself, that they might come to Christ.

Furthermore, all predictive prophecy in the Bible is undermined by introducing free will as a causal factor in history. Consider the problem God would have faced with his prediction that the Messiah would be born in Bethlehem in Judea, when the pregnant mother of Jesus was living in the wrong town, up north in Nazareth. According to Luke, to get this couple down to the right town, God moved the entire Roman Empire from Augustus Caesar down to the local Roman bureaucracy in Palestine so that everyone would go to their cities of origin, where the records were kept of their families.

Let us for a moment imagine how many freewill choices would be involved in moving these people from north of Palestine to the southern city where the prophet said Jesus was to be born. Suppose they had decided to start a week later. After all, such a census would take many months to complete even if everyone without exception complied as asked. Then, because Mary was pregnant, they might have decided to leave her with her sister Elizabeth, with Joseph traveling alone to represent the whole family. Or they might have decided to stop along the way at Samaria or Bethel or on the outskirts of Jerusalem. Or they might have decided to go on to the next town when they saw how crowded the little city of David was when they finally did get there. Any one or more of these decisions would have ignored the highly predetermined body chemistry of the young mother-to-be (of which the participants knew virtually nothing), and the baby would have been born in the wrong town, or worse, somewhere on the road between towns. This seriously damages the familiar Christmas story.

It seems that in order to fulfill this one prediction in the Old Testament about Bethlehem, God needed to have control over every atom in Mary's body and every atom in the entire Roman bureaucracy. God had to know in advance how every freewill decision in the sequence would turn out. Nothing less could guarantee the success of this one prediction.

The Arminian may object with *C. S. Lewis that God, being "outside of time," simply saw the events coinciding down the road and made the prediction on the basis of his foreknowledge, much as we would have foreknowledge of how a film ends by seeing a preview of the film. The Calvinist is then moved to ask who created this "future" that God is able to see in advance? Does God get his knowledge of the world like an empiricist does?

The reason I can see a preview of a film is that someone has already fixed the story on the celluloid for me to examine empirically. If the future already exists in some sense in the mind of God, is this true and certain knowledge? Or is it merely uncertain knowledge of what might possibly happen *if* Caesar and Mary and Joseph happen to choose to make certain freewill decisions? If so, it is merely knowledge of multiple abstract possibilities, not of real events. How could even God himself make a prediction on the basis of uncertain knowledge of a future as yet unsettled? On the other hand, if it is certain knowledge, how could any of the decisions made to bring it about in history have been otherwise?

I do not see how an Arminian can respond rationally to this type of question without moving further away from Christian orthodoxy—which is what recent Arminians are doing (much like the Socinians of the 1600s). To put it another way, how can God have certain knowledge of an uncertain future? Some will say that we are simply finite, and there is an undeniable limitation of our understanding. But this problem of the status of God's knowledge of the future is a logical problem of the incoherence of the freewill theory, not a problem of finiteness.

It will be established in chapter six that fallen people labor under a far more serious disability than mere finiteness. Our finitude is never treated in the Bible as a "problem" at all. Instead, we are viewed as being in some sense enslaved to the results of the Fall of Adam and Eve, and this affects our spiritual competence both to understand the human dilemma and to respond to God's interpretation of it (Rom 8:6-8; 1 Cor 2:14-15).

We now turn to the claim that we must have a free will because we are made in God's image. This raises the whole question of human nature—what constitutes us as "human"?

Further Reading

The literature on the free will versus determinism problem is immense. Every introductory philosophy text has a chapter called "Free Will and Responsibility" or something similar.

The attitude of the Reformers may be gathered from Luther's *The Bondage of the Will,* printed conveniently by Westminster Press with Erasmus's *Diatribe on Free Will* as the single volume *Luther and Erasmus: Free Will and Salvation.*

For the way in which the presupposition of human autonomy has corrupted the apologetic endeavor of Christendom for the last 1800 years, see Cornelius

Van Til's *A Survey of Christian Epistemology* (Nutley, N.J.: Den Dulk, 1969). In Van Til's *A Christian Theory of Knowledge* (Grand Rapids, Mich.: Baker, 1969), chapter four contains a valuable survey on how the church fathers compromised their testimony in preparation for the medieval synthesis.

For the source that destroyed the last vestiges of freewillism in my own thinking, read the last chapter, "God and Evil," in Gordon Clark's *Religion, Reason and Revelation* (Nutley, N.J.: Presbyterian & Reformed, 1961).

Recent Arminian thought is found in *Grace Unlimited* (Minneapolis: Bethany House, 1975) and *The Grace of God, the Will of Man* (Grand Rapids, Mich.: Zondervan, 1989). Both are collections of essays by a considerable list of scholars and are edited by Clark Pinnock.

For a secular demolition of traditional compromised apologetic methods, see *God and Philosophy* (New York: Harcourt Brace, 1966), by Antony Flew. In paragraphs 2.34-40 (pp. 43-47), he challenges Christians to take the idea of a Creator seriously, arguing that if they do, the need to defend autonomy will probably force them out of belief in God altogether.

Edwin Hatch gave the Hibbert Lectures of 1888, which were printed as *The Influence of Greek Ideas and Usages upon the Christian Church* (London: Williams and Norgate, 1890). Chapters six and seven discuss the dependence of the early church fathers on Greek sources for their doctrine of free will.

3

What Makes Us Human? Humanism & Christianity

*H*umanism *typically begins its interpretation* of human experience with humankind as the reference point for understanding reality. The autonomy of human thought is simply presupposed, and everything else is expected to fall into line with this dogma. Such a procedure necessarily generates a wide variety of theories as to what human nature is, since the would-be autonomous investigator can fix on anything that catches the attention to arrange the data around. We will review here seven of these humanisms as described in a recent book on the topic, and then analyze the author's treatment of Christianity to find out how he came to treat Christianity as a type of humanism.

Seven Theories of Human Nature
In a helpful little book of this title, Leslie Stevenson outlines the principal concepts of humanness that have influenced Western thinking so far. He treats them chronologically, examining the Christian view second, following Platonism. He ends with a discussion of how we might benefit from each of them. In other words, Stevenson treats the Christian theory as one among several

humanist visions that we might consider as possible grist for the mill in our analysis of human nature. Although he notes that Christianity claims we are made in God's image, the theological content and philosophic implications of this doctrine are not clarified from the Bible. If they were, it would be clear to his readers that Christianity is not just another possible view, but a unique and exclusive standpoint that makes the others either false or irrelevant. The most the Christian theory could allow would be that humanist theories might say valuable things and offer relatively correct insights, provided the facts to which they draw attention are placed in a Christian perspective. We will consider each theory in turn, identifying its distinctively humanistic viewpoint. Though Stevenson treats them in their chronological order, here we will look at Christianity last.

1. *Plato.* Plato defined our humanness in terms of wisdom, which was ultimately to be understood in terms of our place in society. According to him, the ideal society is one that balances the requirements of the physical and spiritual worlds of the body and soul. Only the truly wise are truly human, and the truly wise society would have to be something like the one described in his *Republic.* For Plato, the unifying principles of wisdom are found in the soul, a preexistent spiritual entity that is temporarily imprisoned in the material body. The soul has had previous lives, and although it has forgotten most of its previous knowledge, this innate store of wisdom can be accessed by *paideia*—the discipline of a child. The word *education* comes from the Latin word the Romans used to translate the Greek term. It means to "lead out" the best in the pupil, to uncover the truth buried in the human soul. Meanwhile, the body limits the soul and makes demands of its own related to its tendency toward decay and chaos. Knowledge, then, consists of a combination of the innate ideas of the soul with the particular experiences of the body. Thus, the unity of truth is found first in the soul, but finally in an eternal world of ideas located in the upper reaches of the great chain of being itself. Diversity is located in the temporal (and less real) particulars of the world of matter.

For Plato, the world of experience interprets itself in terms of principles of unification and diversification found initially in the human soul. Finally, however, they are actually properties of the great one-and-many, which is the vast evolving ladder of being itself. Plato's humanism consists in an organizing principle that was later enunciated by Strato of Lampsacus: "The principles of the world lie themselves within the world." Or, in the words of Democritus of Abdera, "Man is a microcosm," containing the whole world in principle within his own consciousness. Therefore, "one should respect one's own opinion the most," because it "stands as the law of one's soul." He expressed the autonomy of human "reason within the soul" by saying that it "derives its pleasures from itself." Humanism thus best expresses itself in the assertion that humanity is the measure or standard of all things. Modern Western humanism has been derived from Greek humanism through the renaissance of ancient learning in the Middle Ages. Man is essentially reduced to an autonomous moment of consciousness in the evolutionary flow of being.

2. *Freud.* *Sigmund Freud was a chemical determinist who sought to understand human behavior in terms of prior experiences. To organize the data he gleaned from therapy sessions, he postulated three main elements of the inner life: the *id,* the *superego* and the *ego.* The *id* is the innate complex of irrational drives that well up from the body and are largely unknowable. The *superego* is (roughly) the memory of past moral laws, cultural norms and judgments, together affecting what is loosely called the "conscience." The *ego* is the basic sense of self struggling to become free from the other two and to assert its independent significance. Well-adjusted people show an increasingly autonomous ability to balance the irrationalist influences of the id against the rationalistic elements and demands of the superego. Although Freud arrives at this by a very complex and twisted path of psychoanalysis, the essence of humanness is the autonomous person who has balanced needs against wants and can handle the adjustment of life to the shifting environment.

Freud's humanism involves a very self-conscious repudiation of dependence on other people, and especially on that most illusory person of all, God. His concept of the well-adjusted person reminds us of the Stoics' ideal of conformity to nature. In both systems, the person who is most in harmony with the evolutionary flow of being is the person who is most human. All human problems are caused by psychic history, especially the earliest experiences of childhood. These experiences can be dredged up during analysis, and the therapist can then help a patient understand them in order to come to terms with them. Human nature is a bundle of complexes to be understood through a long and expensive process of psychological archaeology. We are basically chemical machines seeking to adjust to our circumstances, and are happiest when fully adjusted. In this view, human nature has again been reduced to one of its functions—adjustment to its inner and outer environment.

3. *Marx.* *Karl Marx was an evolutionistic atheist who defined humanity as the animal who is conditioned by society, particularly by economic conditions in recent history. He asserted that human beings are the only animals who are conscious of their own evolution; therefore, they can modify and control that evolution. To bring our progress under control, we must modify our economic state according to our understanding of the principles of *dialectical materialism.* The future we seek is a workers' paradise on earth in which social and economic justice is founded on the unselfish labor of the individual to meet the needs of the many. The tendency of Marxist societies is for the interests of the individual to disappear into the demands of the state. Almost the only thing Marxist societies do with any vigor is persecute Christians.

Marx's humanism began with his doctoral thesis on the materialism of the Greeks. To this atheistic stance, confirmed by his study of Feuerbach, Marx added an essentially occult principle called the *dialectic.* This was originally a living principle of teleological forward motion in the World-Spirit, an integral part of Hegel's rationalistic idealism. Marx appropriated it and made it a property of matter itself, thereby eliminating any sense of a spiritual world. He presupposed that only matter exists, just like the early Greek materialists on whom he wrote his doctoral thesis. Marx's dialectic is basically an occult life-force inherent in matter that somehow points in the direction of progress as conceived by the Victorian English socialists. Despite his strident antagonism toward religion and his claim to base everything in his worldview on organic evolution, Marx actually stole his ideals of justice and of a provident society from Christianity by secularizing the Christian concept of the kingdom of God. His social altruism was tinged with a very Victorian desire for social justice for the working classes. Nobody can derive such an ideal from naturalistic evolutionism.

The Victorian era was characterized by the churches' struggle to develop a Christian socialism to bridge the gap between the haves and the have-nots.

This inequity had been greatly aggravated by the demographic shift of workers to the cities as part of the industrial revolution in England. Victorian socialism was originally a fruit of the Christian ideal of concern for the poor and disadvantaged. It began in the early attempts of Methodist ministers to encourage the workers to band together into trade unions for the purpose of demanding justice and better working conditions from the coal mine and factory owners. It was the efforts of Christians that forced the Victorian capitalists to face the human needs of their workers, mostly against their will.

Then came the secular socialist revolution on the continent and the Bolshevik movement in Russia. Once protected by a police state after the revolution of 1917, the Marxist leaders progressively slaughtered sixty million people over the next seventy years in the Soviet bloc alone, mostly because the victims were perceived as threats to the power elite of the Communist Party. Communism has been the direct cause of more useless and unjust human deaths than any other movement in history. (Pol Pot's program in Cambodia is a case in point.) For Marx, humans are just clever monkeys seeking a workers' paradise on earth, yet predetermined by economic forces. Once more, human nature is reduced to the evolution of economic factors.

4. *Skinner.* B. F. Skinner was raised in a Presbyterian home, but he seems to have retained only one thing from his Calvinistic background: he secularized Calvin's predestination into a form of mechanical determinism. Skinner held that all of our actions are strictly determined by previous states of affairs in our body chemistry, much as a woman is predestined to have a baby on a particular day once she gets pregnant. External stimuli also cause us to react in certain ways so that all of our actions are the result of responses to stimuli to the brain from within and without. The study of our humanness is simply the study of these stimuli and the kinds of responses they produce. If we change the stimuli, we can change the responses, training the pigeon or the teenager to behave differently. In other words, we modify behavior by modifying the stimuli. No explanation of the workings of human behavior can be made through postulating an inner "mind" or "soul" or "will," or any such internal state. This would be unscientific, since internal states cannot be observed—and therefore cannot be subjects of empirical study.

Skinner's humanism is apparent not merely in his atheism, but in his materialist epistemology. This involves a typical and rather naive form of empiricism which posits that only that which can be observed by the senses has scientific status. This has created endless dilemmas for behaviorists who, following Skinner, have tried to explain the rise of philosophical abstractions in the brain, such as the intricacies of language. (Skinnerians have had little success in adequately meeting the objections of linguistic philosophers such as Michael Polanyi and others.) Skinner's approach to human nature is a good example of an arbitrary reductionism—a human being is just a collection of responses to stimuli.

5. *Lorenz.* *Konrad Lorenz is another example of a scientist who tries to limit our understanding of what counts as an explanation by a set of arbitrary constraints found in his own biological discipline. He sees human beings as just another species evolved from prior animals and motivated by an inner state of aggression. This aggressive drive is variously channeled to produce social structures as well as individual behavior patterns.

The question naturally arises as to what produces and controls this process of channeling. How did it start? We can see readily enough how aggression can provide the diversity of human behavior, but whence its unity? How can considerations of aggression (or of mere stimulus and response) explain the coherence of a person's worldview? Consider the highly diverse mythological systems found in the literature of the Greeks, in the stories of the dreamtime among the Australian aborigines and in the vast Hindu literature of India. How is it that all three reveal the same complex of philosophical questions being asked and answered? These very different religions all deal with the famous *one-and-many problem, with the problem of creation and with the nature of life after death. Whence this pervasive unity in human thought? At face value, there seems to be nothing helpful about trying to reduce humanity to "just another aggressive beast." Its "just" not enough. Lorenz's humanism is nothing but the evolution of the animals writ large.

6. *Sartre.* *Jean-Paul Sartre, along with *Albert Camus, dominated the French existentialist scene well into the late fifties. As a naturalist (and an atheist), Sartre held that the world somehow explains itself to the observer. He concluded that there is no ultimate meaning to human existence apart from our individual commitment to a chosen ideal or course of action. We

create our own meaning, thereby offsetting our meaningless (or "absurd") lives by projecting our personal vision of significance onto the world by means of our metaphysically autonomous choices. This existentialist vision claims that we individually create our own natures by these autonomous choices. Our existence (vindicated as "authentic" by our choices) precedes our essence. There is no prior essence or human nature to which we are ontologically bound to conform either in ethics or teleology. Finally, Sartre said that humanity may be defined as "the project to be God." This, he contended, is what the claim to metaphysical autonomy really amounts to.

Sartre's humanism does more than put human consciousness at the center of the universe: it makes every successive human choice to be the creative origin of meaning. Thus, all human decisions have the same value morally. So when Sartre signed the Algerian Manifesto in 1957, most of his students abandoned him because he had taken a stand with the rest of the French intellectual world that the war with Algeria was an objectively unjust war, when moral objectivity was supposedly absurd on his own basis. Even Sartre's inconsistency with his own philosophy was finally absurd. Human nature is just an irrational choice that *my* choices must somehow mean something, when nothing really means anything.

All six of these representative theories about the essence of human nature presuppose that the theorists can autonomously make sense of experience without the background of a revelation from God. The principles for understanding the world of experience are looked for in the world itself.

7. *Christianity.* Stevenson begins by correctly stating that Christianity explains human meaning and significance in terms of our being created by God in his image to fulfill his eternal purposes. But this would require that final meaning come from God. Such a worldview is *supernaturalistic,* presupposing that there are two levels of reality, God and his creation—rather than just one, which is variously called "Being," "the One" or "the cosmos." The created world, and therefore mankind as a part of this creation, is only intelligible in terms of God and his prior interpretation of his own creation. The universe is incapable of interpreting itself, for it cannot be intelligible to itself in terms of itself alone. Contrary to Strato, the principles for understanding the world come from God and not from the world. God asks Strato of Lampsacus the

same question he asked Job: "Where were you when I made the world?"

However, Stevenson does not get too far along in his evaluation of Christianity before the syncretism begins. He says, "The most crucial point in the Christian understanding of human nature is the notion of freedom," which he oddly defines as "the ability to love." He then further defines this ability to love as being identical to "the image of God himself" (p. 40). The Christian view of our fundamental problem is that man "has sinned, he has misused his God-given free-will" (p. 41). Stevenson even insists that "although Pelagius was condemned as heretical, the doctrine of human free will must still remain as an essential element in Christian belief, difficult as it is to reconcile with the theory of the complete sovereignty of God" (p. 44). (It is refreshing to see someone observe correctly that the freewill theory is the basis of Pelagianism.) Stevenson further adds to the confusion over this "essential element" by quoting Ephesians 2:8 ("For it is by grace you have been saved, through faith— and this not from yourselves, it is the gift of God"), which he follows up with a puzzling assertion: "Yet, *just as clearly,* the Christian doctrine is that man's will is free; it is by his own choice that he sinned in the first place, and it must be by his own choice that he accepts God's salvation and works out its regeneration in his life" (p. 44, my emphasis).

There are two errors here. Although Stevenson says that free will is "just as clear" in the Bible as grace is, he gives no scriptural grounds for this claim. The second error involves the assumption that if a choice really belongs to an individual, it cannot be predestined at the same time. But how does he know this? He simply assumes that the Bible's view of human freedom really means metaphysical autonomy from divine predetermination, making predestination false. It is no wonder, then, that he repeatedly draws attention to the fact that free will and divine sovereignty cannot be brought into logical harmony. He correctly warns his readers that

> the standard thing to say, of course, is these are "mysteries" rather than "contradictions," that human reason cannot expect to be able to understand the infinite mysteries of God, that we only believe in faith what God has revealed of Himself to us. But the trouble with this kind of statement is that it can appeal only to those already disposed to believe, [and] it can do nothing to answer the genuine conceptual difficulties of the sceptic.

Stevenson clearly understands the dilemma, but he has no answer to the problem. Yet this contradiction is not found in the Bible, but rather in the perverse determination of so many Christians to combine the Bible's revelation of God's sovereignty with the false assumption of free will. Like many other freewill theorists, Stevenson points out that exhortations to repent and believe fill the Bible (p. 44), but he offers no evidence that this proves the freedom of the will. He might try to escape this criticism by asserting that the term *Christianity* usually includes the essential teachings of orthodox theology, as well as what the Bible makes explicit. If so, he would thereby equate Christianity with its most common syncretistic error: the acceptance of tradition on an equal footing with Scripture. This in turn would mean that, despite its tremendous influence, Christianity really has nothing unique to offer the world. I doubt if Stevenson wants to go that far.

Stevenson's humanism is basically the same as the others he has considered. When he describes Christianity, he simply imposes his own views on the description, converting Christianity into another form of autonomist humanism. He never questions the central assumption of the autonomy of human consciousness that is common to all the positions he describes. Even Skinner, who, as a psychological determinist, formally rejects free will, still reasons as if he can comprehend the world of human behavior without God's prior interpretation. But this dogma of the autonomy of the human intellect is the breaking point with a consistent concept of God as Creator.

The Biblical Idea of Freedom

The Bible does not define freedom in terms of an ontological property of the will or intellect; much less does it discuss how to balance human freedom against the encroachments of a sovereign Creator. For the writers of the Bible, freedom is one of three things, which may be summarized as follows:

a. It is originally the freedom of the captive who is recaptured or purchased back (redeemed) from the enemy. We see this concept in the freedom of God's people after the exodus and then as enjoyed in their own land. This is the sense that the Pharisees intended when they boasted to Jesus that they "have never yet been enslaved to anyone" (Jn 8:33 NASB).

b. Second, freedom is the condition of being spiritually free from demonic and idolatrous religious influences when we are obedient to God's Law. Parallel to this is slavery or bondage to sin and its results because of our disobedience.

c. The third meaning is the one emphasized in the New Testament, which combines the previous two from the Old Testament. Sinners are thought of as being enslaved to sin in two senses. Sinners are first under the law's moral condemnation, from which they can be freed in Christ through justification. Then, as sinners under the law's judgment, they are slaves to sin itself, for sin is thought of as a moral power within us (Paul calls it "the flesh") that renders us incapable of spiritual obedience and from which we can be freed only through regeneration and sanctification. The first of these is a forensic relationship of guilt from which we are legally declared free when the law has been satisfied. The second is a moral incapacity from which we are progressively freed by the enabling power of the Holy Spirit as we grow in grace.

Jesus therefore says that mere descent from Abraham does not guarantee freedom, political or spiritual. Only "if the Son sets you free, you will be free indeed" (Jn 8:36). Paul says in Romans 6:17-18 that it is only when we are "set free" by the obedience of faith do we become "slaves to righteousness." Only the power of the Holy Spirit in the life of the believer can free us for continuing obedience to God (2 Cor 3:15-18) so that we will continually be renewed by God's power into the image of Christ (Rom 1:1-2). Paul describes himself as a "bond-servant of Christ Jesus" precisely because he had been freed from the dominion of sin by accepting the dominion of Christ. For Paul, freedom is simply the state of being ethically obedient to God. It is an ethical relationship, not an innate ontological attribute. Only in willing enslavement to God's will are we truly free in the biblical sense. Only then can our being be fulfilled, our choices righteous, our knowledge truth and our destiny joy.

The theme of freedom through redemption from sin is found throughout the Bible in many contexts, and the mere fact that the New Testament spiritualizes and internalizes the earlier conceptions of freedom does not alter their permanent literal value as showing how God cares about political, economic, sexual and racial injustice. The fully articulated doctrine of God's kingdom must include the total picture of the redemption of fallen societies and of civilization, which is a major focal point of the prophets. Nevertheless, biblical freedom at any level is tied to faith and obedience as the fruit is to the root. It is a function of ethical submission to our Maker. The philosophical antithesis of biblical freedom is the delusion of metaphysical autonomy and the resultant slavery to sin that it guarantees.

What Is Man That Thou Art Mindful of Him?

All of the views described by Stevenson tend to reduce human nature to one limited aspect of reality. Humans are "just" economic animals, "just" bundles of reflexes, "just" moments of autonomous awareness in the flow of being. They are reductionistic, not comprehensive, in their vision of human reality. They each attempt to describe human nature in terms of a particular scientistic or reductionistic worldview.

Every worldview, whether religious or philosophical, must say something about our place in the universe. Accordingly, the Bible also has an anthropology. Stevenson is right to identify our creation in God's image as central to the Christian's vision of human nature. But the concept must be filled out from the Bible, and the arbitrary assertion that the image must include a free will that is logically incompatible with God's own attributes is not a good start. What *does* the Bible say about the *imago Dei?

In Psalm 8:4-8, we are reminded that we are very important to God. In his wisdom and mercy, he has made human beings "but a little lower than God" (RV) and crowned them above the rest of the creation. God made Adam and Eve to "have dominion over the works of [his] hands," however imperfectly this task of vice-regency has been carried out. Clearly, the psalmist considers the gift of dominion to be a special mark of our humanity. Job asked the same question in a state of deep anguish and depression (Job 7:17-18). He realized that he was a sinner, but he also knew he was nowhere near as bad as his treatment at God's hands indicated. He never once tried to pretend that these things were just accidental; rather, he insisted that God had done it all.

Job had been incredibly prosperous, but now he had to declare, "The LORD gave, and the LORD hath taken away; blessed be the name of the LORD" (1:21 KJV). However, the full force of the disaster had not yet hit him. He was not yet ready to curse the day he was born, although that would come soon (3:1-19). It is important to note that Job's question about what it means to be human is prompted by the terrible things that descended on his relatively innocent soul. King David gives an answer to this question in Psalm 8 that expands the context and leads the questioner back to Genesis. But a crucial perspective has been established in this psalm: God intends to glorify himself through the creation of humankind, making them kings of creation despite the disabilities of the fallen human condition.

The Genesis account records God's blueprint for humanity: "Let us make man in our image, after our likeness: and let them have dominion. . . . So God created man in his own image, in the image of God created he him; male and female created he them" (1:26-27 KJV). While the exact nature of the image is not spelled out in this initial passage, several elements are certainly implied in the details that follow, in the accounts of the creation of Adam and of Eve and their subsequent fall. Certainly their creation as two people to complement each other's gifts was immediately recognized by Adam himself upon Eve's creation. Not only was she made of his own substance (2:23-24), but she was, unlike the animals, able to share the task of personal dominion as his equal, as his colleague ($k^c neḡdô$, v. 20).

We also observe that the task of dominion was itself an element of the image, although it was relational, not ontological. That is, it could be lost without Adam and Eve becoming less human. Some attributes of the image were essential to Adam's humanity, and were therefore shared equally with Eve. These included, among many others, the natural attributes of personality such as rationality, the use of language, the ability to make tools, the conceptions of time and numbers, a sense of purpose and the capacity to give and receive love. In Colossians 3:10 and its parallel passage in Ephesians 4:23-24, we discover four relational elements of the image that are said to be in process of being renewed in the born-again life: righteousness, holiness, truth and knowledge. The first relates to our acts, the second to our innermost heart, the third to our mind and the last to our ongoing experiential acquaintance with God as we learn to respond to him in the flow of life. However, there seems to be nothing rigid about these distinctions.

An important element of God's image in us is our awareness of God. This is something no animal displays. When a dog is in trouble, it does not pray— it just runs away. John Calvin called the innate consciousness of God's presence the "seed of religion" and the "sense of divinity." *Blaise Pascal observed that there is a "God-shaped hole" in the human heart that only God can fill, and St. Augustine confessed that "our hearts are restless until they find their rest in Thee, O God." This awareness of God takes on an added significance when we note the relation of the divine being to ethics. In the New Testament, the words for "consciousness" and "conscience" are the same Greek term. Our innate sense that God is there flows over naturally into an awareness that he is also the "Judge of all the earth" who will "do right," as Abraham said in Genesis 18:25. Paul makes much of this inner sense of right and wrong in Romans 1 and 2, basing God's future judgment of the unsaved upon it.

Two passages teach that even after the Fall, the image of God is still present to distinguish us from the animals. In Genesis 9:6, the death penalty for murder is based on the image of God in fallen humanity. Likewise in James 3:9, the unruly tongue is rebuked for cursing "men, who have been made in God's likeness." It seems, then, that there are elements of the image that survived the Fall (the ontological elements), and elements that were lost (the relational elements). We are seriously crippled in spiritual matters by the Fall, but we never cease to be human. Even the monstrous apostates described in Jude verse 10 are merely said to be "*like* unreasoning animals" (10). They are not said to *become* animals. The ontological elements remain to define us as human beings, while the relational elements are renewed in regeneration and growth in grace.

When God created Adam, he also had the future incarnation of Christ in mind, for Jesus was "the Lamb that was slain from the creation of the world" (Rev 13:8). In other words, Adam's nature was created in such a way that the person of the Son of God could have perfect personal expression through him in the Lamb's incarnation. Accordingly, Jesus is called "the image of God" in 2 Corinthians 4:4. Again, in 3:18, Paul describes our progressive transformation into the image of Christ. Other passages also use this model of our growth in Christian virtues as we are being renewed into the image of Christ (Rom 8:29; Gal 4:19; 2 Pet 1:4; 1 Jn 3:2).

So, What *Is* the Meaning of Life?

Since we are creatures, our meaning originates in the eternal intention of God for his creation. No finite thing has any meaning apart from its place in God's plan. This holds true for atoms, flowers, pencils or the history of Romania. It also holds true for my personal meaning as an individual human being in God's plan. The Good Shepherd knows each of his own sheep by name (Jn 10:3). This is the biblical response to the persistent question "What is the meaning of life?" The meaning of everything is logically identical to God's intention for it. Every fact and thing and relation and event in the creation has a place in God's eternal plan, right down to the toss of a coin as the soldiers gambled for Jesus' tunic (Jn 19:23-24), thereby literally fulfilling a tiny prediction in Psalm 22:18, a prophecy by then about a thousand years old.

So, to experience the meaning of life fully, we must trust and obey God as he unveils his eternal purposes for us day by day. Only the God of the Bible can dispel Sartre's sense of absurdity, fill Pascal's God-shaped hole and give us Augustine's peaceful heart-rest of eternity even as we live in time. Only then can we realize that we don't need to devote ourselves to aggression, to the establishment of a dictatorship of the proletariat, to the struggle up the great chain of being or to manipulatively conditioning other people's behavior. Instead, we can experience God's renewal of his image in us as we learn to trust and obey him, thereby stepping day by day into those "good works, which God prepared beforehand, that we should walk in them" (Eph 2:10, NASB).

Throughout all the biblical references to the image of God, its loss in the Fall and its restoration in Christ, not a hint appears that the image necessarily includes anything recognizable as free will. The Bible simply does not use the idea of free will as an explanatory category at all. *Autexousia,* the right and ability to exercise one's own authority, is a Greek myth designed originally to secure human beings some dignity and protection from the arbitrary absurdities of the gods.

Clutching at Straws

The freewill theorist may object that though the Bible does not mention free will, it does not mention cats either. This surely does not prove cats did not exist in the ancient world, for we know they did: the Egyptians worshiped them in their temples. Neither is the Trinity mentioned by name, but we know that it is a good summary of what the Bible teaches about the three Persons of the Godhead. So why not free will too?

This argument is inconsequential. To begin with, the question is not whether the term *free will* appears in the text of some translations (for it certainly does), but whether we can reasonably exegete the libertarian concept from those texts that might seem to contain it. We will see in chapter nine that this cannot be done. Also, the doctrine of the Trinity is a mere summary of the six basic propositions that make up the idea: (1) the Father is God, (2) the Son is God, and (3) the Holy Spirit is God, while (4) the Father is not the Son, (5) the Son is not the Spirit, and (6) the Father is not the Spirit. Each of these six truths can be explicitly exegeted from particular texts. The first three describe the unity of God's deity, while the last three describe the diversity of the three persons of that deity. Collectively, these propositions make up the essential framework of the doctrine of the Trinity. No such group of doctrines necessitates the conclusion that the Bible teaches the theory of free will.

Conclusion
We have seen that despite the many false views of human nature circulating in the world of ideas, the image of God is indeed an important part of the biblical doctrine of human nature. But the image of God does not involve us in the notion of free will or imply the Arminian idea of free will. For the writers of the Bible, freedom is a fruit of the renewing presence of the Holy Spirit in the soul; "and where the Spirit of the Lord is, there is freedom" (2 Cor 3:17).

We turn now to the next important epoch in the Bible's development of human nature, the Fall in Genesis 3.

Further Reading
Seven Theories of Human Nature (New York: Oxford University Press, 1974) by Leslie Stevenson is a helpful secular survey.

One of the best early books on human nature is John Laidlaw's *The Bible Doctrine of Man* (Edinburgh: T & T Clark). My copy is dated 1895, but it has been reprinted recently. Laidlaw has a valuable refutation of the tripartite theory, but he assumes free will without proof, then concludes correctly that on the basis of this axiom that the origin of evil is a mystery.

Gordon Clark's *The Biblical Doctrine of Man* (Jefferson: Trinity, 1984) is especially helpful, while C. S. Lewis's *The Abolition of Man* (London: Macmillan, 1947), Anthony Hoekema's *Created in God's Image* (Grand Rapids, Mich.: Eerdmans, 1986) and G. C. Berkouwer's *Man: The Image of God* (Grand Rapids, Mich.: Eerdmans, 1962) are also instructive. Lewis had an Arminian view of free will and is mainly concerned with the maintenance of classical Christian educational standards for the preservation of a safe human society. He describes the pagan alternative in *That Hideous Strength* (New York: Macmillan, 1987).

All the standard systematic theologies have a section on anthropology, including the volumes by Charles Hodge, Herman Hoeksema, Louis Berkhof and J. Oliver Buswell. Many Reformed (Calvinistic) theologians are not clear on the idea of free will, however, and sound partly like Arminians. Gordon Clark wrote an exposition of the Westminster Confession titled *What Do Presbyterians Believe?* (Philadelphia: Presbyterian & Reformed, 1965), which contains a commentary on chapters four and nine.

The influential *Institutio Theologicae Elencticae* of Francis Turretin is now being published in English, with two volumes currently completed as *Institutes of Elenctic Theology* (Phillipsburg, N.J.: Presbyterian & Reformed, 1992). There is an excellent discussion of false theories of free will in the first volume (pp. 659-85).

4

Apostate Autonomism: The Fall & the Autonomist Theoria

*M*odern liberal scholars want us to believe that the Bible's accounts of the creation and the Fall are just ancient myths, enshrining deep insights into the human condition but having no significant historical content. For example, Leslie Stevenson suggests in his *Seven Theories of Human Nature* that the story of the Fall is not an account of a real event, although he seems to allow that it is full of philosophical implications (p. 41).

Strictly speaking, however, the Bible itself seems to intend that we understand the decisions made in the Garden of Eden as real events that set the scene for the entire history of humanistic thought down to the present day. From Isaiah's defense of monotheism in his refutation of idolatry to Paul's account of the slide of fallen culture into moral chaos in Romans and his demolition of the Hellenistic religious worldview in the Areopagus address found in Acts, we are given clear illustrations of this history, and they all presuppose the literal truth of the Genesis story. They are all in agreement with the biblical view of sin and its results.

Before the Fall

Genesis 2 expands on the brief statement regarding the appearance of human beings found in 1:26-31. This second chapter tells us that God put the man he had created into a protected garden to look after it. Adam immediately began the task of understanding the environment around him, starting with the classification of the more accessible animals. None of these animals was much like Adam, however, and we are told that God created Eve out of Adam's own being to be "a helper suitable for him" (2:18-22). The two of them then pressed on together with the task of establishing the kingdom of God on earth in the form of this little Edenic "pilot plant." Presumably, if they had not gotten so badly sidetracked, success in the garden would have been followed by ventures into the larger world as their family grew—as God's righteous kingdom unfolded under their capable stewardship. But in the course of their labors, they encountered an intruder in the garden.

God had told them that they could eat from all the trees in the garden except the one in the center, referred to as the "tree of the knowledge of good and evil" (v. 17). God had apparently decided to place in a prominent spot a material example of what he meant by a moral sanction, by the difference between right and wrong. They were specifically told not to eat the fruit of this particular tree. The sanction was as certain as the identity of the tree itself; if they ate its fruit they would certainly die (vv. 16-17). Death would be certain because God had made it inevitable. Another tree nearby, the "tree of life," seems to have had the potential for conferring physical immortality on them, but they may not have ventured that far before the Fall. In the significance of the two trees, God had defined and illustrated what he means by "good" and "evil." Obedience and all that flows from it is good, and disobedience together with all that flows from it is evil.

When the serpent raised the issue of the moral sanction with Eve (and we are told in 3:6 that Adam was with her at this moment), the discussion began with an apparently innocent quest for clarification. If what God had said was clear enough to Adam and Eve, it was not so clear to the serpent. The Hebrew for "every tree" (KJV) in verse 1 is ambiguous and might mean either "all" the trees or "any particular" tree. In her answer, Eve introduces *two modifications* in the supposed interests of clarification. Her response ("God has said, 'You shall not eat from it or touch it, lest you die,' " Gen 3:3 NASB) contains two errors.

First, God had not said that they could not touch the tree. There was nothing in his command to prevent them from cutting it down to make a house from the wood, examining the chemical composition of the leaves or using the flowers for decoration. They were merely told not to eat its fruit. God did not remove it from scientific study or industrial use. It was still within the scope of their stewardship responsibility. Eve's simple addition to what God had commanded brought the whole meaning and scope of their vice-regency into question.

Second, God had said that in the day they ate from this tree, they would "surely die." The Hebrew idiom is one of repetitive emphasis (literally, "dying, you shall die"). It was as if God was explaining that death would be experienced as a process terminating in an event. The process was predetermined to start the moment they ate the forbidden fruit and would continue until the result was completed. But Eve weakened this statement of divinely ordered certainty into a mere possibility, a mere contingency ("*lest* you die").

These two alterations, one an addition and the other a diminishment, carry very heavy philosophical freight. The error of adding to or taking away from the words of the Lord is addressed again in Deuteronomy 4:2 and Proverbs 30:5-6. In the very last chapter of the Bible this danger has still not been forgotten. There we are again warned not to diminish or add to the Word of God (Rev 22:18-19). Adding to God's words implies that they are not sufficiently clear as they stand, and removing some of them implies that our minds are capable of autonomously deciding that God may possibly be wrong about some details. Even before taking the fruit, Eve had already begun to shift her reference point from God's interpretation to her own. She had already begun to live by bread alone rather than by every word coming out of the mouth of God. Eve made herself the origin of meaning for selection from and application of God's words to her own situation. She separated the *meaning* of the words from the *text* of the revelation itself. From that point on, the would-be autonomous mind of humanity would cheerfully allow that a text may be God's, but would also assert that "we all have our own interpretation" of what it means—the text may be objective, but its meaning is subjective. The doctrinal downgrade had begun.

At this point, Satan provided a departure of his own. He began with a question, but now that he had established that God's interpretation is only one of many, he expressly contradicted what God had said: "You will not surely die" (3:4). The supplementary justification for this opinion is equally interesting. He appealed to something he claimed that "God knows," but had not disclosed. God had apparently hidden from Adam and Eve that when they ate the fruit, they would experience a true enlightenment. This in turn was expanded to mean that they would become like God himself in their knowledge. This is the first example of what we might call "the gnostic principle of religious truth." That is, alongside any public and literal revelation God might give, there is always a secretive religion that is necessary for the truly spiritual interpretation of the literal revelation. The serpent led them to believe that beside what God had admitted up front, there was also an interior secret they needed to know so they could be "like God," knowing truth autonomously, with themselves as the reference point, *just as God does.* Satan thereby invited Adam and Eve to enter into the autonomy of theoretical thought, to become their own origin of meaning, to be the first to interpret their own experience of reality. They could give themselves permission to create their own reality by choosing their own future. Humanity would at last come of age.

There Are Only Two Worldviews

The two contradictory propositions "You will surely die" and "You will not surely die" imply two entirely different and incompatible *theorias,* or ways of looking at reality. We cannot explore all their ramifications at this point, but their disjunction on the question of human autonomy must be attended to here.

The first proposition implies that God has already determined what the future will be for anyone who eats the forbidden fruit, for God controls the future. And God has predetermined that the soul that sins "shall surely die." The future is fixed for sinners by God.

But the future is also fixed for those who are obedient, for those who live by every word of God's revelation. They will also experience a predetermined future of ever-expanding blessings as they enter by their obedience into the experience of unfolding all the possibilities of God's creation as ordered by his eternal and creatorial Logos. They will experience the manifold wisdom of God as they reflect on the thoughts of their Lord in their own minds. Every choice they make will freely express their desire to worship and serve their Creator. Their hearts will freely conform to the revealed will of God, fulfilling the aspiration of the Stoic philosopher to be in full harmony with nature. But instead of the fallen world with which *Marcus Aurelius sought conformity, Adam and Eve would have lived in loving conformity to an unfallen and thus sinless Cosmos in which their intellects would have been informed only by the Logos himself. For them, progress would not have been a struggle up the great chain of being with the survival of the fittest, but a true workers' paradise in which the gifts and aspirations of all would have been fulfilled in the happy productivity of all. The little family in the Garden of Eden would have been eventually expanded by simple obedience into the mighty civilization of the kingdom of God on earth. In this scenario, *freedom* means ethical submission to God and the resulting blessings of personal fulfillment. It does not mean the autonomy of the will, an idea never encountered in the Bible.

The second proposition, "You will not surely die," implies that the future is a realm of pure possibility to be determined by human beings from existential moment to existential moment. The first implication of this proposition is not only that God's revelation is not perfectly clear, but that it is at least partly false, if not simply ludicrous. In this view, what God really wants is Adam and Eve to grow up to maturity by autonomously reinterpreting their experience with themselves as their own origin of meaning. God does not really control and determine Adam's future. Rather, God has actually limited himself to give Adam room to move freely. Freedom means self-determination, not submission to an arbitrary external standard. True discipline must come from "within." True enlightenment is the existential moment-by-moment realization of metaphysical autonomy. Therefore, people should live by the maxims "Know thyself" and "To thine own self be true," for the unexamined revelation is not worth believing.

The subsequent Bible history is an account of what happened from God's point of view as things unfolded out of this initial act of disobedience. The following centuries of humanistic philosophy were implied in that original act of defection from the coherence of the revealed Logos. From that point on, fallen thought would necessarily emerge according to an unavoidable internal dynamic.

Absolute Rationalism

To be certain that God was wrong about "surely dying," Adam would have needed exhaustive knowledge and a correspondingly exhaustive control of the future—omniscience and omnipotence. Thus, humankind would have had to be divine. For them to know even one thing would have involved knowing everything, for in a finite universe everything is relative to everything else and can only be understood in terms of the surrounding world. The human consciousness would have to be capable of making all the facts of experience coherently intelligible in terms of its own innate, logically explicated interrelationships. All of these relationships are in principle intelligible to the human mind.

But this approach would imply and require an ultimate rationalism. The observer presumes that the world is ultimately one, and its unity accessible by logic. In the period just before Socrates, this position was articulated by Parmenides with his assertion that "Being is One." He based his analysis of reality on an early expression of the law of contradiction: "Being exists, and non-being does not." Parmenides thought that being is an ultimate unity, in principle penetrable by the human mind by the use of logic.

Absolute Irrationalism

At the same time, the assumption that God does not really control reality would necessitate that, in and of itself, the creation is largely indeterminate. No one could predict what the future might bring, because no one (including whatever gods there be) could know what a truly free will might decide. We would need to keep an open mind, of course, for every freewill decision is in principle unpredictable. If we were to experience the future as a realm of pure possibility, it would seem that both God and humanity together would be surrounded by an indeterminate being-itself. Any predictive proposition about the future might turn out to be falsified by events. With William James, we would face a "blooming, buzzing confusion," and even the laws of logic could turn out to be just pragmatic conveniences of the moment, mere conventions of Western culture. And if all facts were relative, what would they be relative *to* at any moment? And behind whatever order we managed to identify, and ahead of the kaleidoscope of current time-bound choice making, would lie the vast realm of indeterminate being-itself, the ultimate mystery of it all.

This approach implies an ultimate *irrationalism. The observer assumes that behind the world lies an ultimate many, manifesting itself through the chance variations of the data. This position was articulated in the period before Socrates by Heraclitus, who postulated that "everything flows," and that therefore "you can't step into the same river twice, for new waters are ever flowing in upon you." For Heraclitus, being was an ultimate diversity, a chance warfare of oscillating opposites.

The Problem of the One and the Many

Because she started with herself as the finite origin of meaning, Eve stepped automatically into the fundamental dilemma of finite consciousness. She actually chose a reference point that needed to be an absolute unity and an absolute diversity at the same moment. An absolute rationalism requires an absolutely coherent and unified being as its subject, and an absolute irrationalism implies an absolutely incoherent and diversified being as its subject. Being-itself must be both an ultimate one and an ultimate many at the same moment of observation. Yet both cannot be simultaneously correct, for there can only be one "ultimate." And in order for this newly chosen finite reference point to be sufficient in practice, it is forced to interpret reality first in terms of an ultimate unity, and then in terms of an equally ultimate diversity.

For the succeeding millennia, epistemology oscillated between the one and the many, between rationalistic and irrationalistic movements and opinions, finally settling into an existential fog when the possibilities of reason and the probabilities of the data had been canvassed. Ontology tended to project itself onto God himself, alternating between various forms of pantheism on the one hand, hoping to do justice to the one, and polytheism on the other, in order to explain the many. Ethics likewise fixed on a set of rigid standards at times, and on a policy of permissiveness at other times. Our sense of purpose first tried a series of monarchist states, then dissolved into a succession of wandering tribes. A fulfilled teleology was pushed off into the dreamtime, to

Valhalla, and finally to the ultimate and inevitable socialist workers' paradise, the kingdom come on earth, finally brought to realization by a humanity that had come of age.

The problem of unity versus diversity would manifest itself in every field of human endeavor as successive civilizations sought to fulfill their own public vision of the ideal society. At the same time, those in power would seek to use the state to fulfill their own private visions of happiness. This usually meant war between local tribes and between totalitarian states. History, like philosophy and religion, became little more than the story of the sequence of unsuccessful efforts to bring unity to the state and meaning to the individual, the alternation of the dominant one with the uncontrollable many.

Because a finite reference point is always insufficient to cope with ultimacy, the one and the many can never, in principle, be reconciled at the finite level. In other words, sinners cannot save themselves epistemologically. They can never settle on whether reason or facts must have precedence, or whether God is one or many. Their best and biggest political programs tend to develop into totalitarian dictatorships. Sometimes a pragmatic balance between the one and the many could be held for centuries, as it was in the Harappa culture of the Indus valley from about 2500-1550 B.C. But the price was stagnation, and the system would eventually become prey to aggression from without.

The Great Chain of Being

Once it was realized that the problem is in principle insoluble, the question ceased to be how to solve it and moved on to how to contain it. The problem concerning what counts as a true revelation still remained, but it was thought that perhaps this could be handled by an appeal to the realm of the spirits. With this hope that spirituality might succeed where the intellect had failed, the occult became the recourse of a confused humanity. Mysticism took over where the mind had fallen silent, and it was hoped that we would be lifted to a higher plane, experiencing higher dimensions. A newer and more comprehensive vision was needed to replace the original primeval revelation that all had shared since Eden and the flood.

The biblical model of the new primeval solution was the historical tower of Babel, a world program of unification around a common symbol system.

At the top would be the tokens of our aspirations for higher realms. Worshiping at the top of the tower, untrammeled by more solid realities, humanity could aspire to explore strange new worlds of the occult.

God's answer to this new leviathan was simple enough: destroy the unity of the symbol system, and all would grind to a halt as culture fragmented into survivalism in the Gentile jungle. The disintegration of modern liberalism as it encounters the acids of postmodernist criticism repeats this process in the modern university during our own decade.

Despite this ancient failure of a political unification of humankind, there is one vision of importance that reappears again and again among the bubbling mass of boring and repetitive revelations from the spirit world. All the higher powers, all the ancestral and familiar spirits, all the ascended masters and all the gurus and avatars are in harmony about one thing. Whether we listen to a Victorian séance or to Edgar Cayce, to the Mahabharata or to the Upanishads, to stories of the Golden Age of Greece or to the myths of the Babylonians, to Madame Blavatsky or to *A Course in Miracles,* "reality" turns out to be a series of eternally repeating cycles of evolving being, a perpetual efflux of the many from the one and back again, a vast consecutive chain of being ever unfolding from itself and returning upon itself, from eternity to eternity. The "wizards that peep, and that mutter" of Isaiah 8:19-20 (KJV) and the wise daemon that Socrates depended on all seem to have the same ultimate vision of what being is. In his famous survey of mysticism, Aldous Huxley gathered up the representative visionary pictures from the religious past into the unified vision he called *The Perennial Philosophy* (1945). (Arthur Lovejoy examines its impact on Western philosophy in a work titled *The Great Chain of Being* [1957].)

Satan knows better than anyone that the problem of who or what is ultimate cannot be solved by any compromise, but that one side or the other must be completely vanquished. Therefore, at any cost, he must find ways to use God's creation against him, lest that frightening prophecy about the seed of the woman crushing his head finally come to pass. The consensus of his followers has always been that if the problem of the one and the many cannot be solved, it can certainly be contained simply by turning it upon its head, so that the absolute One occupies the top rung of the ladder and the absolute

Many the bottom rung. By this simple move, a great scale of nature, a chain of being, a tree of life, can be constructed to maintain the continuity between the two incompatible ultimates. Such a structured vision of being-in-general can be made to include all particular beings, each having a definite place on the scale. Adam can be placed on the middle rung, with Eve on the rung just below him. This vision of reality can then be assumed to be the order of creation.

The assumption of metaphysical autonomy that caused the apostasy of Adam and Eve finally led to a new *theoria,* a worldview or way of beholding reality that is not only required by the suggestions of the serpent in the garden, but seems to surface repeatedly throughout the ensuing religious occultism out of which fallen philosophy has since developed. In Eden, the divine theoria was replaced by the demonic theoria. From then on, apostate autonomism would lead by its own internal dynamic to faith in a demonic worldview.

It is this sinful worldview that Paul described as the great human problem in Romans 1, which he confronted in the sophisticates of Athens and to which he gives the gospel of Christ as an answer in 1 Corinthians 1 and 2. The kingdoms of Israel and Judah confronted it in the ancient idolatries of the Canaanite tribes. Paul confronted it in his own day as the cultural philosophy of Hellenism. Luther confronted it in the Roman Catholic *hierarchy. Missionaries confront it in Hinduism. Today's evangelicals encounter it in everything from the fantasy novels of Charles Williams and C. S. Lewis to the occult visions of the New Age, and even in the hierarchicalist defense of the subordination of women in the more conservative churches.

Naturally, Philo combined it with his first-century Judaism, the pseudo-Dionysius, Erigena and then Thomas Aquinas combined it with early medieval theology, and today's Christians combine it in syncretism with elements of the Reformation gospel. It is invariably assumed rather than proved—and is much too useful to question. Even a solid, commonsense evangelical such as C. S. Lewis constantly used it as the bridge from revelation to the unbeliever's imagination.

There Are Only Two Religions

It turns out in the long run that questions concerning philosophy, worldview and religion are all addressing the same topics. The problems of one are the problems of the others. In particular, the religion that evangelicals used to think of as a private realm of personal faith and devotion turns out today to be the public arena of church versus state, just as it was in the Middle Ages. The points at which the state most seriously threatens Christianity are still education, revenue and public justice. These kinds of issues never change as long as the one faces the many in fallen cultures. As the tide of the Christian moral consensus ebbs around us, the occult basis of the non-Christian worldview is increasingly exposed, and syncretistic believers discover that they have been fishing from someone else's jetty all these years.

In humanistic philosophy, the areas of ontology, epistemology, ethics and teleology (or, being, knowing, morals and purpose) are all uniform in their testimony against Christian orthodoxy. They all faithfully reflect their dependence on, and contribution to, the apostate worldview or the demonic theoria. They all operate out of a relativistic, pragmatic and immanentist starting point in assuming that the human mind is ultimate. They agree with Strato of Lampsacus that the principles for understanding the world must be found in the world itself, and not in a God "outside of time." We dare not get our presuppositions from the Bible, lest some alert pagan notice that we are all standing in the same created universe, and accuse us of circular reasoning, as if only the skeptic can have objective truth.

In humanistic religion we are told on the one hand that all views are equally legitimate, but on the other hand, that evangelical orthodoxy must be excluded at all costs. New Age Wicca is an acceptable form of religion to be studied in a state school, but Calvinism is not. Eastern yogic meditation can be used, but not Christian prayer. The point, of course, is that *every form of human spirituality may be comprehended and tolerated as part of the apostate world vision (the demonic theoria) except historical Christianity.*

At least the really self-conscious humanists have one thing right: they know who the ultimate enemy is. They recognize him by the fish on his T-shirt. They use his son Calvin as the worst possible case of what happens when the Bible is made the *basis* of education instead of just one traditional option to be interpreted humanistically.

Arminianism and Calvinism

We have seen that these two historical terms are just convenient labels for two very different approaches to Christian doctrine that have taken various forms, some more consistent and some less, in the history of the churches. My point in the foregoing analysis is to provide a context for the reader to decide where the Arminian departure from the Reformation doctrine of God, human nature and grace really leads. It is my view that Arminian thought is best understood historically, as a compromise of the Reformation gospel with the humanistic motif of the autonomy of the human consciousness flowing out of the ancient pagan learning that had just been rediscovered in the Renaissance and that was soon to come to maturity in the Enlightenment.

As a compromise position Arminianism is necessarily unstable, for its underlying assumptions about reality are compromised by the Greeks' one-and-many problematic. Accordingly, Arminians, like Catholics, invariably tolerate chain-of-being thought and even (like the pseudo-Dionysius, who was a Neo-Platonist, or C. S. Lewis, who was not) write as if it were essential to Christianity. Those compromised with this vision are also less able and less willing to criticize the hierarchical views of human relationships in society, church and family that have always flowed from the assumption of a great chain of being.

In the next five chapters we approach the question of the degree to which Arminianism actually reflects a defective form of the gospel as originally understood by the Reformers, and, as J. I. Packer once put it, as found in the Bible "in plain text after plain text."

Further Reading

For the way in which Christians have developed compromised and therefore inconsistent forms of Calvinism, see Cornelius Van Til, *A Christian Theory of Knowledge* (Grand Rapids, Mich.: Baker, 1969) and *A Survey of Christian Epistemology* (Ripon, Calif.: Den Dulk, 1969).

For a discussion of what a "worldview" is and how it influences a culture, see E. M. W. Tillyard's *The Elizabethan World Picture* (New York: Random House, 1969). This marvelous little book was designed to explain to English literature students how the chain-of-being vision controlled the intellectual atmosphere in the days of Shakespeare. Tillyard and C. S. Lewis were colleagues during Lewis's Oxford years, so this work provides a great shortcut to understanding Lewis better too.

Two excellent books on the principal worldviews are Brian J. Walsh and J. Richard Middleton's *The Transforming Vision* (Downers Grove, Ill.: InterVarsity Press, 1984) and James Sire's *The Universe Next Door,* 2nd ed. (Downers Grove, Ill.: InterVarsity Press, 1988). Francis Schaeffer's *Escape from Reason* (Downers Grove, Ill.: InterVarsity Press, 1968) was important because it showed evangelicals how the worldview of the Christian West had changed. Its cultural manifestations and results were canvassed with illustrative material in the book and video series *How Should We Then Live?* (Old Tappan, N.J.: Revell, 1976).

5
Salvation as God's Choice to Save: All Is of Grace

*B*efore we consider the five key doctrines of the Calvinistic view of salvation, we will compare Charles Haddon Spurgeon's vision of the gospel with the doctrines actually taught by the Remonstrants and the Arminians with whom John Owen contended in the seventeenth century. Spurgeon has been chosen not only because he was a solid Calvinist and highly evangelistic in his presentation of the gospel but also because he is both far enough behind us to be a hero to most evangelicals, and yet modern enough to have realized that Arminian theology had no power to resist the secularization of doctrine already visible in the British Baptist Union in the 1870s and 1880s. Spurgeon realized what the modern liberal movement really meant for the life of the churches. He saw clearly that theological liberalism was capitalizing on the Arminians' plea for a broad doctrinal toleration among evangelicals, bringing about a Babylonian captivity to the Enlightenment. Their ideal was a Christianity without binding creedal formulations of any kind.

Charles Spurgeon and "God Saves Sinners"
What did Spurgeon think the essence of the gospel was, and what did he think

of the freewill theory? Once when seeking a short summary of the Reformation gospel message, Spurgeon hit upon the expression "God saves sinners." For him, this was the hinge on which all else swung.

God, sovereign in eternity, wills or decrees (that is, he plans, intends, decides and foreordains) to save some of those who are to be enslaved by sin through the fall of Adam. This means that it is God who initiates the program and the process of salvation, rather than the sinner. Salvation is therefore by grace alone, since the sinner, being finite, does not have the ontological standpoint in eternity even to plan saving acts, let alone the sovereign power to effect them. On his own divine initiative from eternity, God interferes in history to initiate and consummate all that is necessary to save rebel souls.

Salvation is a *gift,* and the sinner contributes nothing but the empty hand that reaches out to receive it. Even this simple act of faith itself is by divine initiation, not by autonomous self-generation. Saving faith is itself a gift, not a natural capacity by which we simply decide to focus on Christ as an object of trust like we do with other objects (e.g., a chair, our parents, the telephone). From the first feeble stirrings of a desire to know God in some vague sense, through all the steps necessary to link a soul savingly to God through Christ, and all the way to our final glorification in the presence of the Father, "all is of grace." "Salvation is *of the Lord!"* (Jon 2:9 KJV).

God saves. God does not merely do enough to make salvation *possible,* leaving it to us to work our way up, to "merit the merits of Christ," to do our part to make the merely possible become the actual. Every link in the chain of redemption is forged on God's anvil from start to finish. Even God cannot achieve an end without a means. In order to secure the predestined end, he foreordains each step and causal link, sovereignly acting to see that each cause and effect occurs. I have already shown that he had to move the entire Roman military bureaucracy several years earlier to make certain that at the end of the empirewide census, one particular pregnant girl was in the right town at the right moment just so the Messiah would be born in Bethlehem and not up north in Nazareth! The entire Roman bureaucracy was predestined to keep in step with the body chemistry of one unknown Jewish girl in the far outer reaches of the first-century Roman Empire.

As far as the atonement is concerned, in dying on the cross as our great high priest, Jesus actually achieved and secured on our behalf the salvation of every one of his sheep, of every one of those that the Father had given him out of the world, of all those upon whom he had set his electing love from before the foundation of the world. He had to secure every step in the process, every microscopic means, however detailed, to secure the end result intended. Nothing could be left to chance—there could be no chance in a *created* cosmos— so none of his promises could fail (Josh 23:14).

God saves sinners. Sinners are rebels, averse to all good. They are slaves to sin, with darkened minds and unclean consciences, suppressing one part of the truth by the selective use of other parts, by playing off one truth of God against another. In short, sinners are practicing unrighteousness. It's all a game to see how the rebels can vindicate and secure the fundamental rationalist-irrationalist presupposition of metaphysical autonomy (see Romans 1 and Ephesians 4).

These, then, are the creatures who the Arminians claim always respond to the gospel from a standpoint of neutrality. The whole doctrine of grace is here vitiated at a stroke, for sinners capable of so good an act as the self-revolution of accepting Christ surely have reason to boast.

We shall see in the next chapter ("Depravity and Election") specific Scriptures that explicate the real state of the sinners and why God's intervention is so necessary to turn the rebels around. Sinners are not represented in Scripture as neutrally awaiting a chance to put themselves in the right, but as determinedly and deliberately in headlong retreat from God and his holiness. Sinners work hard for their wages, and those wages are richly deserved: the Bible says that "the wages of sin is death" (Rom 6:23).

Free Will a Slave

In his famous sermon and tract "Free Will a Slave," Spurgeon gives a classic account of the Reformation doctrine of the bondage of the will, quoting Luther's book on the first page. His text is John 5:40: "Ye *will not* come to me, that ye might have life" (KJV, my emphasis). He first points out that humans by nature are dead both *legally,* being under the sentence of death as sinners, and *spiritually,* not having the life in Christ that is requisite for being able to come to Jesus. Finally, they are dead *eternally,* for there is no other remedy if Christ be rejected. He observes from the outset that "because there happen to be the words 'will' or 'will not' in it, [the Arminians] run away with the conclusion that it teaches the doctrine of free will." But the adjective *free* can no more be applied to the noun *will* than electricity can be said to be heavy. "The will is well known by all to be directed by the understanding, to be moved by motives, to be guided by other parts of the soul, and to be a secondary thing." He therefore equates the will throughout his sermon with the person acting as a whole. For Spurgeon, the will is not an independent mechanism in the head, but a function of a *character*.

God saves all who come to Christ, says Spurgeon, and Christ receives all without exception who come to him. He speaks of universal atonement as "a wilful falsehood," and describes the idea that there are some in hell for whom Christ shed his blood as a "nonsensical Gospel." He says that the question in this text is not whether sinners *can* come to Christ, but whether they *will* come. "You will notice that whenever you talk about free will, the poor Arminian in two seconds begins to talk about power, and he mixes up two subjects that should be kept apart." By nature, no one wills to come. In the parable, "even the ragged fellows in the hedges would never have come unless they were 'compelled.' "

> Anyone who believes that man's will is entirely free, and that he can be saved by it, does not believe the fall. . . . Why, beloved, the fall broke up man entirely. It did not leave one power unimpaired. . . . The will too is not exempt. . . . Your will, amongst other things, has gone clean astray from God. . . . You will not come; but then your will is a sinful will.

To demonstrate the incompatibility of the freewill theory with grace, Spurgeon observes that

> you have heard a great many Arminian sermons, I dare say, but you never heard an Arminian prayer—for the saints in prayer appear as one in word, and deed, and mind. An Arminian on his knees would pray desperately like a Calvinist. He cannot pray about free will; there is no room for it. Fancy him praying, "Lord, I thank thee that I am not like these poor presumptuous Calvinists. Lord, I was born with a glorious free will; I was born with a power by which I can turn to thee of myself; I have improved my grace. If everybody had done the same with their grace that I have, they might

all have been saved. Lord, I know thou dost not make us willing if we are not willing ourselves. . . . It was not thy grace that made us to differ. . . . I made use of what was given me, and others did not—that is the difference between me and them." That is a prayer for the devil, for nobody else would offer such a prayer as that.

This sermon is typical of other occasions when Spurgeon had occasion to mention free will. The point throughout is that the will is not an independent entity, but a manifestation of the whole person, of the fallen *character*.

The Remonstrants After the Synod of Dort

As mentioned in a previous chapter, the Remonstrants were the original followers of Jacobus Arminius who put together the most serious theological challenge the Dutch state church had yet faced. Some of them wanted more radical changes than others, but all hoped for a considerable liberalization of the standards of doctrine expected of ministers in that church. The heart of their theology was their conviction that free will is incompatible with Calvinist soteriology. In these early days it was not yet apparent to many where this seemingly innocent starting point would lead the Reformed churches, but the next twenty years would make everything clear.

Frederic Platt's article is not the only commentary on the Arminian tendency to prepare the way for far worse defections from orthodoxy. James Orr, a moderate Calvinist of the era just before Platt, makes a key observation on Arminianism in his *Progress of Dogma:* "The lustre of its great names—Episcopius, Grotius, Curcellaeus, Limborch—and its elaboration in imposing tomes, of the dogmatic material, cannot hide its flattening down of all the great doctrines, and its growing tendencies in an Arianising, Pelagian, and Socinian direction" (p. 297).

But Platt's comments are more far-reaching. When they were written in 1906, the liberal views that were to become modernism in the twenties were already confident of victory. Historical scholars like Platt exhibited more willingness then to admit that their Arminian tradition was an important stage of liberalization than we find among more conservative Arminians today. The simple truth is that modern evangelicals under the influence of Arminian thinking, being drawn away from their nominally Reformed roots, have for-

gotten the effects that these views have had in the past. The following comments from Platt may remind them of some sobering truths.

Frederic Platt's Admissions

In the course of his article "Arminianism" in Hastings's *Encyclopaedia,* Platt
explains that the Arminian view of God involves God's "owing something to
the creature," and that our relation to God is essentially democratic, balancing
human rights over against God's rights. He notes that

> the introduction into these relations of the Arminian principles, resulted
> in a criticism that seemed irresistible; for the moment that the idea of equity
> was admitted to a place in the consideration of the relations of man and
> God, the old absolute unconditionalism became untenable. . . . Arminian-
> ism was always most successful when its argument proceeded upon prin-
> ciples supplied by the moral consciousness of man. . . . It regarded man
> as free and rational; sin had not destroyed either his reason or his freedom.
> . . . He had the ability to believe. . . . Thus the freewill of man was regarded
> as conditioning the absolute will of God.

Platt explains how "Arminianism became the form of reformation theology
which most easily allied itself with the advance of knowledge and with the
humanism of the new learning." He also notes that "in the Netherlands . . .
a liberal spirit was showing itself in a general uneasiness under the yoke of
the Symbolical documents, [which] found special favor with the Arminians."
He speaks of "the growing tendency towards Rationalism and *Latitudinarianism into which Arminian theology frequently drifted" and refers to "the
association of Arminianism with Deism and Naturalism."

At one point Platt seems to be conscious that he is giving away the family
jewels by these admissions and hurriedly tries to make amends with a pragmatic excuse: "But that this drift represented any *necessary effect* of the Arminian movement is disproved by the fact that it was the Arminian system
of thought which lay at the theological sources of the great Methodist revival
in the United Kingdom during the 18th century" (emphasis mine). This claim,
however, is false. No doubt the original Oxford Holy Club was predominantly
Arminian in its thinking, but it was not the Holy Club that started the revival.
The revival in England became Arminian only after it was started by the

Calvinistic Whitefield, because Wesley insisted on attacking Whitefield's preaching on election. The Methodists of Wales continued to follow Whitefield in the matter of grace. In America, the revival was under way even before Whitefield arrived, having been started not by Wesley, who by his own admission was a hopeless failure in Georgia, but by Calvinists like Jonathan Edwards. By its later stages in the Second Great Awakening, Calvinistic evangelists such as Asahel Nettleton were confronted with a very different type of thinking in the person of Charles Finney and his "new measures."

The phrase *necessary effect* is misleading. There are different kinds of necessity, and physical causation is only one kind. There is also the responsibility of the person who opens a locked security door and leaves it ajar for the likelihood that someone will sooner or later walk through it. The internal requirements of a system under the pressure of a desire for consistency is also a type of necessity. I have referred to it in this book under the term *internal dynamic*. Platt has no right to document the flow of a natural tendency so effectively, only to draw back from facing the fact that, granting the premises, the results are close to inevitable.

Platt continues with his account of the results of Arminianism by admitting that subsequent ethical thought was also not based on the "external authority" of the Bible but on the "inward compulsion of conscience." He seems to accept the common humanistic interpretation that the Reformation was primarily a battle between the individual human conscience and the authority of the pope. But Martin Luther did not say at Worms, "My conscience is the final authority," but "My conscience is captive to the Word of God," a totally different thing. We shall return to these issues in the last chapter, which deals with the location of ultimacy.

Enough has been said here to indicate that Platt wants us to understand that Arminianism is at heart a form of humanism: "Arminianism was always most successful when its arguments proceeded upon principles supplied by the moral consciousness of man." Incidentally implied is that, in practice, Arminianism spiritually feeds off its association with elements of a compromised Reformation orthodoxy. Platt demonstrates this conclusively, however uneasy a modern evangelical may be with his account. Filling it out with stories of the spiritual accomplishments of godly Arminians has no bearing on the final outcome. The Calvinist has every right to point out that godliness is followed by spiritual blessing because God is faithful to his promises in these areas, even though the recipients of these blessings may not always have all their theology straight. God meets his promises to Arminian believers too.

The Five Points of Calvinism

The Synod of Dort responded to the five areas of the *Remonstrance* in the same order the Remonstrants had arranged their material. That is, they stated their position on each point in turn, stating also the negative that they were refuting, so that it would be understood what they did not mean as well as what they meant. It is convenient to rearrange the order of the areas of doctrine to correspond with the mnemonic *TULIP*, which stands for *total depravity, unconditional election, *limited atonement, irresistible grace and perseverance of the saints. The last is often called "eternal security" today, and many Calvinists prefer "particular redemption" to "limited atonement."

Total depravity refers to the complete, comprehensive and radical nature of human fallenness, as explained in the Augustinian vision of the seriousness of sin. The mind and the will in particular are both slaves to the sin nature. This means that the intellect is only capable of being logical and reasonable as long as the basic fallen presumption of autonomy from God is not being threatened. This assumption is also the essence of the will's presumed awareness of its own self-determination.

On the other hand, the Arminian definition of the will's freedom is a freedom to choose either of two alternatives with equal facility. When they use phrases like "real freedom," "genuine self-determination" or "free agency," they simply mean that the will acts in autonomy from any previous causation. They always allow a variety of influences to affect the will, but in the final analysis, the will can always rise above any conditioning factors.

The case of the development of Remonstrant thought between 1610 and 1618 illustrates perfectly how a theological inconsistency caused by one's evangelical past can persist for years, resisting serious criticism. Meanwhile, the inconsistency creates a tension between the logical requirements of the thought processes on the one hand and one's desire to hang on to elements of orthodoxy on the other. Simon Episcopius composed the first version of the *Remonstrance,* and like Arminius he was loath to part with eternal security. He wanted more research on the topic and left it hanging. But the rational requirements of the freewill hypothesis demand that if we have free will before our conversion, we could hardly be deprived of it by regeneration! Just as we were free to believe as unbelievers, we must surely be free to disbelieve as believers. So the Remonstrants gave up the perseverance of the saints by the time they got to Dort. The Arminians were free at last from the Reformation doctrine of God's sovereignty in salvation.

This phenomenon was among the first in the history of Arminianism to illustrate the fact that compromised systems are unstable and tend without powerful restraint to slip into modes of greater consistency. It is the theme of this book that this tendency remains today in evangelical Arminianism, continuing to press for further and further departures from Reformational orthodoxy. I have already noted that Clark Pinnock's freewill theism illustrates just such a tendency. The most powerful restraint is probably the desire of Arminianizing teachers to continue to be thought of as evangelical despite their disintegrating theology. Their students are not so squeamish. For every inconsistent teacher there are several of their students who are quite willing to drive the truck of heresy through the holes the master has left in the semiorthodox fence. Thus a "moderate" shift in one generation becomes a virtual revolution in the next, as the demands of rationality are pressed against artificial restraints called "tensions."

Unconditional election is the idea that God elects or chooses those whom he will save without regard to any merit or condition on their part. All sinners equally deserve death—there are no grounds in the human soul, in fallen human nature, or in human nature's interactions with the truth of the gospel to commend a sinner to a holy God. Therefore, if God chooses any for salvation, it must be for reasons found ultimately in God, not in the sinner. In particular, God does not decide who is fit for election by means of a sneak preview of a film he does not write or produce himself, in order to gather the knowledge of our future acts of saving faith that will enable him to choose those whom he "foreknows" will of themselves choose Christ. This would really mean that God looks for some future distinguishing mark in the sinner to enable him to choose the truly spiritual ones. It seems strange that modern Arminians cannot see that this means election on the basis of foreseen merit.

Dort therefore insisted that if grace be grace, there can be no merit or a humanly supplied condition preceding God's eternal election. That God may have reasons of his own for choosing me for salvation and not my father (who, as far as I know, died an atheist) may well be so, but it is certain that I did not supply him with those reasons.

The conditional election envisioned by the Arminians has some odd results, not the least of which is its invitation to a theory of merit. Platt is quite right to point out that the Jansenists were Augustinians, while their implacable opponents, the Jesuits, were essentially Arminians. The Jesuits correctly saw that the Roman system of merit and reward could not survive the criticism of Jansenist theology, which was really a form of Calvinism. The entire sacramental system was likewise threatened. But it was the military authority of the pope, not the give-and-take of the marketplace of ideas, that spelled the death of the Jansenist movement. Likewise, papal authority guaranteed the victory of the Jesuit type of Arminianism over the residual (and finally merely nominal) presence of Augustinianism in the Roman communion. Although St. Augustine is still widely respected, and some of his influence remains through Thomas Aquinas, no real revival of Augustinian thought has been possible in the Roman church since the destruction of the Jansenists.

Limited atonement teaches that God intended the death of Christ to be a substitutionary sacrifice to actually *effect* the salvation of only the elect. Christ did not merely generate an abstract lump of atonement that would then be made available to everyone without distinction who happens to request it. No doubt there are side effects and secondary purposes in the death of Christ that have reference to the nonelect, but these are not ultimately saving effects. They may mitigate the effects of sin in individuals and in society as a whole, but they do not finally save sinners from their sin. The term *common grace* is used by Calvinists to describe the nonsaving effects of the atonement. This means that there are genuine acts of divine mercy in history toward the nonelect, but these acts nevertheless fall short of securing their salvation. It is called *common* grace because it is common to both believers (before their salvation) and unbelievers alike. After our regeneration, common grace merges into, and is indistinguishable from, *special grace* (also called *saving grace*) in the believer's experience.

This is why many Calvinists dislike the application of the word *limited* to the atonement. They feel that it is the Arminian who limits the atonement, not the Calvinist. The Arminian theory means the death of Christ was so limited in its power that it is in fact not effective at all. For the Arminian, the thing that makes the death of Christ effective is not God's decree, or Christ's dying, or even the Holy Spirit's regenerating, but the free will of the sinner in choosing. Christ's dying makes people savable but does not actually save any particular person. Thus Jesus should have said, "You have chosen me so that I could choose you" (Jn 15:16). How free will can be reconciled with "you did not choose me, but I chose you" is not explained by the Arminian system.

There is a sense, then, in which everyone (except the universalist) limits the atonement one way or another. The Arminians limit its effectiveness in that it fails to save everyone, while the Calvinists limit its intention in that it was only designed to save the elect. The consistent universalists make it 100 percent effective by both intent and outcome, for, in their view, God intended to save everyone by the death of his Son, and will infallibly succeed in doing so.

Irresistible grace means that when God decides to save a particular sinner whom he has chosen, his power is such that he cannot but succeed in getting the job done. The point is not that grace is like some weird mechanical force that rides roughshod over human personality, as if we were blocks of wood. The essence of the irresistible nature of God's grace is seen as an unavoidable conclusion from those passages of Scripture that teach that no one can stop God from accomplishing his plans, simply because he is omnipotent. Nor is it claimed that God's grace is never resisted by the elect. All sinners resist the interference of God's love and movements in their souls, for these gracious acts of God are a threat to the sinner's apostate autonomism. But God is patient, loving and wise, and he does what is necessary to win over the elect. He regenerates the human heart, infusing divine life into it, thus enabling the wicked to believe, even though they were formerly enslaved to the habit of rebellion.

So repentance and faith are both often described as a gift from God in the

Bible (e.g., Eph 2:8-9; Phil 1:29; 2 Tim 2:25). How else could God save a sinner except by overcoming all spiritual resistance to himself? If this did not include the resistance of the human will, no one could be saved, except occasionally by chance, in a world incompetently managed by God.

The Arminian presupposition of a free will weakens the Bible's doctrine of grace to the same degree that it weakens the doctrine of omnipotence. When the Arminian insists that somehow God limits himself at the door of the human will, this can only mean in practice that the sinner must supply something for salvation that God is powerless to supply. That something is the act of saving faith, essentially an autonomous manifestation of a purely natural, innate spiritual competence. In other words, salvation is partly a transcendent act of God's mercy in providing the necessary circumstances and partly an immanent natural achievement of the sinner's spiritual competence.

A Test Question

I first encountered serious Calvinists while at London Bible College during 1965-1966. One Sunday evening I returned from an evangelism practicum at the Highgate Baptist Chapel to find a discussion in progress in the basement of the student rooms at the school I attended. I sat down to listen. It was a concentrated debate between some Arminian students and a senior student, Michael Buss, who later became pastor of the Lansdown Baptist Church in Portsmouth. He suddenly turned to me and said, "What do you think about this, Wright? You're a Calvinist. Tell these people which comes first: regeneration, or the exercise of saving faith?"

I thought about it a second, not realizing where the conversation had been leading. I said "Well, I suppose the order would be that when we are presented with the gospel, and God gives us enough light for us to understand what it means, we put our trust in Jesus, and then God gives us everlasting life. So I guess that saving faith comes first and regeneration, the new birth, immediately after that."

Michael said, "I see. What you mean then is that when you heard the gospel, you managed, contrary to all your past habits, to so revolutionize the bent of your fallen character that while dead in trespasses and sins, at enmity with God, with a darkened understanding and thinking the gospel foolishness, you managed to reconstruct your whole spiritual awareness around a new center, so as to realize that the gospel is your best bet, and so you embraced Christ as your Savior, whereupon God rewarded you for this wonderful effort of spiritual achievement by giving you everlasting life. Is that what you meant to say?"

Totally taken aback, I stammered that no, that was not really what I intended to say.

Michael responded simply, "Well, that's what you *did* say. Think about it."

In 1985 I met Michael Buss again and recalled that conversation almost twenty years earlier. He did not even remember the events of that Sunday afternoon. But I did. That was the day I first realized that I did not really understand Calvinism, and it caused me to do my homework and become a more consistent thinker. God had predestined from eternity that I would arrive back at the college at just the right moment to hear something from someone who had thought it all through, at just the right point in my own thinking on the subject to cause me to follow it up seriously.

The heart of the doctrine of irresistible grace is that we would be wholly incapable of embracing Jesus Christ as our Savior, or of continuing in obedience, if God did not give us the ability—no, the life—to do so. Faith and its obverse, repentance, are supernatural gifts from God. They are not merely the application or redirection of a purely natural ability toward a new object. No, saving faith is absolutely nothing like sitting in a chair or trusting ourselves to an airplane, contrary to the common Arminian illustrations. And God does not grant regeneration as a reward for being so spiritually clever as to accept Christ as Savior. Unless God gives life, sinners can never truly believe. We just don't have what it takes.

Perseverance of the saints means that the truly regenerate are given, along with all the other spiritual blessings, the gift of perseverance to the end. God makes certain that he upholds his children in their faith. God actually does all that is necessary in every individual case to really *save* the elect, not just to make their salvation possible, leaving it up to them to make it certain. When Peter warns us to "make [our] calling and election sure" (2 Pet 1:10), he is not telling us to secure them ourselves, but to make ourselves certain of them. It is we who need to be certain, not God's choices in eternity. Another version puts it this way: "Be all the more diligent to make certain about His calling and choosing you" (NASB).

Eventually, the doctrine of free will forces those evangelicals who think they are Calvinists merely because they believe "once saved, always saved" to give up even this last lonely vestige of Reformed theology. Consider: if we have free will as unregenerate people that God does not take away from us at the new birth, then we have it still. But this means we can give up Christ at any time, just as freely as we accepted him in the first place. And if we have it now, we will presumably have it forever. This in turn means that in eternity, even after thousands of years in God's presence, we could still sin and blow the whole program! It also means that even Jesus, being truly human, and therefore having a human free will like we all do, could not only have sinned while on earth, but could still do so in the future. An Arminian may not like this conclusion, but there is nothing he can offer to offset it without modifying his vision of free will. On the other hand, if we do not have free will in the resurrection state, it cannot be essential to our human nature, and so cannot be an essential part of the image of God in us. And if it is not essential then, it cannot be essential now.

In the interest of consistency, the Remonstrants gave up the perseverance of the saints as the Synod of Dort approached. This was both honest and unavoidable, and is still so today. Only those who believe in limited atonement have a rational right to the doctrine of eternal security. To believe in just one point of Calvinism is inconsistent Arminianism.

The Real Difference

The real difference between Arminianism and Calvinism is the determination of Arminians to combine their Christian testimony with the rationalist-irrationalist presupposition of autonomy. Only rarely do we meet with attempts to prove free will—for most it just remains an assumption. Unfortunately for those evangelicals caught up in this confusion, it is also the fundamental assumption of humanism. Calvinism tries to bring all of our assumptions to the bar of Scripture by bringing every thought into captivity to Christ (2 Cor 10:5). The negative side of the Calvinist apologetic against Arminianism is basically just the extrapolation of the challenge to Arminians to be consistent to their basic presupposition while yet trying to maintain the biblical gospel. It just cannot be done, for more and more must be given up.

The Arminian has no right to expect the Calvinist to allow the freewill theory to pass uncriticized, as if it has some kind of privileged immunity from examination. Once it is identified as such, a presupposition is in the class of "all thoughts" that must be brought captive to Christ. We must continually ask whether our presuppositions are in harmony with the other great doctrines of the Bible on God, human nature and sin. If Arminians remember what Luther said at Worms, they must be ready to make their consciences captive to the Word of God, and this must necessarily include their presuppositions also.

We must recall as well that both Calvinists and Arminians are always imperfect saints who are in need of self-examination at many levels of understanding. It is important to distinguish the consistency of a theology from the inconsistency of the one who may profess it. None of us is fully consistent in practice. All believers need to strive toward increasing consistency both in thought and deed, emulating the full consistency of Jesus himself, the fully loving and fully rational incarnate Logos. It is the holiness of the man Christ Jesus that the Christian seeks in personal growth in grace, while seeking to "be transformed by the renewing of [the] mind" (Rom 12:2). The compromised believer locked into a syncretistic union with some form of apostate autonomism is in no position to challenge the fallen mind. The essential weapon has been left behind.

Arminian attempts to prove free will from the Bible will be dealt with in chapter nine. The following four chapters are intended as an outline of the principal arguments from Scripture for each of the five points of Calvinism. We will turn first to the biblical evidence for the doctrines of human depravity and the election of grace.

Further Reading

For Spurgeon's views, see Iain Murray's *The Forgotten Spurgeon* (Edinburgh: Banner of Truth Trust, 1978).

For an introduction to the five points, see David Steele and Curtis Thomas, *The Five Points of Calvinism: Defined, Defended, Documented* (Phillipsburg,

N.J.: Presbyterian & Reformed, 1963). Loraine Boettner's *The Reformed Doctrine of Predestination* (Philadelphia: Presbyterian & Reformed, 1966) is also a good place to start.

For an introduction to the way the Puritans preached on the attributes of God, read the chapters "On God's Knowledge" and "On the Power of God" in Stephen Charnock's *The Existence and Attributes of God* (1682; reprint, Grand Rapids, Mich.: Baker, 1979). Charnock was a disciple of, and co-preacher with, the great John Owen in his final years, and is one of the best Puritan doctrinal writers. May the Lord give us all the grace and patience to devote some time to these mighty treatises on the divine attributes.

6

Depravity & Election: Spiritual Incompetence & Divine Sovereignty

*F*rederic Platt is helpful in explaining the Arminian perspective on natural human abilities. He observes in the Hastings *Encyclopaedia* article that the *Remonstrance* expressed a clear commitment to the seriousness of the Fall, along with a view of a prevenient grace that amounted to "a restored freedom of the human will as an element of the Divine decrees and in opposition to the assertion of the absolute sovereignty of God" (1:808). Platt wants us to see the movement as "a *via media* between 'determinism' and 'Pelagianism.'" He identifies two things as determining its later influence: its concern for justice and "the emphasis it lays upon the human in the redemptive relations between God and man." Accordingly, "Arminianism held that depravity was a bias, which left the will free and man responsible for his own destiny through the choice of faith or unbelief. The Adamic unity of the race was preserved, but its inherited tendencies to evil were met and neutralized by the free and universal grace communicated to the race in Christ—the second Adam."

In this way prevenient grace is transmuted from its original Augustinian content of the grace needed before a slave to sin could will to believe into the idea of "the universal diffusion of the influences of the Holy Spirit." Grace is therefore not "the solitary cause of salvation," for it must be supplemented by "the cooperation of free will." The bottom line is that grace cannot be effective without the cooperation of a factor acting autonomously or independently from God. It is the sinner who supplies that factor.

Platt's reference to a concern for justice is actually a reference to God's obligation to respect certain human rights, a notion that will be dealt with in chapter ten ("The Problem of Evil").

Syncretism and the Search for the Middle Ground

Platt exhibits the common hope of Arminians today that there must be some middle ground between the dependence on human ability so characteristic of the Pelagians and the full divine sovereignty of the Reformers. The result is a rejection of both "extremes" in the interests of a syncretism of grace with human ability. Yet there is no practical difference between the autonomy of humanism and the autonomy of Arminianism. One happens to be inherent and requires no conversion, while the other is granted to everyone by prevenient grace before conversion. The result for the individual is identical in each case. All are practically free and able to become believers whenever they will. In the Arminian syncretism, as in secular humanism, autonomy is limited only by human finiteness.

In syncretisms of Christian principles with non-Christian principles, the claim is often made that a balance of some kind is being sought in order to avoid extremes. The result is frequently a loose compromise between incompatible first principles. At first, following the evangelistic concern to communicate with the world of unbelief, points of contact are sought with the non-Christian mindset. The points of contact actually identified in the Bible—the restraining effect of common grace, the image of God in everyone, the conscience and the use of logic—are minimized or deemed insufficient. Non-Christian elements are then pragmatically selected from secular systems, creating a compromise with non-Christian philosophies. The plea is that we can "use them in the Lord's service" to "reach the lost," to make headway in "the real world." The primary achievement of syncretistic thinking is a mixed theology incorporating incompatible positions. Contradictory presuppositions are arbitrarily held together under the plea for balance. The unbeliever immediately recognizes it as self-contradictory.

When Arminians speak of a balance between God's sovereignty and our responsibility, they really mean between sovereignty and free will. The fact that the two propositions "God is wholly sovereign" and "We are responsible for our choices" are not in any logical conflict is not even noticed, let alone demonstrated. If they can plead for balance they can appear quite reasonable while preventing their assumption of autonomist freedom from being questioned. Then, in order to protect these internal contradictions from close examination, appeal is regularly made to terms like *mystery, paradox* or *antinomy.* But there is a price to pay for this move: if we believers can contradict ourselves, so can the unbeliever, and the whole apologetic enterprise is negated at a stroke. No further rational defense of anything is then possible, whether Arminianism or the gospel itself.

Someone is wrong here. Either God is fully sovereign in salvation, or his sovereignty is limited by our free will. The doctrine of total depravity states that fallen human nature is morally incapable of responding to the gospel without being caused to do so by divine intervention (1 Cor 2:12-15). Once the soul is sovereignly regenerated, it willingly responds in saving faith to God's command to repent and believe the gospel, but not before. Only those who have been "born from above" can "see the kingdom." To regenerate the heart is to regenerate and free the will also, a will previously enslaved to the fallen nature, committed to the autonomist principles of the Fall and averse to God. Assuming an autonomous will logically separates the will's actions from the causal elements and moral influences of the character, thereby setting God's sovereignty over against our responsibility. Paul, however, believed that it was God who was at work in the Philippian believers (Phil 2:13). If we manage to will and then perform the good, it is only because God has first been at work in our souls, giving life to the dead, regenerating a will that now desires to know God better and to follow his Good Shepherd.

There is no question for the Calvinist that the human will is real, and that our choices are truly significant for the future. But by "truly significant" the Arminians mean "truly autonomous." The Calvinists mean that any one link in a chain is just as important as any other link. The whole chain is useless if even one link is missing. Our choices are necessary causal links in God's chain of means. It is not the *reality* of the will that is in question, but its *independence* from the rest of our fallen nature and its *capacity* to choose autonomously against God's eternal purposes.

Depravity: The Scriptural Evidence in Five Steps

The following section covers a selection of the more decisive verses in the Bible for the Reformed position on the depravity of the fallen heart. Some exposition is included to bring out the force of selected verses, but the reader is referred to John Gill's *The Cause of God and Truth* or David Steele and Curtis Thomas's *The Five Points of Calvinism: Defined, Defended, Documented* for more material. I am convinced that if this material is not enough, together with the texts for the other points of Dort in the following two chapters, the question cannot be resolved by appeal to Scripture at all, and other factors must be addressed.

I would encourage the reader to work through these passages with an open Bible to ensure that nothing has been treated apart from its context. At the same time, we must all pray that the Holy Spirit will search our hearts for evidence that our exegesis is controlled by assumptions and presuppositions of which we are not fully aware, because they bias our reading of God's Word. However, the issue is not whether we can be unbiased or not, but whether we are aware of our presuppositions. Do we realize how they affect us, and are we also willing to see them judged in terms of Scripture? These steps are substantially similar to those used by Steele and Thomas in their outline.

1. *Since the Fall of Adam and Eve, all are born spiritually dead in their sin nature, and therefore require regeneration to a life they do not naturally possess.* See Genesis 6:5-7; Psalm 51:5, 58:3; Jeremiah 17:9-10; John 1:12-13; 3:5-7; Romans 5:12; 8:7-8; Ephesians 2:1-3, 8-10; Colossians 2:13.

Romans 5:12 is in the middle of the famous passage in Paul on the two Adams, which has a parallel in 1 Corinthians 15:45-49. The essential point is that death passed to all because of Adam's sin, and it is added that "all sinned." Recalling the Genesis 3 account, the death referred to in 2:17 began as a state of spiritual death the day they took the forbidden fruit and terminated years later as physical death.

Ephesians 2:1-3 (NASB) speaks of the preregenerate sinner as being "dead in . . . trespasses and sins," starting out as an "object of wrath" who needs to be made alive by God. In verses eight to ten this is said to be "by grace . . . for we are [God's] workmanship." This is not the language of synergism, let alone of syncretism.

The verses in Psalms 51 and 58 only confirm that this sin nature is original to our conception. It is not acquired, but manifests itself "from the womb," causing sinners to go astray as soon as they are born.

John 1 and 3 introduce us to the language of "new birth." This is not a product of the human will—either our own, or that of another person (such as a husband or priest)—but rather is "of God" (1:12-13). It is not when we see what the kingdom is all about and decide to believe that God regenerates us. We cannot even see the kingdom until we are born again (3:3), and only then is it manifest that we have been so born "from above."

That God considers the entire moral life of the unbeliever to be problematic is indicated by the comprehensive language in Genesis describing the state of civilization before the flood: "The wickedness of man was great on the earth, and . . . every intent of the thoughts of his heart was only evil continually" (Gen 6:5 NASB). These terms are not consonant with degrees of spiritual life more or less acceptable to God. There must be a corresponding sense in which there is no spiritual life present at all.

2. *Being fallen, the natural heart and mind is sinfully corrupt and unenlightened.* See Genesis 6:5; 8:21; Ecclesiastes 9:3; Jeremiah 17:9-10; Mark 7:21-23; John 3:19; Romans 8:7-8; 1 Corinthians 2:14; Ephesians 4:17-19; 5:8; Titus 1:15.

Jeremiah 17:9 states that the human heart is deceitful above all things and so thoroughly corrupted by its sin that it cannot be understood by anyone. Then verse ten explains that at least we can depend on God to evaluate the heart justly and to reward each of us according to our deeds. The salient point is that the heart is too confused to be intelligible to itself. It is totally incapable of self-understanding. To Socrates' advice to "Know thyself," Jeremiah would have replied, "How? It's beyond you."

In Mark 7 Jesus explains that external sources of ritual impurity are nothing when compared to the corruption and evil that proceed from within a person's heart. It is our very nature that is the root of our sin problem, not external circumstances. It is also Jesus who says in John 3:19 that unbelief, an internal state of the heart, is what secures God's judgment upon us.

Romans 8:7-8 describes the spiritual incapacity of "the carnal mind," a Pauline term for the unregenerate heart. This is then confirmed in 1 Corinthians 2, where we discover that the natural mind does not accept spiritual things (i.e., the gospel) because such a reception requires a spiritual discernment that it does not have. The unregenerate mind is simply incapable of this knowledge.

Ephesians 4 contains one of the most negative evaluations of the unbelieving mind in the Bible. The mind of the Gentiles is empty, lifeless, ignorant and blind. Paul adds in Titus that "their minds and consciences are corrupted."

3. *Because the whole of nature is involved in the Fall and its results, sinners are slaves to sin.* See John 8:34, 44; Romans 6:20; Ephesians 2:1-2; 2 Timothy 2:25-26; Titus 3:3; 1 John 3:10; 5:19.

In John 8:44, the phrase "of your father the devil" (NASB) is a reference to the Hebraic concept of the father "begetting" offspring, and therein communicating his own nature to them. In other words, bad trees bring forth bad fruit. Jesus has just pointed out to these same hearers that those who commit sin on a continuous basis are "slaves of sin" (v. 34). Paul uses this very phrase in Romans 6:20, and something similar in Titus 3:3 (serving lusts and pleasures as slaves).

Second Timothy 2 ends with a description of conversion as sobering up after a bout of intoxication. The need is for the gift of repentance to enable those captured by Satan to escape this intoxication, during which they "do his will." Presumably, they will only escape if this gift is *given* to them.

4. *No one escapes the unrighteous tendencies of the sinful Adamic nature.* See 1 Kings 8:46; 2 Chronicles 6:36; Job 15:14-16; Psalm 130:3; 143:2; Proverbs 20:9; Ecclesiastes 7:20, 29; Isaiah 53:6; Romans 3:9-18; James 3:2, 8; 1 John 1:8-10.

Second Chronicles 6 and 1 Kings 8 both state that there is no one who does not sin. Proverbs 20:9 appeals to the conscience to make the same point.

Isaiah 53 is the key Old Testament passage on the nature of the atonement.

It states that in going astray like lost sheep, we only demonstrate our desire to run our own lives as if God had no right to interfere; we have followed our own paths.

Romans 3:9-18 is a chain of quotations from the Old Testament intended to show what God thinks of sinners in general. "There is no one who does good, not even one."

First John 1:8-10 teaches that the claim to be sinless is nothing but self-deception. Such self-deception involves calling God a liar, since it is by his Word that we know his moral standards and what our failure to reach those standards really involves.

The most natural conclusion from these verses is that the effects of sin are universal and involve our radical nature. We are not dealing here with a superficial quality, but with the fundamental bent of the unregenerate soul.

5. *Left to themselves, those dead in trespasses and sins have no spiritual ability to reform themselves, or to repent, or to believe savingly.* See Job 14:4; Jeremiah 13:23; Matthew 7:16-18; 12:33; John 6:44, 65; Romans 11:35-36; 1 Corinthians 2:14; 4:7; 2 Corinthians 3:5.

Jeremiah 13:23 is the well-known comparison of sinners, who are unable to change themselves, with leopards, who cannot get rid of their spots.

Matthew 7 recounts Jesus' warning in the middle of the Sermon on the Mount that the bad tree cannot bring forth good fruit. It is this fact of the unchangeable regularity of character that makes it possible for him to conclude that "by their fruits you shall know them," that is, the false prophets.

First Corinthians 2:14 and 4:7 together confirm that by nature we are incapable of changing our own spiritual darkness, because only God can make such a difference in the soul. It is therefore completely illogical for us to ascribe our spiritual improvement to our own efforts, particularly to a natural autonomy of the will.

The terms *absolute depravity* and *complete inability* are needed to press the point that no part of human nature, whether the mind, the emotions or the will, have escaped the corruption of the Fall. When Adam fell, all of Adam fell. The will, as a motion or function of the fallen soul, participates in our fallenness. Therefore, although the unregenerate may wish in the abstract to be good in some private sense, they cannot will the good as God sees it, for that would be to give up their would-be autonomy. The moral aspirations of the unregenerate soul are limited spiritually by its commitment to the principles of the Adamic nature. This is the reason that repentance, as the correlative of faith, is consistently referred to in the Bible as a gift from God, just as faith itself is a supernatural gift.

Arminian Misconceptions Clarified

Some people, upon noticing the adjective *total* in the Reformed doctrine of the depraved state, have jumped to the conclusion that Calvinists teach that the Fall has extinguished all vestiges of the imago Dei and that fallen people are no better than animals. It is true that some Lutheran theologians have taught this, but all the Calvinists I have read hold that while we have lost certain relational elements of the image, qualities such as rationality and conscience, although enslaved to sin, remain to secure our humanness. There is no doubt that the Fall was serious, but it was not such that sinners are always as bad as they could conceivably be. Even *Adolf Hitler could have been much worse than he was. This is due to God's common grace, which restrains the sin of the sinner, thus enabling that "blessed inconsistency" with apostate autonomism that makes civilization possible.

In order to survive as creatures in God's world, even the most depraved are capable of behaving themselves to a degree convenient to themselves. But this is not repentance, nor is it saving faith. It is worth observing that the more consistently Hitler tried to work out his theories, the more his world progressed into chaos and the less those theories corresponded to the realities of the surrounding war. He spent the last months of the war firing and replacing German generals who voiced any rational opposition to his ridiculous orders, and finally found nothing better to do than blow his own brains out in his concrete bunker while Berlin was being destroyed above him.

Many assume that if we are incapable of faith, we cannot be blamed for our unbelief. J. I. Packer states, in his well-known "Introduction" to Owen's *Death of Death,* that one of the basic presuppositions of the original Arminians was that "inability limits responsibility." The assumption underlying this notion is that if we are not autonomously free, we are not free in any sense and so are not responsible. But the unregenerate sin quite willingly. In fact, they love their sin (Jn 3:19) and cheerfully wallow in it (Rom 1:32). No one (least of all God) forces sinners to sin against their will or their better judgment.

Sinners are always suppressing their consciences, and the Bible makes it clear that they will be judged by the light they have. We all sin against what light we have, some of us more, some less. No one, whether Hindu or Muslim, lives up to the light that exists even in his or her religion. We will be condemned for rejecting the light we do have, not for our inability. The Bible clearly bases responsibility on degrees of knowledge. In the final analysis, all sinners who go to hell go in spite of all the light and truth they ever had. There are no facts and no arguments in favor of going to hell!

It is popularly thought that the teaching of total depravity will discourage sinners from repenting even when they know the gospel. But again, this presupposes that the unregenerate heart is quite able to repent whenever it wishes and merely needs encouragement and opportunity. This, however, is the point at issue. The Reformed view is that if the hearer is elect, God will eventually use the preached Word to regenerate the sinner, turn the heart to the Savior and give the gifts of faith and repentance. It is the Word in the sovereign hand of the Spirit of God that regenerates, not an autonomous will.

Paul indicates this when he says of the Thessalonians that when the Word came to them in the gospel, it was accompanied by the power of the Spirit, thus producing a regenerating effect (1 Thess 1:5). Consequently, they could know that they were elect. Had it come "simply with words," it no doubt would have been ignored by sinners dead in their trespasses and sins.

The Puritans taught that the faithful preaching of depravity allows the unbeliever to see how serious sin is. The slave in chains must cry out to the Lord for deliverance from bondage to sin and its inevitable results. Carnally secure and spiritually snoozing sinners often need to be startled out of their deadly complacency, and God may often use warnings and judgments to arrest sinners in their tracks. The Bible is full of such examples. On the other hand, how can it be an act of love to fail to warn sinners clearly of their danger? This underscores the Calvinistic emphasis on the necessity of powerful and effective evangelism.

Before turning to God's merciful decision to save at least some of those fallen in Adam, we will allow one of history's most vociferous anti-Calvinists to speak a clear word on conversion as the Calvinist understands it. It is a remarkable fact that the gifted Charles Wesley wrote around 6,000 hymns, many of which have survived to the present. A number of them have been forgotten, including his rather angry attacks on various Calvinistic opinions. One famous hymn, however, is a rousing testimony to the wonder and power of God to save helpless sinners in bondage to sin. All Calvinists sing it with gratitude to God for this brother's wonderful gift of expression and sensitivity to the reality of God's sovereignty in releasing us from bondage to our sin nature. This was Charles Wesley's testimony:

Long my imprisoned spirit lay, (a prisoner)
Fast-bound in sin and nature's night. (the bondage of the sin nature)
Thine Eye diffused a quickening ray; (the light of the Logos)
I woke; the dungeon flamed with light! (true enlightenment)
My chains fell off, my heart was free. (release from slavery)
I rose, went forth, and followed Thee. (the obedience of faith)

Here we have a truly regenerate Arminian describing his own conversion in fully Calvinistic terms. Of course one could always reassert the presupposition of autonomy and insist that the "quickening ray" was prevenient grace, while "I rose, went forth" was merely an act of free will, but this does not seem to have been the thought of Wesley at just that moment. Otherwise it might have read like this:

Long my mistaken spirit lay, (mere ignorance)
Confused by sin and absent light. (lack of opportunity)
Thine Eye diffused prevenient grace; (universal mercy)
I suddenly realized my plight. (smart lad, this)
I had freewill, my autonomy! (just like before the Fall)
So I just got up and followed Thee. (just like that)

This seems to me to be a somewhat different gospel from the one professed by Wesley, but it is fully consistent with Arminianism. It is included here to illustrate the fact that even a true and valid personal experience of God's grace can then be quite sincerely misinterpreted when bent into the shape of a false presupposition. Then, when that assumption is not in view, the regenerate consciousness reports the truth without distortion. Charles Wesley certainly did.

The Election of Grace

1. *The choice is God's.* It would appear, then, that if the sinner's case is as naturally hopeless as Charles Wesley was apt to describe it, only God himself would be able to solve the problem. The Creator must mercifully intervene to save these rebels even as they slide cheerfully into the pit. From eternity, God willed, decided, planned, intended and *chose* to save some sinners. We do not know what his reasons were for not deciding to save all sinners, but he was certainly under no obligation to do so. To *elect* is to choose, and *election* is therefore God's choice of who will be saved. If God had not chosen to save some and do what was necessary to save them, no one would be saved.

It is the prerogative of a sovereign Creator to do what he wills with his own property. God's attributes always work in harmony, and here God's wisdom conforms to his knowledge and eternal purposes. Sinners owe the Creator everything, starting with their mere existence, and have no intelligible rights in respect to their Creator. As Paul puts it, "Does not the potter have a right over the clay, to make from the same lump one vessel for honorable use, and another for common use?" (Rom 9:21, NASB). Paul would reject Frederic Platt's concern that God recognize equity between God's rights and ours.

2. *Election as conditional.* We have already seen that *irresistible grace* does not mean that sinners do not resist, but that God eventually overcomes their resistance and fulfills his eternal purpose to save those individuals. One Arminian preacher that I know surprisingly described grace as "the love which pursues and conquers the object of its choice." But this is a Calvinistic definition. Platt, on the other hand, is very clear that grace for the Arminian "made the salvation of nobody actual, but rendered the salvation of all possible, the result being in every case conditioned by faith." He reminds his readers often that "the supreme principle of Arminianism is conditionalism." That is, grace is always resistible because it is dependent on the will of the sinner. Until the sinner wills otherwise, thereby supplying the condition upon which God can act further, God's hands are tied.

3. *A limited omniscience?* We have also noted already that God's election, or choice of a sinner, for the Arminian, is based on God's foresight of saving faith. That is, God looks forward in time to discover whether a particular sinner will believe or not. God gets his information about the future in much

the same empirical way that we would if we were able to see a preview of a film.

This, however, is a puzzle for those who believe in omniscience. If God is truly omniscient from eternity, he cannot logically be thought of as gathering new information about the world by empirical observation. In any case, where does he get the film to preview? It does no good at this point to imagine with C. S. Lewis that God is somehow above or outside of time, much like an observer on a high hill is able to see that two cars on a mountain road are going to collide around an approaching corner. The problem is not that God transcends time (which all Calvinists and most Arminians believe) but that if he made the mountain to observe, he must also have created an observable future. But this means it must already be in some sense a divinely fixed reality that cannot be otherwise. Even God cannot have certain knowledge of an uncertain event. God's foreknowledge may not actually *cause* events, but it cannot be uncertain knowledge and must include foreknowledge of causes as well as of events. Are not causes themselves "events"?

4. *God's knowledge is certain knowledge.* The Calvinist concludes that if God is omniscient in any intelligible sense, his knowledge must ultimately be knowledge of his own eternal omnipotent plan. Nothing less than God's own omnipotence could undergird his exhaustive knowledge of all beings. Only God can control the future, because only God controls the present. This is why it was so unreasonable for Adam and Eve in the Garden to allow the contingency that Satan might possibly be right and God wrong. To begin with, God could only be right about this claim on the future if he actually controlled the future to such a degree that he could secure the intended result. To deny this control is to be forced into one of two remaining possibilities. The rationalist alternative is that Adam controls the future to such a degree that he can be sure God is wrong ("You will not surely die"). The irrationalist alternative is that nobody controls the future, so the future is an indeterminate realm of pure possibility. Neither alternative can be avoided by the would-be-autonomous sinner; thus, heathen philosophy has oscillated between them ever since.

It is no doubt true that God's knowledge includes what would happen or be true upon certain conditions. That is, God knew what would be the state of the history of postwar Japan if President Truman had decided not to drop nuclear bombs on Nagasaki and Hiroshima. He also knew with infallible certainty that Truman would actually decide to use the bombs. Knowledge of logically possible but unfulfilled conditions is quite consonant with knowledge of which conditions will actually occur. God must necessarily have both if he is omniscient.

Underlying much confusion on this topic is the subconscious presupposition, the subliminal conviction, that if a human choice is not totally free from causal influences it cannot be a real choice at all. But once more, the assumption is being made that the will must be autonomous to be real. In a created cosmos, every fact and relation and event is part of the created order. It is precisely its place in the great plan of God that gives it reality, significance and, ultimately, its existence in the first place.

The same must be true for the human will, as it surely is part of God's creation. Recall the hundreds of "freewill choices" that led Joseph and Mary to be in Bethlehem on that cold Christmas night, rather than warm in their own home up in Nazareth. Every human choice that led to the inevitable fulfillment of that single prophecy was a real choice. The fact that it was fixed in God's eternal purposes was the very thing that gave it reality.

A glowing light filament is a real event precisely because it is caused to glow by the human act of turning on a switch, coupled with other causes like the flow of electricity in the wire. Likewise, a human choice is a real event and no less my personal choice, although thousands of causal details, some moral, some teleological and some physical, contribute to the outcome. We are actually quite unconscious of most of the factors involved in a choice, even when it is consciously deliberated. I have already explained that an uncaused event is for all practical purposes indistinguishable from a chance event. And chance eliminates omniscience, omnipotence, purpose and ultimately knowledge itself from the divine as well as the human consciousness. Therefore, it seems that for anyone to be saved, God must act himself to choose to save sinners and then choose the sinners to save.

The Biblical Evidence for Election

The following verses are relevant to the study of divine election: Exodus 33:19; Deuteronomy 7:6-7; Psalm 65:4; Isaiah 46:9-11; 55:11; Daniel 4:35; Matthew

11:27; 20:15; 22:14; 24:24, 31; Mark 13:20; John 15:16; Acts 13:48; 16:14; 18:10; 18:27; Romans 9:11-13, 16; 11:29; Ephesians 1:4; 2:10; Philippians 2:12-13; 2 Thessalonians 2:12-14; 2 Timothy 1:9; Titus 1:1; 1 Peter 1:1-2; Revelation 13:8; 17:8, 14; and many others.

These verses are a small selection of nearly 150 texts on election, predestination, foreordination and similar terms. This is not a small topic in the Bible, if the sheer number of references says anything. We will look more closely at an even smaller selection.

When Jesus said to his disciples in John 15:16, "You did not choose me, but I chose you," he hardly meant, "I decided to choose you because I realized you would choose me." The condition that the Arminian would have the believer supply is expressly excluded in verses such as John 10:26: "You do not believe, because you are not of My sheep" (NASB). If Jesus were an Arminian, he would have said, "You are not of my sheep because you do not believe." Throughout John's Gospel, Christ's sheep are the elect whom he has chosen out of the world, whom the Father has given him out of the world to be his very own. Peter calls them "a chosen people" (1 Pet 2:9) and "a people for His name" (Acts 15:14 NASB). Jesus was simply following the Old Testament language when he called them "the elect" in the gospels.

Exodus 33:19 begins a series of verses in the Pentateuch that assert that God decides whom he will save—not because they are good enough, but in order to vindicate and express his glory. Deuteronomy 7:6-7 says that God did not elect the Israelites because they supplied a condition, but that he loved them because he loved them. That is, the condition was supplied by God's will alone.

Isaiah 46:9-11 states that God will do everything he plans and his every intention shall be fulfilled. When he plans something he always gets it done—this is what omnipotence means.

Acts 13:48, 16:14 and 18:10 are important verses for showing how the doctrine of election undergirds evangelism. The first states that all who had been ordained to eternal life believed when Paul preached at Antioch. This indicates that Luke considered evangelism the provision of a predestined opportunity for the elect to come to faith, not the provision of a "chance" for some indeterminate number to autonomously believe. In 18:10 God promises

Paul that he will be safe in Corinth even though there are no Christians there, because "I have many people in this city." This seems to refer to the as-yet-unregenerate elect he had there to whom Paul was about to announce the good news. When Lydia "attended unto" (KJV) the gospel, Luke ascribes this to the prior fact that God had "opened her heart" (16:14). This type of language is inexplicable if we assume that God waits for sinners to provide a condition before he can act in mercy.

Romans 9 is the most famous chapter on election in the New Testament. Here we are told that the destinies of Esau and Jacob were chosen by God "before the twins were born or had done anything good or bad" (see vv. 10-14). Next, Paul presents Pharaoh as an example, showing that he is a case of God's raising up a ruler and hardening his heart simply to show his divine power. Therefore, God has mercy on whomever he wills and hardens whomever he wills. All this is to prove that "it [that is, election] does not, therefore, depend on man's desire or effort, but on God's mercy" (v. 16). When Paul is finished expounding this theme, he sums it up with an all-encompassing conclusion: "The gifts and the calling of God are irrevocable" (11:29 NASB).

Romans 9 looks so distinctively Calvinistic that Arminian exegesis has had a hard time coping with it. Arminians' usual interpretation is to claim that the Esau and Jacob of verses 10-14 are not individuals but groups elected to the privileges of the gospel (as "children of the promise") or perhaps to the privileges of service, but *not* to salvation. And of course, from these privileges they may by free will defect.

There are two reasons this is impossible. The first reason is exegetical; the second is a matter of logic. First, the text plainly says that they had not done good or evil (v. 11). This could not be said of a group, whose defection from circumstances of privilege is a matter of doing evil. It can only be said of the unborn individuals. The next verse then says that the choice was made "by him who calls" (that is, by God), in order that the process might be apart from works. But the whole point of the Arminian theory of election on the basis of foreseen faith is that election is based on something the individual *does*. Despite the Arminian gloss, the passage speaks of the individuals concerned by name and nowhere is a group mentioned, nor is election to privileges mentioned. Both these notions are smuggled in to avoid the

Calvinistic force of the verses.

Ad hoc exegesis is hardly enough to do justice to this great chapter. The reader can consult John Piper's *The Justification of God* (Grand Rapids, Mich.: Baker, 1983) for a full exegetical treatment of this part of Romans 9, not to speak of the works of the great Reformed commentators such as John Murray, Charles Hodge, Robert Haldane, William Shedd and Martyn Lloyd-Jones on Romans.

Before looking at the second reason, we should notice that in 2 Thessalonians 2 Paul says that the Thessalonians were elected personally, not just as part of some undefined group. He says that he is bound to give thanks for them because God chose them from the beginning (of time) to be saved through sanctification of the Spirit and belief in the truth of the gospel (v. 13). Here we have several important elements of the Pauline doctrine of election. Election is of individuals to salvation, not merely to the abstract possibility of salvation (cf. Rom 8:29). The choice is God's, not ours, and such a choice must be fulfilled by certain means also chosen by God. God has also chosen that salvation will be accomplished through sanctification and faith in the gospel as truth. Here we have the means to the end clearly defined. Finally, Paul has a specific group of people in mind, namely, the Thessalonian saints to whom he writes. There is nothing impersonal or indefinite about who is in the group of these elect. The elect here spoken of are specific believers personally known to the apostle.

The second reason that groups could not be referred to by Paul as distinct from individuals is God's omniscience. It is true that a finite human being might choose a group of people without knowing exactly who is in the group, just as I can have the abstract idea of the concept of a triangle without knowing all the existing real triangles in the class represented by the idea. This is because I am finite, obviously. But God cannot choose an abstract or merely "possible" future group of people, whether to salvation or to certain privileges without knowing every particular individual who makes up the group. An idea in the mind of God is not, like mine, distinct from the parts that comprise it. God is omniscient and not only knows the abstract idea of a dog, but he also knows all and every existing dog from eternity to eternity that make up the class. Therefore God cannot choose a group for any reason without also choosing who will make up that group. Jesus only confirms this by his illustration of the Good Shepherd who knows the entire class of his sheep by name (Jn 10:3).

The only way to escape this argument is to deny that God is omniscient, which is to abandon the Christian view of God. The Arminians did this in the 1600s after they distanced themselves from the Reformation on the subject of salvation. They did so again in the 1800s after the first flush of Wesleyanism had passed, and they are doing it again today under the cover of evangelicalism and by referring to God in terms of his *openness*.

Even if it can be said that in one sense faith is a condition for justification—and the phrase "justification by faith" has often been understood to mean this—it does not follow that God does not cause the faith. In fact, in order to secure the justification of any individual, God would need to supply both the condition as well as the forensic effect of justification. This is precisely the point Augustine was making when he prayed that God might ask whatever he wanted, if only he would give what he had asked. The Bible expressly states that faith (and/or repentance) is a gift of God in Ephesians 2:8-10, Philippians 1:29 and 2 Timothy 2:25, to list a few places.

When God decrees that there will be a condition attached to a future eventuality, he must also necessarily decree to supply that condition, in order to secure the result. Means must be provided to ensure that the ends will be achieved. How else could a rational being guarantee anything in the future? Even God cannot produce an end without a means, and Reformed thought has pointed out that even when God acts on the soul itself to inspire Scripture or to regenerate the soul, he uses his Word as an instrument or means.

Conclusions

1. Total depravity means in particular that the human will is not an independent choosing mechanism in the head, but an integral part of the fallen human nature, in bondage to sin because the sinner is in bondage to sin. To paraphrase Antony Flew, "If the first point of Dort is in, autonomy is out."

2. Depravity may also be referred to as "total inability," "spiritual slavery," the "dominion of sin" or "moral incapacity," depending on what result of sin is being emphasized.

3. The First Point of Dort must be preached not only because it is true and part of the gospel, but in order to unseat the carnally secure and so to "discover close hypocrites," as the Puritans were wont to put it. In the 1600s, *close* meant "securely hidden," and *to discover* meant "to reveal by uncovering."

4. Election cannot be based on any condition the sinner supplies because the sinner is "fast bound in sin and nature's night" and cannot lift a finger toward his own salvation without supernatural grace to enliven the will. Sinners must be *made willing*. Only then, "if any man will," may he come to Jesus and receive life.

We turn now to the question of how grace guarantees the perseverance of the saints.

Further Reading

For explanations of election, the systematic theologies of W. G. T. Shedd and Charles Hodge have full and clear chapters. The recently reprinted volumes of Francis Turretin's *Institutes of Elenctic Theology* (Phillipsburg, N.J.: Presbyterian & Reformed, 1992) should also be consulted. The term *elenctic* refers to its apologetic content in refuting such enemies of the Reformation as the Socinians.

John Calvin's first commentary on a book of the Bible was on Romans in 1539. I have also had reason to value John Piper's carefully argued study of election in Romans 9:1-27, *The Justification of God* (Grand Rapids, Mich.: Baker, 1983).

Luther's *The Bondage of the Will* is conveniently published by Westminster Press (Philadelphia: 1969), in the same volume as the *Diatribe on Free Will* by Erasmus. See also the large and helpful discussions in the volume titled *Sin* by G. C. Berkouwer (Grand Rapids, Mich.: Eerdmans, 1973).

For the five points of Calvinism expounded effectively from the Gospel of John, see Kenneth Good's *God's Gracious Purpose* (Grand Rapids, Mich.: Baker, 1979).

J. I. Packer has republished his introductory essay on Owen's *The Death of Death in the Death of Christ* in his recent *A Quest for Godliness* (Wheaton, Ill.: Crossway Books, 1990).

7

Grace & Perseverance: Salvation & Its Security

In order for a rational being to achieve certain ends, it is necessary for a whole chain of causes and effects to be brought together coherently. First, the purpose to be accomplished must be conceived. Then the materials for the project must be gathered or otherwise made available. Next, a chain of causes commensurate with the achievement of such an end must be designed. Finally, each cause must be sequentially brought about or done so that the end or plan is actually realized.

God is just such a rational being. The Bible makes it clear that he planned the world from eternity and wholly within his own nature (theologians call this the divine decree). Then God created the cosmos as the material stage for the drama to unfold in history. In this way, his eternal purpose to glorify himself by the salvation of the elect and the judgment of unbelievers would be fulfilled. By his providence, he then secured each cause and effect, aiming the whole as well as every detail toward the intended end. He allows nothing to happen by chance, or in error. He has no need to experiment with abstract possibilities: "I am God, and there is no one like Me, declaring [and therefore knowing] the end from the beginning" (Is 46:9-10 NASB).

Who, then, can reasonably doubt that God will actually achieve the designed results he intended when he created the world? If you have even a shadow of doubt about this, I urge you to peruse carefully the opinion of the prophet Isaiah, especially noting 40:10, 13-14, 25-26, 28; 41:4, 20-23; 42:5, 8-9; 43:1-7, 13; 44:6-8, 24-28; 45:5-7, 18-25; 46:8-13; 48:3; 55:6-11. It is unimaginable that this prophet could have thought that Jehovah's plans could be thwarted by any human alternative. No doubt sin interrupts God's purposes in an understandable temporal sense, but it cannot divert it or prevent its final fulfillment.

When we say that "God is a rational being," we do not mean that our finite human consciousness can comprehend or encompass all that he is or does. Nor do we mean that we have a natural right to know everything that God is doing or why he does what he does. God is under no obligation to tell me everything I want to know. By God's *rationality* we mean that God does not contradict himself either in his internal relations or in his revealed Word (2 Tim 2:13; Tit 1:2; Heb 6:18; 1 Jn 2:7). We also mean that it is God's internal rational coherence that is the ultimate standard of what is reasonable, not the autonomously directed human mind. It follows necessarily that when God plans to do something, he designs the means in such a way that it is commensurate with, or corresponds with, the end to be achieved. God does not design means that fail to get his will done.

The Glory of God

The ultimate reason for creating the world (rather than not bothering to create at all) is clearly given in the Bible. For example, Revelation states, "Thou hast created all things, and for thy pleasure they are and were created" (4:11 KJV). The great theologian Jonathan Edwards wrote a careful essay on this topic called *A Dissertation on the End for Which God Created the World.* This end of course is the manifestation of God's glory to another being, and for this a finite creation is necessary. Edwards mentions Isaiah 43:1-7, 48:11, 60:21, Romans 11:36, 1 Peter 4:11, and those passages in which something is being done "for his name's sake," which are taken by Edwards to be synonymous with glorifying God. What is meant, then, by something existing "for the glory of God"?

The word for *glory* in the Old Testament is *kābôd,* which originally meant "heaviness," "importance" or "significance." It came to mean magnificence when applied to such objects as the sun or the symbols of royalty displayed by a king. Hence, it could be used to describe the magnificent appearance of an angel or the radiance of God himself, as in a vision. Therefore, to glorify something means to add to something's magnificence or to display favorably its attributes. In particular, to glorify God is to express his attributes of significance and greatness through obedience and worship. And this involves knowing accurately what they are.

The New Testament word translated "glory" is *doxa,* which has two meanings in Greek. The first is "opinion," a meaning never used in the New Testament itself, but common in other Greek literature. The word comes from the root of the word that means "to seem or appear," because one's opinions are controlled by how things appear to be. The second meaning was translated as the Latin word *gloria,* which means "a magnificent appearance," as of the sun or a king in his royal raiment. When used in reference to someone's reputation, it means "importance," "greatness," "renown" or "significance." Therefore, to "glorify God" means to exhibit and express the greatness of God's attributes in the creation, usually by worship and obedience. Since the highest element of the creation is our human nature in God's own image, we are the part of creation that glorifies God most of all.

When the Bible speaks of the creation "glorifying God," it means that God's attributes and significance are being displayed by elements or events in the creation itself, often through praise. The phrase "for the glory of God" therefore means "for the display and expression of God's attributes" in the finite cosmos, especially in the history of the unfolding of human redemption from sin, "things into which angels long to look" (1 Pet 1:12 NASB). An important part of worship is the enjoyment of the contemplation of the divine attributes and the way they have been displayed and given meaning to God's people during the drama of redemption. The task of the theologian is therefore highly important in clarifying and teaching the people of God what these attributes are.

God Did Not Need to Create

Since the three Persons of the Godhead exhaust each other's being and consciousness (there is no less or more of God in each Person than in another), God enjoyed perfect love and communication within his own being in eternity. That is, before he created, God did not need someone to love, because he was entirely self-contained. The three Persons of the Trinity were satisfied with each other's being and love. Rather than creating to meet a need or deficiency in himself, God created the finite cosmos in order to express his attributes to and for finite beings.

The creation was in fact an act of love. As creatures, we are the recipients of this act of gracious love extending beyond God's own being. Again, this was solely an act of God's will, not of some internal necessity within his being. In other words, God is the ultimately free being. *Free* here does not mean an uncaused, capricious or chance freedom, but a will free to act creatively in harmony with all of God's other attributes. God's free will is an expression of the divine character. In turn, this means that once we know something of his attributes, such a God can be trusted. We can have faith in God because he is reliable—his attributes are rationally coherent.

Theology and Worship

For Christians, the glorification of God both in personal meditation (or study) and communal worship requires that we have a correct understanding of God's attributes. This is why correct theology will be found behind sound worship. In fact, constructing a correct theology, a correct *theoria,* a correct "beholding" of God, is the prerequisite for the body of Christ to worship God adequately. Otherwise, the word *God* tends to be the name of an idol we have made and does not refer to the Yahweh of the Bible. As E. H. Bickersteth realized as he observed the rise of Arianism among the more liberal Anglicans of his own day, when the doctrine of the Trinity is rejected, one cannot worship properly with the Book of Common Prayer, since it sets forth a trinitarian God and a correspondingly trinitarian form of worship. In his famous *Rock of Ages,* later reprinted as *The Trinity,* he shows exactly why the worshiping believer must see God as triune. It is not enough to "believe in God"—the *kind* of God we believe in determines the kind of worship we give.

In a critique of the Arminian view, we must ask whether justice is being done to God's attributes when they are being minimized or distorted or set into conflict with one another, simply to protect an extrabiblical assumption. It seems clear that this is what has happened in the most recent developments in evangelical Arminianism. When such attributes as God's omniscience and omnipotence are being denied in the interests of preserving the purely imaginary human attribute of metaphysical autonomy, how is God better glorified?

Likewise, it seems clear to the Calvinist that God's glory is not enhanced by the notion that he may in some cases fail to achieve his eternal purpose to save sinners. Such an idea necessarily involves God's using means that are not commensurate with, and incapable of achieving, the ends that he has decreed to fulfil. Divine omnipotence would need to be replaced here by the divine incompetence, and the divine omniscience by the divine nescience, that is, the divine ignorance. It is singularly difficult to see how such attributes can be the basis of what Paul calls "a reasonable worship." Could Paul's phrase in Romans 12:1-2 also include, "We praise thee O Lord, that thou hast only the vaguest idea of how things will turn out"? Or, "We bless thy name O Lord, that thou art able to make clever guesses about the future"? What is mere belief without an adequate worship? This dilemma will be further illustrated when we examine what the Arminian offers us in place of the perseverance of the saints.

Irresistible Grace

When God sets out to save someone, he succeeds in doing so. His saving power cannot in the long run be set aside by the creature, for saving grace is finally irresistible (Jn 6:39). God regenerates each elect person so that he or she invariably responds willingly to the gospel. The preached Word is always accompanied by "the working of his mighty strength" in the case of the elect (Eph 1:19-20; compare 1 Thess 1:4-6). The many means to the end of saving each one of the elect are always so effected that the end always successfully results. The means are infallible because God is infallible. The natural resistance of the fallen nature is invariably overcome in each case.

If God had elected to save everyone without exception, all would certainly be saved. But God never had the slightest intention of saving everyone. That is what the doctrine of election means in the first place: God chooses some, but not all. Since all sinners deserve the wrath of a holy God, they have no just claim on salvation. If any sinner is saved at all, it will be *sola gratia* ("by grace alone"), as the Reformation heroes took pains to remind the church.

Regeneration Is Not an Experience

The new birth must be carefully distinguished from the experience of conversion. Regeneration of the soul is a supernatural act of God whereby he gives life to whomever he will. When the gospel is heard by one of the elect, the Holy Spirit takes that word and applies it savingly to the heart, ensuring the begetting of eternal life within that soul. That is, the gospel comes to the elect not "in word only," but also in the power of the Holy Spirit so that the elect become "imitators of . . . the Lord" (1 Thess 1:4-6).

The newly good tree now brings forth good fruit, and saving faith is the earliest identifiable result. It might take some time, but eventually God overcomes any and all resistance to the initial exercise of faith in Christ, and people come to believe in Jesus as their Savior. The initial infusion of the resurrection life of Christ into the human soul is an event, not a process. The new life is necessarily either present or not present, which means that at some point, it must be newly present for the first time. This act of God is therefore an event, not a process. The exercise of saving faith will inevitably follow eventually in each case of regeneration.

I say "eventually" because everyone's experience of the conversion process is unique to that person's needs as God sees them. It is quite possible for a person to hear the gospel for the first time in an evangelistic meeting and come to faith while the preaching is in progress and be saved that very night. Afterward such people may testify to a relatively sudden experience in which it is not possible for them to experientially distinguish between their conversion and their regeneration. For them, this distinction is only theological, because their struggle against irresistible grace is relatively brief—everything comes together in a matter of minutes. Others have an extended battle over many years, involving many issues and various levels of seeking and of sinful resistance to Christ. But in every case the Good Shepherd pursues that sheep until it is found. Francis Thompson's famous poem "The Hound of Heaven" is about this extended spiritual pursuit. Conversion is for these people a long experience of many crises and events. But in every case the result is the same, for whether conversion is fast or slow, eventually God wins, and the lost sheep is home at last.

So regeneration is an act of God and is instantaneous, taking place deep in the innermost subconscious reaches of the heart, and is therefore nonexperiential. It is accurately compared in the Bible with natural birth. A woman does not "experience" fertilization until the developing egg begins to have biological effects that are unmistakable. What she is "experiencing" is the development of a new life within—the process of pregnancy. Accordingly, *conversion is our human response to the movements of the new life within.* This takes time, and is consciously experienced. When people give their testimony, they are describing their conversion, their experience of God's working in their life. Of course no one can be exactly certain when they were regenerated, although often our opinion of the time must be close to the truth of the case, because our awareness of the effects of the gospel are often quite clear. We may presume in such cases that those giving testimony are recounting the effects of the gospel being sovereignly applied to their spiritual needs.

One thing is made very clear in the Bible: regeneration is *not* brought about by "the will of the flesh, nor of the will of man, but of God" (Jn 1:13 NASB). Other passages also incidentally drop hints that the saints are those who "through Him are believers in God" (1 Pet 1:21 NASB) because only those who are "appointed for eternal life" believe (Acts 13:48). James too says in passing that "he chose to give us birth through the word of truth" (1:18). God tells Paul that before the gospel was even heard in Corinth, the elect were already chosen: "I have many people in this city" (Acts 18:10).

However, these facts have not prevented theologians from using words like *regeneration* in a much wider sense, and John Calvin himself preferred to use it as a synonym for the entire renewal process of the Christian's life and spiritual growth.

Key Verses on Irresistible Grace
See Deuteronomy 30:6; Ezekiel 36:26-27; Matthew 11:25-27; John 1:12-13; 3:3-8, 27; 5:21; 6:37, 44-45, 64-65; Acts 11:18; 16:14; Romans 8:30; 1 Corinthians 4:7; 2 Corinthians 3:6-8; Galatians 1:15-16; Ephesians 1:11, 18; 2:1-5,

8-10; Philippians 1:29; 2:12-13; 2 Timothy 2:25-26; Hebrews 9:15; 1 Peter 1:23; 2 Peter 1:3. Of these passages, some are of particular interest here.

Deuteronomy 30:6 states as a promise of God that he will "circumcise your hearts," a reference to God's future regeneration of the elect in Israel. Later prophets (as in Ezek 36) show that God will certainly (irresistibly) fulfill that promise. This is something that God must do, for no one can perform such a spiritual operation on their own hearts. True, God commands his people to "circumcise therefore the foreskin of your heart" (Deut 10:16 KJV), but the context shows that it is simply a command to repent ("and be no more stiff-necked"). If the command to repent and believe is accompanied by the regenerating power of God in an individual case, that person is both enlightened and regenerated to life by that very command. Commands are one of the forms of God's Word that are most often used by him to produce repentance and faith.

John 5:21 says that the Father has the power to raise the dead (how much cooperation from the dead does God need to do this?) and the Son likewise "gives life to whom he is pleased to give it." In the next chapter, Jesus promises that every one of those in the category of "all that the Father gives me" will certainly come to Jesus, and all who come will certainly be received by the Lord (6:37). Its hard to see how mere human resistance could effect this result. In verses 44-45 Jesus warns not only that no one may come unless the Father draws him or her but also that those who are drawn will be finally resurrected to life with the Son. In verses 64-65 Jesus adds that he was able even then to tell who would believe in him, and the difference again is explained by the Father's enablement of the sinner. This enablement is not the mere influencing of people in general, but the pulling or dragging of individuals to Jesus by God's power. There is no question concerning the meaning of the Greek here, and the Arminian attempts to weaken it to "wooing" or a mere "influence" that can be resisted indefinitely are singularly unconformable to the language of John 6.

Ephesians 1:11 says that God works out (operates, energizes) everything by the power of his own will. This then becomes the foundation for the strong statement concerning irresistible grace found later (2:8-10). The promise here is not merely that Christians have the possibility of performing good works on the basis of God's grace, but that God has predestined that we will *actually walk* in those good works.

In Philippians 1:29 Paul states that the ability to believe is a gift of God, and in 2:12-13 he bases our ongoing experience of working out our own salvation on the prior working of God in our souls: "For it is God who works in you to will and to act according to his good purpose." Our working is essentially the outworking of God's "inworking" gift. Here our sense of responsibility for persevering is based squarely on the prior activity of God. There can be no doubt that the mere promise of God's continued working in our lives has always had the effect of encouraging the saints to greater efforts of faith and activity. Any number of believers can testify to the energizing effects of just such verses in their own growth in the Lord. This is why unbelieving historians are so puzzled by the tremendous activism of the Calvinistic communities they write about. They confuse predestination with an enervating fatalism and cannot then understand how the Calvinist ever manages to accomplish anything. They express amazement that Calvinism has produced such great evangelists, businessmen and politicians.

Is the Divine Purpose Always Accomplished?
The question of whether God as a rational being is really capable of designing and effecting means of such a kind as to accomplish his intentions comes to a head a passage like Ephesians 1, where God's eternal purpose for the elect is clearly stated.

In 1:4 the purpose of election is stated: "He chose us in Him before the foundation of the world, that we should be holy and blameless before Him" (NASB). At any moment in history this verse must minimally refer to those specific believers alive at the time. In 1:9-12, God's eternal will is said to be that all things might finally consummate in Christ, in whom "we have obtained an inheritance, . . . that we . . . should be to the praise of His glory" (NASB). He even specifies a guarantee in the form of a "pledge" given in order to secure the "redemption of God's own possession" (1:14 NASB). This seal of the Holy Spirit must be given to specific individuals and is also presumably irresistible, since it is based on the reliability of God's promise. As Paul puts it in Romans 9:19, "Who resists his will?"

These few passages are decisive in themselves and also prepare us for the last point of Dort. It follows necessarily that if God has foreordained and chosen who will be saved and has irresistibly worked by his grace in their lives to secure their regeneration and good works, then the truly regenerate saints cannot finally be lost. As the Puritans used to put it, the true saints persevere to the end and so are saved. Today we commonly refer to their being "eternally secure" in Christ. What evidence do we have in the Bible for this conclusion? It certainly sounds reasonable, granting the other points. But is it true?

When the early Arminians tried to hang on to the idea of eternal security, they found it impossible without the other four points of Reformed soteriology. Likewise, we may now establish that the doctrine of perseverance follows naturally, once the other four are established.

The Perseverance of the Saints

Jesus tells us in Matthew 24:13 that those who persevere to the end shall be saved, but who is included in this class? Some have sought to limit this reference to an elect group at the time of the great tribulation referred to in 24:21-22. In this view, the perseverance would consist of lasting to the end of the tribulation, or until Christ comes again to set up his kingdom on earth. Matthew 24:22 states explicitly that the time of the tribulation will be kept short so that the elect can actually survive it. If it were allowed to continue, there would be no one left alive on earth. Matthew 24:29-30 states that the Second Coming will take place "immediately after the distress of those days." Thus it is clear that the tribulation will be terminated by Christ's coming itself.

While this question is of some interest in connection with the nature of the tribulation period, the principle of perseverance is not affected by it. The description of the coming tribulation does not start in Matthew 24 until verse 15. Verses 4-14 seem to apply to the whole time of the present age, before the tribulation starts in earnest or intensifies toward the end of the age.

The term *perseverance of the saints* was used by the Puritans because it was being contrasted with the idea of apostasy. Arminians always argue that the fact of apostasy among professing believers (and we all know of such cases) proves that a real Christian can be lost. But there is no way an Arminian can prove that any particular apostate was truly regenerate in the first place.

John says of certain false teachers who apostatized that "if they had belonged to us, they would have remained with us; but their going showed that none of them [really] belonged to us [in the first place]" (1 Jn 2:19). So a person giving up the faith merely provides the observer with evidence of unregeneracy.

Arminians (and Roman Catholics) insist that we cannot know with any certainty who the elect ones are. In other words, it would be mere pride for people to imagine that their salvation is in any ordinary sense secure or certain. In fact, the Council of Trent (which met intermittently from 1545 to 1563) actually states that Christians who claim to know whether they are going to heaven are anathematized as heretics. We will know who is going to heaven only when we get there, and claiming assurance of salvation is a mortal sin. The elect of whom Jesus speaks are on this basis a smaller class than the regenerate because regenerated believers can lose their salvation by the same free will by which they accepted Christ in the first place. This is a perfectly reasonable conclusion from the presupposition of free will.

Scriptural Proof of Eternal Security
The following passages provide evidence in two steps that true believers cannot be finally lost.

1. *God's elect are known to have eternal life the instant they believe.* See Matthew 18:12-14; John 3:16, 36; 5:24-25; 6:35-40; 10:27-30; 17:11-15; Romans 8:1, 29-30, 35-39.

2. *God will keep his people faithful.* See Romans 8:37-39; 1 Corinthians 1:7-9; Ephesians 1:5, 13-14; 4:30; 1 Thessalonians 5:23-24; Hebrews 9:12-15; 10:14; 1 Peter 1:3-5; 1 John 5:4, 11-13, 20; Jude 1, 24-25.

Two Key Passages
Some of the passages above show quite explicitly that eternal life (not merely the possibility of it) is in the possession of every believer from regeneration onward. Others seem clearly to base believers' security on God himself, whether on his power or his promises, without any reference to a believer needing to shore up that power by his own response to and continuance in the gospel.

In 2 Corinthians 1:22, Ephesians 1:13-14 and 4:30, we find references to a seal of personal ownership being applied to our souls by the Holy Spirit himself that presumably cannot be erased. To imagine erasing a supernatural seal from our own souls is rather like trying to imagine our just deciding never to dream at night. We simply do not have that kind of control of our own inner natures.

A full treatment of this topic, including the careful refutation of all imaginable Arminian arguments against it, took John Owen over six hundred pages in his massive study *The Perseverance of the Saints* (1654), which was completed in a hurry when the Parliament asked him to do another project on Socinianism. (Nevertheless, it remains the definitive work on the topic and should be studied carefully.) However, we will concern ourselves here with two decisive passages that give direct proof of the eternal security of the regenerate: John 10 and Romans 8.

1. *John 10.* This is the well-known passage on the Good Shepherd and his sheep. It opens with the image of the sheepfold and with warnings against fleshly attempts to circumvent truth and grace. Jesus points to the individual care of the Shepherd for his sheep and draws attention to the fact that the Shepherd knows each sheep by name (10:3). Then he adds that these sheep know and recognize the voice of their own Shepherd (vv. 4-5). This seems to indicate that for Jesus, the elect are supernaturally affected by the preached Word in such a way that they are especially enlightened to respond to it. In other words, God causes the elect to recognize their Savior in the gospel.

Then, having identified himself as the door to the fold and as the Good Shepherd himself, Jesus moves on to the supreme sacrifice of giving his life for the sheep. In verses 14-15 he brings together the two truths that he knows his sheep and that they know him. He then links this mutual recognition to the mutual recognition of the first and second persons in the Trinity. This recognition can hardly be an inaccurate or merely probable knowledge.

Later in the passage, Jesus again confronts his enemies in the crowd (vv. 22-30). He warns them that they have not become believers in him because they are not in this group called "my sheep," and he therefore does not know them as his own. If they were his sheep, they would recognize who Jesus is. He identifies his sheep with the final elected saints, a concept familiar to first-century Jews because of the writings of the prophets: "I give them eternal life, and they shall never perish; no one can snatch them out of my hand" (v. 28). This verse makes three points about the sheep. First, they are given eternal life now, not the mere possibility of a future eternal life. Second, they can never be lost ("shall never perish"). Finally, no one can remove them from the Son's safekeeping. "No one" must presumably include the saved person, Satan and any other possible candidate for challenging the Good Shepherd's keeping power. These three things alone guarantee the eternal security of those sheep. It specifically excludes the common Arminian comment on this verse: "No one else can take us out of the Father's hand, but we can take ourselves out." "No one" must exclude ourselves, too, unless God did not intend us to take *all* of this text seriously.

2. *Romans 8:28-39.* This passage includes an extended proof of the security of the believer in Christ. It first states that believers can be confident that everything is worked together by God toward the good of those who "love him, who have been called according to his purpose" (v. 28). Then follows what the Puritans called "the Golden Chain" of divine acts to secure the salvation of the elect (vv. 29-33). This group is labeled "those God foreknew" (v. 29).

At this point the Arminian says, "There it is! The ones who are predestinated are those whom God *foreknew would believe.* Election is based on God's foreknowledge. The same thing is stated in 1 Peter 1:2: 'chosen according to the foreknowledge of God.' What could be plainer?"

Well, the Calvinist thinks the Arminian's exegesis could be plainer. The verses quoted here do not state that election is *based on* foreknowledge. The passage in Romans says that the class of those labeled *the called* and "whom he foreknew" is coextensive with the class labeled *the predestinate,* and the second says that election is according to foreknowledge. This says no more than that election is in harmony with foreknowledge and has the same subjects, not that foreknowledge must precede election, as the Arminian theory requires. It may in fact be teaching the Calvinist view that God's foreknowledge is simply foreknowledge of his own chosen plan in each person's case. After all, the text says that "those God foreknew he also predestined" (v. 29). It is clearly persons, not mere events or generalities, that God foreknows.

The matter of the coextensive classes is much more interesting, as Paul continues with the idea in verse 30: "All those in the category of the predestinate, these and these only, and all of these, were the subjects of the call just mentioned. And those in the class of the called, these and these only, are those whom he declares righteous or justified, upon their exercise of saving faith. Then those in this class of the called are the ones whom he brings to glory; these, all of these, and none else but these" (my paraphrase). So the classes of the called, the predestinated, the justified and the glorified are precisely coextensive. If you are in one group, you are necessarily in all the other groups, because they are the same people exactly. For Paul, it is simply a matter of defining clearly the contents and limits of these classes.

This chain of reasoning is completely devastating to the Arminian position. Even if the Bible did contain verses teaching free will, they would make no difference to the exegesis of these verses in Romans 8. "The Golden Chain," as the Puritans called it, is complete in the inclusiveness of the classes described, not just in the mere listing of individual links mentioned. (Illumination, sanctification and resurrection are other links of the chain, but are here omitted.) "Those God foreknew *he also* predestined"—each link in the chain is described in these terms. Finally, as if his favorite term had been inadvertently omitted, Paul completes the chain by calling those glorified in verse 30 "the elect" in verse 33 (NASB).

The precise destiny of the predestined ones is to be "conformed to the likeness of his Son" (v. 29). This, incidentally, is a description of the process of sanctification, which we might perhaps have expected to have been mentioned between justification and glorification in verse 30. The destiny of the elect, then, as well as their destination, is predestined. All the links are in place, joining those who are effectively called with their final glorification. Without holiness, no one shall see the Lord, says Hebrews 12:14.

But Paul is not finished with his case. He invites his readers to draw the appropriate conclusions too. "What, then, shall we say in response to this?" he demands (v. 31). The first thing we must say is that although they are indeed sinners, the elect can have no objection raised against their salvation at the final judgment, because God himself is the one who justifies them, having heard the testimony of his Son, their advocate (v. 34). Then he lists some things that might conceivably induce the elect to be separated from God's electing love.

After a predictable list (vv. 35-37), he says he is convinced that nothing dead, nothing alive, no angelic powers, no demonic entities, nothing now existing, nothing that might exist in the future, at the upper reaches or at the lower reaches of the philosophers' great chain of being, nor any other created thing, can separate the elect from God's electing and predestining love.

This is a totally comprehensive list—and would include human free will too, were we to grant it to the Arminian for the sake of the argument. No further proof of eternal security could be asked for, although much more could be offered. The reading list on page 142 indicates that John Gill deals with some twenty verses more than I have covered here, and most of them make Arminianism impossible.

Conclusions

1. It follows irresistibly from the other four points of Dort that the truly regenerate are eternally secure in God's eternal electing love.

2. Nothing in the creation can separate the elect from their destiny in glory.

3. "Praise be to the God and Father of our Lord Jesus Christ, who has blessed us in the heavenly realms with every spiritual blessing in Christ" (Eph 1:3). "All" spiritual blessings must include the blessing of perseverance, lest all the others be neutralized and not be blessings after all. Without the grace of perseverance, none of the others could be finally effective. The plan of a rational being cannot be incoherent. His means must conform to his ends.

4. God, being both rational and omnipotent, cannot fail in any of his purposes (Is 43:13). "This is the will of God, your sanctification," says Paul in 1 Thessalonians 4:3 (NASB); thus, this will of God must necessarily be fulfilled in the conformity of God's sheep to the image of the Good Shepherd. The means of a sovereign God must necessarily achieve the end he plans.

5. The later Remonstrants, presupposing free will, were quite right to give up the idea of the saints' perseverance. It cannot be consistently maintained without the other four points of Dort, and it cannot be rationally maintained upon the assumption of free will. Modern evangelicals who claim to be Calvinist on the ground of believing in "once saved, always saved" have no logical right to their belief in eternal security and are simply inconsistent Arminians.

Further Reading

For the greatest exposition and defense of the perseverance of the saints, see John Owen's *The Saints' Perseverance Explained and Confirmed* in volume eleven of the Banner of Truth Trust (London, 1966) edition. This is a large work (over six hundred pages), but it should be consulted. Chapter three, titled "The Immutability of the Purposes of God," is a good place to start, as it is only twenty pages long. Most of the book is a response to the Arminian arguments of John Goodwin, one of the few Arminian Puritans.

For a careful exposition of key verses supporting perseverance, see also the relevant portions of John Gill's *The Cause of God and Truth* (brought out in four parts from 1735 to 1738; reprint London: W. H. Collingridge, 1855). Gill has been evaluated by careful Reformed critics as having *hyper-Calvinistic elements, but this makes no noticeable difference to his treatment of "Arminian verses." In part one, over fifty passages are examined.

For a modern source on perseverance, see G. C. Berkouwer's *Grace and Perseverance* (Grand Rapids, Mich.: Eerdmans, 1958).

For the connection between true doctrine and the devotional life, see Bishop E. H. Bickersteth's classic *The Trinity* (reprint Grand Rapids, Mich.: Kregel, 1957). This is possibly the most helpful book on the Trinity published in the 1800s.

8

An Effective Atonement

*E*vangelicals are traditionally used to a view of salvation based on a generalized Arminian type of theology. They are therefore not used to thinking analytically about exactly how the atonement works. But it may reasonably be asked, "Exactly how does the death of someone two thousand years ago have any effect on me in the twentieth century? How can the cross be a saving instrument?" No one can be a Christian for very long without asking this kind of question, and the Arminian gives a very different answer from the Calvinist.

The Arminians prior to Dort wanted to modify the Reformed conception of the atonement by claiming that the cross did not actually save any particular person. The death of Christ, said the Remonstrants, satisfied the justice of God in such a way that it rendered all people savable without actually making anyone's salvation certain. It rendered God propitious toward everyone. As Platt, in his article "Arminianism" in James Hastings's *Encyclopaedia of Religion and Ethics,* puts it, "The Arminian held that the Atonement was universal. It was of infinite value, designed for all, accomplished for all. It made the salvation of no man actual, but rendered the salvation of all men possible, the result being in every case conditioned by faith." Again, "The supreme principle of Arminianism is conditionalism" (1:811). We supply the condition that God needs before he can act by our own freewill decision.

Theories of the Atonement

The fact that Christ saves us through his cross is no doubt the heart of the gospel. Exactly how this mechanism works, however, has produced several theories in the course of church history.

The earliest theory of the atonement was called the *ransom theory*. That is, since one of Jesus' own ways of describing his central task was "a ransom for many," it was thought that he must have offered himself as a ransom or payment to Satan as the rightful owner of the sinner. The captives could then justly be freed. Eventually it was realized, however, that not only did Satan have no rights over even sinners, but that God could have sovereignly freed them if he so wished, and the devil could not have done anything about it. A ransom is only paid because one is powerless to get back the captives any other way. It was correctly concluded that it was actually the Son who paid the ransom to the Father's justice, not to Satan. "Ransom" was just a figure of speech for a satisfactory payment, and in this case the payment was sacrificial.

This clarification led to the *satisfaction theory,* which saw the atonement as a payment to redress the cosmic imbalance caused in the moral structure of the universe by sin. Athanasius and Augustine both spoke clearly of God's justice requiring satisfaction on account of sin, but St. Anselm refined the theory in the high Middle Ages in his *Cur Deus Homo?* ("Why did God become man?"). He explained satisfaction as requiring that God's honor be maintained by the sinner having to correct the blunder. But it was humanity as a whole who caused the dishonor, so humanity must make the amends. Only God is able to do this task, so he became man to do it on our behalf, in the person of his Son. The necessity of the Incarnation is thus explained. The sinless Savior, as the God-man, generates infinite merit by his perfect sacrifice, and this merit is then freely available for the faithful. The ransom is paid to God's honor, to his justice. Although it is by no means complete, this view of the matter is far closer to Scripture, pointing to the sinner's need for a substitute.

The *penal substitution theory* is a further refinement of the concept of satisfaction. The Bible makes it clear (for example, in Is 53; Rom 3:21-26; Gal 3:13) that Jesus died for sins not his own, in order to be the sacrificial substitute for the real sinner, taking upon himself the sinner's punishment. "In my place condemned he stood, . . . sealed my pardon with his blood" (Philip Bliss, "Man of Sorrows"). He offered up a perfect life, being in his own person the Torah incarnate. His blood indicated that he really died in the sinner's place and that this substitutionary death really satisfied God's justice. Only a perfectly loving God could do such a thing, and only a perfectly just human being could be the means. Substitutionary satisfaction thereby fulfills all the symbolism in Scripture about the need for a sacrifice. This was the view of the Reformers.

Subjective theories are also suggested by some of the Bible's language. The *moral influence theory* contains undoubted truth but requires a theory of penal substitution to undergird it. Jesus' dying on the cross draws out our heartfelt response precisely because he is doing this *for me!* Not in a million years could I ever satisfy God for my own sins.

After the Reformation, the Socinians developed the notion that Jesus died to express in his martyrdom an example of gratuitous obedience. The atonement was not necessary, but it was an example of God's moral concern with sin. Their view seemed so feeble to the great Arminian Hugo Grotius that he addressed the issue in a book of his own.

The Governmental Theory of the Atonement

According to the new Arminian theory developed by Grotius, God accomplished the atonement by setting forth Christ as an example intended to illustrate what sin actually deserves. Sinners are supposed to conclude from this that in order for the world to be run properly, they must be obedient to God morally. Thus this theory is called the *governmental theory*. As Platt makes clear, it was invented as an alternative to the Calvinistic idea of Christ's dying as a penal substitute for the sinner. It has been pointed out by other scholars that Grotius's view is really a form of the moral influence theory, since its saving power lies not in its being a price or punishment paid on sinners' behalf, but in its being merely an example provided by God to induce faith and repentance by revealing how frightful is sin and its just deserts.

That there is indeed a moral influence intended by God in the death of his Son cannot be reasonably doubted. But to reconstruct the entire working of the atonement around this idea is to place too heavy a strain on the concept, while ignoring other elements in the atonement that figure even larger in the Bible than any degree of moral influence.

The moral power of the cross to influence sinners toward God is well illustrated by a famous hymn:

> When I survey the wond'rous Cross
> On which the Prince of Glory died,
> My richest gain I count but loss
> And pour contempt on all my pride.

But this does not negate, nor is it an adequate substitute for

> They turned their eyes away
> And treated him with scorn;
> But 'twas their griefs upon him lay,
> Their sorrows he has born.

> Like sheep we went astray
> And broke the fold of God,
> Each wandering in a different way,
> But all the downward road.

> How dreadful was the hour
> When God our wanderings laid
> And did at once his vengeance pour
> Upon the Shepherd's head!

How glorious was the grace
When Christ sustained the stroke!
His life and blood the Shepherd pays
A ransom for the flock.

These last four stanzas are from the same Isaac Watts who wrote the first and more famous stanza. Watts had no difficulty inviting the flock to sing of both substitutionary sacrifice and of its moral influence virtually in the same breath. Grotius, however, rejected the first while promoting the second.

It is important for our present purposes to observe that in Grotius's view, the actual efficacy of the death of Christ in saving us depends entirely on our response. The death itself is a mere demonstration of divine rectitude, which of itself saves no one. Naturally, the Arminians were quite happy with Grotius's view, while Calvinists like John Owen energetically wrote against it, often trying to demonstrate its affinities with the even less orthodox views of the Socinians, to whom it owed little historically. In fact, Grotius's main work on the atonement is actually intended as a critique of Socinianism.

Modern evangelical Arminians often prefer a moral influence theory because it quite strongly lends itself to graphic illustration in gospel preaching, but the concept of substitution is equally easy to illustrate. As early as Genesis 22 we find predictive elements in the offering up of Isaac. The God-given lamb dies in the place of the sinful son of the father: "And Abraham went and took the ram, and offered him up for a burnt offering in the place of his son" (v. 13 NASB).

Some modern liberals have continued to use the language of "moral influence," but they do not have a rational purpose underlying Christ's death to explain how it could be the act of "redeeming love" they offer it as. It is sometimes pointedly observed that we accomplish nothing for the one we love merely by throwing our life away. The question of the meaning of the cross remains, therefore, for all who do not see the connection between the act and its purpose, beyond the bare fact of an embarrassing prophet falling foul of the authorities because his personal style of messiahship failed to meet the popular expectation.

The bottom line for any theory of the atonement is that the death of Christ was a deliberate act on his part. What exactly, did he think he was doing? The Calvinistic view of the death of Christ seeks to answer this question explicitly.

The Reformed View of the Atonement

Calvinists have always recognized the Anselmic and other classical insights concerning the reason for Christ's death. They have also always emphasized the penal substitutionary elements, based on the recognition that the death of Christ was a sacrifice *necessary* to satisfy the divine justice. This "satisfaction theory" coupled with the substitutionary elements, both stated and implied, led to a complete theory of a limited purpose in the death of Christ and a total efficacy to that end. The result is usually called *limited atonement,* a view found in all the Reformed confessions and catechisms, including the Baptist Philadelphia Confession of 1742.

Positively, the Calvinist view is that Christ offered himself as a necessary satisfaction of God's justice by dying as a substitute for all those whom the Father had elected from eternity for salvation. That is, Christ died for *me* in the sense that God sent his Son to die in my place as one of the elect, bearing my punishment, which would have taken me eternity and then some to pay on my own account. By accepting Christ by faith as my Savior in this sense, I am thereby justified at a particular moment in history. That is, I am declared righteous by virtue of Christ's own righteousness being counted to me by grace. I am freely forgiven all my sins that Christ has paid for literally and in historical time.

God is then free not only to forgive me in history upon my justification by faith without ignoring his justice and personal holiness, but also to apply to me by the Holy Spirit's activity all the blessings secured by Christ's atoning death, including the specific blessing of final perseverance. This spiritual application is experienced by the believer as the process of sanctification. Again, we must distinguish between justification as an *event* on the one hand—a change in the forensic relationship between God and the sinner—and sanctification on the other—a lifelong *process* of growth in personal holiness.

For the Calvinist, the death of Christ actually secured and accomplished the certain salvation of the elect by satisfying God's justice and securing the blessings of redemption on behalf of all those for whom the offering was made.

This is what Jesus' intercessory prayer in John 17 was all about. Its scope is deliberately limited: "I have revealed you to those whom you gave me out of the world" (v. 6).

John McLeod Campbell

In his book titled *The Nature of the Atonement* (1856), *John McLeod Campbell explains how he came to realize that as long as the death of Christ is allowed to be in some sense a penal substitution, one is forced to deal with the issue of why everyone is not saved eventually. Then the only alternative becomes a particular redemption. In other words, because John Owen believed the *nature* of the atonement is substitutionary, his conclusion that the *extent* of the atonement is limited to the elect is unavoidable. Because not all are saved, Christ could not have died as a satisfaction for the sins of all existing unbelievers, for that would require God to punish twice for the same sins in the case of those finally lost. Having recounted John Owen's summary of the case, Campbell concludes, "As addressed to those who agree with him as to the nature of the atonement [as a penal substitution], while differing with him as to the extent of its reference [that it was intended for all sinners], this seems unanswerable" (p. 51).

This is a remarkable admission, but since he was already convinced on other grounds that the atonement was an expression of divine love intended for everyone, Campbell chose to modify the nature of the atonement by denying that it was substitutionary. Because of this radical departure from the Westminster Confession, he was removed from the ministry of his Scottish Presbyterian denomination in 1831. I refer to him here only because he clearly saw and admitted what many modern evangelicals are so unwilling to admit: a *substitutionary* atonement must either save everyone without exception or be seen as a limited atonement in the sense that it was designed to save only the elect.

In an important argument (quoted in full in the next chapter), John Owen shows that if Christ died as a penal satisfaction for all the sins of all humanity, as the Arminian would have it, he died for all the sins of unbelief. If so, then God cannot justly condemn unbelievers to hell, since Christ has rendered satisfaction for this unbelief among their other sins. This is the argument that

Campbell said was unanswerable, and the reason is clear. If the death of Christ is a manifestation of justice and love, the justice must necessarily be satisfied, and the love must terminate on a known object. But if justice is satisfied once, it cannot be required again of the same sinner, even though he or she remains in unbelief. And if love's object is knowable, it must consist of either all human beings or some. If all, then all must be saved, because all are atoned for; if some, then the atonement must have been limited in its intention.

The only way to avoid these conclusions is to deny that Christ died to satisfy God's justice. This Campbell did, claiming that in dying, Christ offered a perfect substitute *repentance,* not a substitute *punishment.* The Presbyterians deemed this a heresy by their standards, and they were right. To abandon the element of substitutionary sacrifice is to abandon the atonement as taught in Scripture and as understood by the Reformers.

Payment for Something Purchased

The language of the Bible, from the sacrifice of animals in Eden to provide skins for Adam and Eve to Jesus' death on the cross, is the language of one dying to save others, of a payment made to secure a specific result. From "When I see the blood, I will pass over you" (Ex 12:13) to "Christ, our Passover lamb, has been sacrificed" (1 Cor 5:7), the lamb dies sacrificially to purchase a reprieve of some kind. Whether this is temporary, as when Abraham offers up the ram instead of his son (Gen 22:13), or permanent, as when Jesus offers "for all time one sacrifice for sins" (Heb 10:12), the substitutionary death inspires expressions such as 1 Corinthians 6:20: "You were bought at a price."

Clearly, the Bible uniformly describes the death of Christ as the sacrificial purchase of salvation. What then was purchased, and for whom was the price paid? Apart from being a rather spectacular martyrdom, what did Jesus' death actually achieve? At this point one must choose between the Calvinist or the Arminian type of answer. We have seen that the Arminians believe Christ merely made God propitious toward everyone, without guaranteeing the salvation of any. The Calvinists believe that Christ satisfied God's justice for the sins of a specific group, for whom a certain salvation in all its contributing parts was secured by a complete purchase, infallibly and forever.

An Omnipotent Savior

When the Bible speaks of Christ as "the Lamb slain from the foundation of the world" (Rev 13:8 KJV) or of Jesus coming "to seek and to save that which was lost" (Lk 19:10 NASB), it points to a specific purpose in Christ's death. What was that purpose or intention, and did it succeed? Fifty quotations (like Heb 9:14 or 28) could be provided to show that the death of Christ was a deliberate act of the Father, the Son or the Spirit, and sometimes all of them together. So what did Jesus expect to accomplish by dying?

We can recall here Charles Spurgeon's observation that the Arminians claim that the purpose of the atonement was universal, but that its effectiveness is limited by our human response, while the Calvinists claim that its intended purpose was limited, but its effectiveness was complete. That is, God only ever intended to save the elect, but he does what is necessary to save perfectly every last one of them, however large or small that number may be.

The difference may be best understood by asking whether an omnipotent God could be expected to fail to any degree in achieving what he intended in his Son's sacrifice. If God is all-powerful and has exhaustive knowledge of the state of affairs in his own Son's death, would he not manage to succeed in designing and putting into action all the appropriate and necessary means to achieve the intended end? And if he intended the salvation of all, could he not then achieve the salvation of all? It would be necessary in the case of any individual for God to do only what was needed to save that person. Being omniscient and omnipotent, he would know what had to be done (that is, he could plan the necessary means) and would be capable of getting it done (that is, he could apply the necessary means). A God so competent would have to be irrational or immoral not to do what he needed to do in order to achieve what he wanted to do. The Calvinist therefore concludes not only that God intended the death of Christ to save only the elect, but also that he could not fail to do so successfully. This then is the doctrine of limited atonement, or particular redemption.

Scriptural Proof of Particular Redemption

1. *The purpose of the atonement was the salvation of a specific group* (Mt 1:21; Jn 3:16; Gal 1:3-4; Tit 2:14; 1 Pet 3:18), *and it actually achieved that*

result (Rom 5:8-10; Eph 2:15-16; Col 1:21-22; Heb 9:12).

2. *Christ actually secured by purchase all the gifts needed for the regeneration and sanctification of this group* (1 Cor 1:30; Eph 1:3-4; 5:25-26; Phil 1:29; Tit 2:14; 3:5-6; Heb 13:12).

3. *This group was known to God from eternity, and the sacrifice was designed for them, and for them alone* (Jn 6:35-40; 10:11, 14-18, 24-29; 11:50-52; 17:1-11; Acts 20:28; Rom 8:32-34; Eph 1:3-12; Heb 2:17; 3:1; 9:15; Rev 5:9).

Matthew 1:21 states, "You are to give him the name Jesus, because he will save his people from their sins." Jesus confirms this purpose later in the gospel narrative: "The Son of Man did not come to be served, but to serve, and to give his life as a ransom for many" (20:28). The former verse says that he will actually save a specific group, and the second says that he will do so by a ransom, which was the purpose of the incarnation. Further, the Greek for the phrase "for many" is *anti pollōn* ("instead of many"). This "many" is the subject of several key prophecies, such as Isaiah 53:10-12: "But the LORD was pleased to crush Him, putting Him to grief. . . . The Righteous One, My Servant, will justify the many, as he will bear their iniquities. . . . He Himself bore the sin of many" (NASB).

Titus 2:14 describes the purpose of Christ's death: he "gave himself for us to redeem us from all wickedness and to purify for himself a people that are his very own, eager to do what is good." This verse contains all the essential elements of a particular redemption. The "us" is the elect of 1:1, and the "gave himself" is the act of oblation on the cross. The purpose was "to redeem us," not merely to make a redemption possible. The redemption will solve the sin problem 100 percent, securing us from "all wickedness" and making us "his very own." Further, we will zealously pursue practical sanctification, as distinct from fulfilling merely the Arminian notion of a "carnal Christian," whose unsanctified life is admittedly indistinguishable from the heathen.

Hebrews 9:12 states that Christ as our high priest actually "*obtained* eternal redemption," as distinct from merely opening up the possibility or chance of redemption, conditional on our efforts of faithfulness.

First Corinthians 1:30 says that Christ is actually "made unto us wisdom, and righteousness, and sanctification, and redemption" (KJV) as a climax.

Here the start, the growth process and the glorious consummation of the whole drama of redemption are all said to be provided to us in Christ. The language is once again substitutionary and very much denotes a successfully completed task.

John 17 contains the great high-priestly prayer of Christ, uttered on the eve of the crucifixion. Is it conceivable that an omniscient God could possibly have intended to offer his Son savingly for those for whom the Son was not even willing to pray? He says that he is praying not for the world, but for those whom the Father has given him out of the world (v. 9). Later he also includes all those who will come to faith in him as a result of the testimony of the apostles (v. 20). This of course is the whole body of Christ thereafter, including me personally. It would appear that the offering and the intercession for those for whom the offering was about to be made must be coextensive in intention. It may be asked by some whether the Father would hear and answer such a prayer. The answer is found in Jesus' confidence in John 11:41-42: "I knew that you always hear me."

These verses are, even by themselves, decisively in favor of a particular redemption. However, the reader is advised to make the effort necessary to read John Owen's *The Death of Death in the Death of Christ,* in which a full and convincing defense of a limited atonement is made. Arminians never seem to get around to reading John Owen. If they did, they would perhaps not be Arminians.

When I first encountered Arminian preaching in my home church in South Australia, a series of Bible studies that year confirmed two things to me. First, there were indeed four or five verses in the Bible that looked like they taught the Arminian idea that truly born-again believers could lose their salvation. In those days I was innocent of serious Reformed exegesis and did not know where to look for answers. On the other hand, there were also dozens of verses that clearly taught the security of the believer. Accordingly, I decided that even if I could not answer the challenge of the few "Arminian" verses, I would continue to believe in eternal security, because the majority of verses were in its favor! This of course, is theology by vote counting. We absolutely *must* do better than this.

The next chapter is dedicated to the proposition that there are no "Arminian" verses in the Bible. No Bible-believing Christian can rationally claim to be a "Calminian."

Further Reading

The decisive defense of particular redemption is Owen's *The Death of Death in the Death of Christ* in volume 10 of the *Works* (and also published separately by Banner of Truth Trust). It is written in four parts, and I was completely convinced before I was even through the first part. I then turned to the last part, which covers objections raised from specific verses, to see what he said about 1 John 2:2 and 2 Peter 3:9. I was very surprised to find that these verses contain nothing of help to the Arminian after all.

In *The Grace of God, the Will of Man* (Grand Rapids, Mich.: Zondervan, 1989), an article by Terry Miethe criticizes J. I. Packer's introduction to Owen's *Death of Death* but does not answer Owen's own arguments themselves.

Typical Arminian treatment of important verses can be found in Grant Osborne's articles in Clark Pinnock, ed., *Grace Unlimited* (Minneapolis: Bethany, 1975) and *The Grace of God, the Will of Man.*

For the meticulous exegesis of dozens of verses used both for and against the Calvinistic view, see John Gill's *The Cause of God and Truth* (London: W. H. Collingridge, 1855). The role of presuppositions in approaching the key texts becomes very clear in this work. One is repeatedly surprised that there are often a number of logically possible alternatives to the common Arminian interpretation, and usually only one of them has any likelihood of being correct.

9

Are There Any "Arminian Verses" in the Bible?

*T**he purpose of this chapter is to discuss* the relationship between the Arminian notion of free will and the interpretation given to certain verses in the Bible by Arminians when they try to explain their position from Scripture in response to Calvinism. I will examine how the Arminians exegete certain Bible verses and respond to their interpretations. I will also address some concerns often expressed by Christians who are newly encountering the doctrines of grace and wonder what to do with what are often called the "Arminian verses" in the Bible.

Serious Calvinists are of the conviction that since God cannot contradict himself (see 2 Tim 2:13, Tit 1:2), there cannot be "Arminian" verses in the Bible. For example, it is either true or false that regenerate Christians cannot lose their salvation. If it is false, the Arminians are right who understand certain verses in Scripture to teach that a born-again believer can so defect or decline from the state of grace as to become effectively unregenerate again and finally lost forever.

If Calvinists are right to believe that God so keeps the regenerate believer that he or she cannot be lost, then there can be no verses of the Bible that teach otherwise. It will not do for people who have not given serious attention to this subject to imagine that they can safely refer to something called "Calminianism." If the Bible teaches both positions, the Bible is nonsense and cannot command the attention of logical thinkers.

Since many modern evangelicals have not seriously studied the matter, they would be advised at the outset to withhold judgment and plead ignorance. This is a lot safer than to believe someone who invites us to acquiesce in the notion that the Bible teaches contradictions and yet must be believed nevertheless.

A Question of Strategy

The Bible is the written Word of God, and as the infallible record of God's interpretation of reality, it is to be accepted without reservation, however difficult it may be to understand. No external evidence of mind or sense or feelings can count against it, for upon the presupposition of its truth all Christian rationality stands or falls.

However tiresome it may seem to some to refute the Arminians verse by verse, it is a task most necessary. It does Calvinists no good to try to convince Arminians of their error as long as the Arminian sincerely believes that the Bible teaches Arminianism and Arminianism only. Why should they give much attention to Calvinists if they think there are verses in the Bible that make Arminianism the only possible choice? It is therefore imperative that Calvinists know exactly what to do with every verse of Scripture quoted against their position. This chapter merely begins this task.

It is *not* necessary, however, for every verse in the Bible to teach distinctly Calvinist doctrine. It is only necessary for Calvinists to be able to show that for perfectly sound and cogent reasons, verse X does not necessarily teach what Arminians think it means. By offering a sensible alternative interpretation, Calvinists demonstrate that that particular verse is thereby removed from the Arminian arsenal. Of course the verse may not teach any particular Calvinistic distinctive, but the point must be established that Arminians have no ground for quoting it in their own favor. This is all that Calvinists are required to do. Once shown that the "Arminian verses" do not obviously teach Arminianism, open-minded investigators might be encouraged to explore the possibility that there may actually be verses in the Bible that make the Calvinistic view of salvation unavoidable.

Finally, it is vital that the Calvinist not only pray all the way through any interaction with Arminians, but also remember that however defective their views may seem to be, Arminians are our brothers and sisters in Christ to whom we owe complete faithfulness and honesty. This whole dispute is a discussion between brothers and sisters in Christ who together seek the face of Yahweh in peace and sincerity. Nothing less will do.

This chapter's method will therefore be as follows: I will first consider some verses that have the words *free will* in at least some translations and then ask whether this is a necessary translation of the verses from the Greek. Two frequently quoted verses will then be closely examined to see whether they favor Arminianism as clearly as is sometimes thought. A final concluding comment will be made about lessons from history.

Freewill Verses?

In the past, Arminian users of the King James Version have not found too much in their favor on this subject. Apart from references to "freewill offerings," the phrase "free will" appears in this translation in only one verse, Ezra 7:13, where we are told that certain people who were "minded of their own freewill" to leave and go to Jerusalem would be allowed to do so. In other words, King Artaxerxes simply declares that those Jewish people who want to emigrate with Ezra to their homeland are free from his restraining them and may go if they wish. The word here rendered "freewill" is from a root meaning "spontaneous," "willing" or "voluntary." It indicates only that the person is acting without the legal or physical restraints formerly placed on them by Nebuchadnezzar. This is proved easily enough by the fact that the word or its root appears sixteen times in the KJV to refer to the "freewill offerings" that were encouraged over and above those prescribed by the Law, such as tithes. The point is a distinction in the Law, not a metaphysical statement about whether the faculty of choice is caused or not. Needless to say, Bible students influenced by Arminian thinking usually realize that they cannot use references to voluntary offerings to prove their theory of human nature.

In order to prove the Arminian view of the human will, it would be necessary to find verses that establish that the faculty of choice (or of the "will") is not only *not influenced or caused to act in one way rather than another by any external pressures,* but also that the faculty of choice is *not caused to act by any causes or psychological influences from within the soul either.* The will must be conceived of as an autonomous choice-making faculty independent of the characteristics of one's nature. Of course, such a curious notion is not even hinted at in the Bible. Strictly speaking, there are no verses in the Bible that teach a free will in the Arminian sense. A request by Calvinists for exegetical proof of the Arminian notion of free will usually brings a stunned silence. Arminians hold this truth of free will to be self-evident, and it usually does not occur to them to "prove" the theory.

At this point, the freewill theory is exposed for what it really is: an extrabiblical presupposition imposed on the Bible from without. If free will is assumed without question every time the idea of will or choice appears in the Bible, Arminians automatically assume that it is a reference to free will in their sense. Suddenly the exegetical silence is broken with a flood of verses referring to will, choice, commands and invitations. We will now look at some of these in order to examine the common method of reasoning from such verses.

The Term *Will*

While the word *will* in English might be a verb or a noun, it normally refers to the universal phenomenon of choice of one course of action over another. Numerous terms in Scripture are translated by such terms as "good pleasure," "will," "purpose," "intention," etc. They refer to the mental activities of planning, deciding and choosing a course of action. Some refer to God's will or purpose, and some to human choosing or planning.

Arminians are so controlled by the presupposition of free will that every time a verse appears using the word *will,* they assume it must mean free will in the Arminian sense, so that they read their theory into the verse. For example, in regard to Revelation 22:17, many Arminians will argue that "whosoever will, let him take the water of life freely" (KJV) must mean "anyone without distinction (any indeterminate someone) who autonomously chooses to do so, or wishes to do so by free will, is invited to take of the water of life."

But the verse says nothing remotely like this in the Greek. It is simply saying "the one wishing, let him take." It does not touch the question of how some come to wish this while others do not. Furthermore, "freely" has no reference to free will, since it is the Greek word *dōrean,* which means "without cost" or "as a gift." Its use in the verse above refers to the fact that Christ has already paid for the blessings of the gospel, "the water of life." It's the gospel that is free, not the will!

Arminians see the word *whosoever* and, because it is an indefinite pronoun in English, assume that it must mean in Greek an undetermined person who acts by free will. But "whosoever will may come" is a phrase from a hymn, not a verse of the Bible. Consider, for example, John 3:16 as quoted from the KJV: "God so loved the world, that he gave his only begotten Son, that *whosoever* believeth in him should not perish, but have everlasting life." Arminians assume a great deal about this verse, some of which contradicts the Greek. They assume that "so loved the world" must mean "loves every existing human being equally and without difference." This is an interesting speculative gloss on the verse, but it requires proof.

The passage states that as a result of his loving the world, God gave his Son, which is usually understood to be a reference to the incarnation and atonement. Then the Greek says "in order that every one believing in him may not perish." There is no word for "whosoever" in the original. On the contrary, far from God's giving his Son to provide a generalized atonement for everyone who exists, the verse states that he gave his Son for the express purpose of saving a specific group. Since this group excludes all unbelievers and is less than all existing human beings, John 3:16 states explicitly that the purpose of God in sending his Son to die was limited to atoning for believers only, that *they* "should not perish, but have everlasting life." This is what Calvinists call a *limited atonement,* in answer to the general or universal atonement taught by the Arminian, Catholic and Lutheran systems.

The issue then for Calvinists is not "whosoever will" but why some will or choose to come to Christ and others do not. Arminians say they come by their innate free will. The Bible says they come because the Father draws some and not others (Jn 6:44). Indeed, Jesus tells us in John 5:21 that the Son gives life to whomever he wants to. The question naturally follows as to how he decides who will receive life, assuming he does not regenerate everyone. Jesus answers this clearly enough in his doctrine of "drawing" (Jn 6) and his description of a category he calls his "sheep" (Jn 10).

In John 10:3-5, Jesus notes that his sheep hear his voice and follow him. In fact, he himself "lays down his life for the sheep" (v. 11), reemphasizing the definite atonement of 3:16. In 10:27-30 Jesus further explains that these sheep always recognize his voice because they know him and he knows them. It is these sheep to whom he is willing to give eternal life (5:21) so that they then will "never ever perish" (*ou mē,* a double negative in Greek), because they are protected in the hand of the omnipotent Father and in the hand of the omnipotent Son.

If Jesus intended in John 10 to give an explicit statement designed to refute Arminianism, he could hardly have made it clearer. In fact, in order to absolutely exclude free will as the spontaneous cause of his people's coming to and believing on him, he explains to his unbelieving enemies that the reason they did not believe in him was that they were not in the category of his sheep: "You do not believe" he says, "*because* you are not my sheep" (10:26). And earlier he had said, "No one *can* come to me unless the Father who sent me draws him" (6:44). Therefore, they *could not believe,* because God had blinded them (12:37-40). If Jesus had intended to imply Arminianism, he could have said, "You are not of my sheep because you do not believe." In fact, he said the opposite.

As if to warn his readers at the outset of the Gospel that they would get no comfort for their freewill notions from him, John says in 1:12-13 that Jesus gave the right to become sons of God to believers, and that these believers are born "not of blood, nor of the will of the flesh, nor of the will of man." Rather, their right and begetting as sons is *ek theou,* or "of God." The Greek word *ek* means "out of" or "from," and here indicates the source or cause of the begetting. Once more free will is excluded, just as family origin is excluded as the cause of a person's becoming a believer, or the will of a husband, priest or guru.

Accordingly, when the apostles had joined him and began to follow him as the Messiah, he gives them a warning: "You did not choose me, but [surprise, gentlemen!] I chose you" (Jn 15:16).

Human Choices

Human choices occur throughout the Bible, starting with Adam's choice to obey God and bring the animals under his governance in the Garden of Eden, as he was commanded to do in Genesis 1:26. The Fall also involved real choices, significant for what followed.

When Arminians see an example of a choice, they automatically assume that it is a freewill choice, because this is required by their presupposition. In the meantime, ignoring for the moment the Arminian complaints about "puppets" and "automatons," Calvinists are both fully aware of many of their own choices and fully accepting of the many cases of choice recorded in the Bible. No Calvinist I ever met or read denies the reality or the experience of human choices. The question is not about the *reality* of the choices, but about whether they are *caused* or not.

Furthermore, Arminians and Pelagians cannot prove the existence of a free will merely because it is so "obvious" to them. I have already noted that no human being is conscious of causation in the brain. In fact, we are not even conscious of the brain at all. We have no awareness of the mechanism of consciousness within us, let alone of the causal factors involved in the mysterious relationship between the brain and the soul or mind. This vast cavern of personal ignorance excludes any certainty that a particular choice was not in fact preceded by causes of which the choice is the resultant effect. Arminians conclude that because they are not *conscious* of causes affecting their will, it must be free of all causes. But the conclusion is not warranted by the premise. In fact, there may always be causes acting on the will of which we are simply unaware. We could never know that this were not so unless we were omniscient. On the basis of the "openness of God" theory, even God himself is ignorant of future freewill acts. Therefore, not being omniscient, he could not know if the will were free in a particular case or not. He would just not know enough.

Our conclusion must be that the reality of choices does not require that our choices be free from all determining causation. The proposition that people have free will cannot be proved because it is supposedly obvious to certain Arminians. Obviousness is a subjective state—it must be translated into conclusive arguments before the point is obvious to someone else.

As for "automatons," I will only point out that no Calvinist I am aware of, including the strict determinists in the ranks, thinks of human beings made in God's image (making dozens of real choices every day, some of them more conscious than others) as automatons. The capacity for choice is an integral part (or function, rather) of our personhood, thus excluding any mechanical metaphors. The question dividing Arminians from Calvinists is about what causes the will to act, not whether the will exists, which both affirm.

Commands

Commands also do not require that people have free will in the Arminian sense. It was the anti-Christian philosopher Immanuel Kant who said, "Ought implies can," not the Bible. Kant was asserting that if there is a moral imperative, it presupposes that people are able to do what is right. Similarly, the Greek philosopher Socrates held the view that because human nature is ultimately rational, to know the truth is to do it. But the Bible knows nothing of such speculations. Instead, it speaks of slavery to sin.

The Bible teaches that good trees bring forth good fruit and that bad trees bring forth bad fruit. In other words, people normally act out their inner characters. Since the Fall of our first parents, we have been inheritors of a fallen nature that naturally produces unrighteousness. In Ephesians Paul says we are "by nature children of wrath," being "dead in . . . trespasses and sins" (2:3, 1 NASB). When we were dead in sins, God made us alive by his grace. In verse 5 Paul is simply repeating the doctrine of Jesus in John 5:21. This supernatural life is expressed in the first instance by the exercise of saving faith in Jesus, but Paul says that this faith is "not from yourselves, . . . not by works" because "it is the gift of God" (vv. 8-9; compare Phil 1:29; 1 Pet 1:21). But if the capacity to believe, to act out of a heart of flesh instead of out of a hardened heart, is a gift from God, it can hardly be the result of a natural free will that everyone is assumed to have merely because they are human beings.

Kant's statement is a presupposition, not a rationally proven conclusion. God, on the other hand, may have many reasons for commanding sinners to do what he knows they cannot do. One reason would be to reveal the seriousness of slavery to sin. That is, he may command righteousness in order to show sinners their spiritual incompetence (Rom 7:14-24). Another reason might be that by convicting the people of their sinful inability to be good, he might thereby induce them to seek God's mercy (Rom 7:22—8:4). Or perhaps he wishes to cause them to act in a way that will bring them into judgment (Jer 50:24).

Again, the command may be accompanied by the Spirit of power, the two combining to regenerate the sinner and so induce faith (1 Thess 1:4-7). Or God may have reasons that he does not (and is not obliged to) tell us. Although he tells us a great deal about his plans and purposes (see, for example, Gen 18:16-21), God owes human beings no explanation of his actions beyond what he graciously gives us in the Bible. We will see in the next chapter what Job's response was to this painful truth.

Invitations

Invitations to come to Christ, to repent and believe, are found throughout the Word of God and are the essence of the appeal of evangelism. Arminians seem to think that God's invitations presuppose the ability to respond in the right way. The Bible expressly denies this ability. Jesus said in the very preamble to "Come to me, all you who are weary and burdened, and I will give you rest" that "no one knows the Father except the Son and those to whom the Son chooses to reveal him" (Mt 11:27-28), for sinners cannot come to Jesus unless the Father actually draws them (Jn 6:44).

John 6 is particularly explicit in this regard. Having identified himself as "the bread of life" (v. 35), Jesus warns his hearers that they have already encountered that bread of life and have not believed in him. Jesus then speaks of a category of people who come to him. He calls them "all that the Father gives me" (v. 37). In John 17:2, 6, 9, 11 and 24, he identifies them again, and he is careful to note that it is these for whom he is praying and not for everyone who exists (vv. 9, 20-21).

It is clear that throughout John's Gospel, invitations are given not merely to condemn those who refuse them, but also to provide occasions for the sheep whom the Father has given to the Son to respond as he draws them. This drawing is infallibly effective in the case of every sheep, for Jesus says, "All that the Father gives me will come to me" (Jn 6:37). No one who comes when they are drawn will be rejected. And no one even tries to come undrawn, for they love darkness rather than light (Jn 3:19).

The irresistible conclusion, then, is that invitations are primarily occasions for the elect sheep to be distinguished from the nonelect goats. The purpose of evangelism is the gathering in of Christ's sheep.

Verses Mentioning Free Will in Some Versions

We have already noted that in some English translations, the term *freewill offerings* is used. There are sixteen of these instances in the King James Version. The same expression occurs twenty-four times in the Revised Standard Version, and many of these passages are similarly translated in the New American Standard Bible, the New English Bible, the New International Version and the Living Bible. The term so translated means "voluntary," as distinct from "prescribed by law," having no bearing on the question of whether a person's will is caused to act or not. Some translations, however, use the word "free will" in other passages also, and these should be considered.

Second Corinthians 8:3 (RSV) says that the believers of Macedonia "gave . . . of their own free will." The Greek word translated as "free will" here is *authairetoi,* which simply means acting "of themselves" or "of their own accord." It does not contain the Greek words for "free" or "will" or anything similar. The point is only that they gave without it being demanded of them. Without external constraints, they gave voluntarily. The further philosophical question of whether their choice had some metaphysical or spiritual causation behind it is not touched. Certainly there was no apostolic command involved. This is a case of Paul commending what the Old Testament calls "voluntary offerings" in over twenty places.

In Philemon 14 (RSV) the same thing occurs: "I preferred to do nothing without your consent in order that your goodness might not be by compulsion, but of your own free will." Paul wants the slave-owner Philemon to be good voluntarily, not because he feels compelled by the sheer authority of an apostle: "that your goodness might not be by compulsion but of your own free will." The Greek phrase is *kata hekousion,* which literally means "according to what comes from (your own) being." The contrast is with the Greek notion of fate *(ananke),* translated "necessity" (KJV) or "by compulsion" (RSV). Paul wants Philemon to forgive Onesimus out of his own regenerate nature, recognizing the returning slave as his brother in Christ and not merely submitting to apostolic authority unwillingly. Again, the question of whether the decisions of a regenerate (or unregenerate) nature are caused or uncaused (the Arminian freewill theory) are not in view here. Paul is not concerned here with the freewill theory, but with getting a loving response from Philemon, whom he believed to be regenerate.

Paul distinguishes in 1 Corinthians 9:17 (LB) between doing something voluntarily and doing it because something has been entrusted to him (or placed upon him as an obligation he cannot refuse): "If I were volunteering my services of my own free will, then the Lord would give me a special reward; but that is not the situation, for God has picked me out and given me this sacred trust and I have no choice." When we compare verses 16-17 from the Living Bible with the New American Standard Bible, we discover that the point again, in the more literal translation, is that something may be voluntary or obligatory, but the issue is not addressed as to whether the process of voluntary choice is caused or not. This question of causation is the aspect of free will separating Arminians from Calvinists.

James 1:18 (LB) also says that God regenerates us by his own free will, but this is God's free will and not humanity's. In any case, the Greek here simply says (as the NASB correctly translates it), "In the exercise of His will He brought us forth by the word of truth." Once again, there is no Greek word for "free will" in the original text.

In conclusion, a comparison of those verses in various English versions where "freewill" or "free will" appear soon reveals that without exception the term can be replaced by such neutral expressions as "voluntary" or "voluntarily." Only people influenced by Arminian habits of language (including evangelical Bible translators) might almost automatically translate the terms *kata hekousion* or *boulētheis* as "free will," thereby prejudicing the translation in favor of Arminianism and creating the impression that the Bible teaches free will. We should not presume that even the best translators are always consistent. Besides, when a Calvinist uses the term *free will,* nothing is conceded to the Arminian theory, but rather it is simply meant that people choose according to their natures or characters. Bad trees freely (unconstrainedly, and out of their own natures) produce bad fruit, and good trees likewise produce good fruit—it is not possible *(ou dynatai)* for it to be otherwise (Mt 7:18).

Another verse that has been translated in a misleading way is John 10:18 (J. B. Phillips). Although this verse does not contain "free will" in most versions, it was quoted to me over and over again by a Pelagian pastor (in radio debates during 1987) as if its meaning were so obvious that only a mind perverted by the absurdities of Calvinism could not see that it taught the freewill theory. But is it all that obvious?

Jesus says that he is in the process of laying down his life with the express purpose of taking it up again (v. 17). This claim that he has absolute control even of the future event of his own death and resurrection is staggering. He then says, "No man taketh it from me [that is, I cannot be killed by mere human beings, even if they are determined to do so], but I lay it down *of myself*. I have power [the authority or right] to lay it down, and I have power to take it again." In other words, to put it as bluntly as possible, "I will die when I want to and rise again when I want to, and no mere man can cause my death one minute before I decide to die." The phrase *ap'emautou* has been variously translated "of myself" (KJV), "of my own accord" (RSV) or "on My own initiative" (NASB) and does not mean, imply or require the idea of an uncaused or autonomously free will.

Again, the question of whether Jesus acted out of a cause or not is not raised here. It is merely said that the time of his death is under his own control at the behest of his Father and that no mere creature can interfere. We may conclude that this verse is a tremendously strong affirmation of divine sovereignty over against human interference, but it says nothing about the free will of sinners. Besides, even if God or Jesus has free will in the Arminian sense, it would still not follow that you and I do.

The curiosity remains that Pelagians and Arminians read their freewill theory into verses that not only do not even mention the word (at least not in the Greek) but do not imply or necessitate the theory either. If Calvinists can show that a particular verse is reasonably capable of being understood in a way compatible with a neutral or Calvinistic sense by normal standards of exegesis, then the passage can be simply removed from the Arminian arsenal. Thus when J. B. Phillips in his groundbreaking paraphrase *The New Testa-*

ment in Modern English rendered John 10:18 as "I lay it down of my own free will," he was translating in a way that showed an Arminian bias. If Phillips had been asked why he used such a term when there was no word for "free will" in the text, he would have said that he chose the simplest common-sense idiom that occurred to him. An Arminian can hardly be blamed for using an Arminian idiom, but nothing is implied or necessitated by this paraphrase that discounts Calvinism.

Presuppositions and the "Obvious Meaning" of the Text

I said at the beginning of this book that presuppositions in matters of interpretation are rather like the International Rules in a game of chess—they control what counts as a possible move throughout the game. No one can produce a presuppositionless argument, since one's starting point is itself a presupposition (and you have to start somewhere!). If one's presuppositions are wrong, only being illogical will save one from moving further and further from the truth. Presuppositions determine how we will proceed, what counts as a "fact," and where we will finish up at the eventual end of the reasoning process.

So when Arminians complain that "Calvinists are always trying to bend the Bible to suit their theory," this only reveals that they are controlled by different presuppositions, making the interpretation of the verses in question look "obvious" in their own eyes. But one person's obvious meaning is another's problem text. Uncovering and questioning the presuppositions that control our expectations about a particular problem soon shows that a serious Bible student should not appeal to so subjective a notion as the "obvious" meaning of a disputed verse.

The rule is this: If the verse is disputed, its meaning is no longer obvious, and it is probably time to do some homework. As we discovered with the well-known verse John 3:16, a brief look at the Greek instantly destroyed its apparently obvious Arminian meaning.

Two "Obviously Arminian" Verses

The number and variety of verses capable of being understood in an Arminian sense is naturally quite large. In John Gill's critique of a popular defense of

Arminianism by Daniel Whitby, well over sixty are examined. We will take notice of only two here, but they are the two often thought to be decisively against Calvinism.

The first verse we will examine is 2 Peter 3:9. Here are two different translations:

> The Lord is not slack concerning his promise, as some men count slackness; but is longsuffering to us-ward, not willing that any should perish, but that all should come to repentance. (KJV)

> The Lord is not slow in keeping his promise, as some understand slowness. He is patient with you, not wanting anyone to perish, but everyone to come to repentance. (NIV)

Calvinists are often told by fellow believers influenced by popular Arminian thinking that "God is not willing that any should perish." The word *any* in this loose representation of 2 Peter 3:9 is assumed to mean "any human being whatsoever."

The simplest response to this curious notion is that if God did not want anyone to perish, he should not have created us with a free will in the first place, because this made the Fall inevitable sooner or later. More to the point, however, we might suggest that God should have done what would be necessary to save everyone, thus ensuring that everyone would not perish. We know that God is quite capable of saving even very bad people and has frequently done so.

Furthermore, even Arminians believe that a time will come when at least some sinners will be fixed in immutable righteousness forever, saved finally and glorified never to sin again. Do Arminians care to allow that once glorified, we no longer have free will? If they say yes, they concede that free will is not finally necessary to our humanness. If they say no, how can they deny the likelihood that a million or so years into eternal blessedness some unfortunate saint will not spoil the whole deal by sinning again? Arminians have no rational assurance that this will not happen. On the Arminian basis, far and long into eternity future, the "great gulf fixed" between heaven and hell may possibly be breached, and some may by free will pass from heaven to hell after all. Jesus presumably did not think about free will when he warned the lost rich man that no one could leave Hades, even if they would (Lk 16:26).

The question to resolve in 2 Peter 3:9 is who the "any" are. Arminians merely assume that it must mean "any human being existing," but there is nothing in the verse to require such an interpretation. The salutation of the first epistle shows that these two letters are addressed to a category identified by the author as the "elect" (1 Pet 1:1). They have been born again (v. 3) and are "kept by the power of God through faith unto salvation" (v. 5 KJV).

Then in 2 Peter (where he says in 3:1 that he is writing this second letter to the same people) he states that God is not constrained by time the way we are (v. 8). In fact, he can take a thousand years to get something done. We are then told that it is not reasonable to measure the time God takes to do something by our standard of "slowness" (v. 9). The truth is that the extended time God takes to save us is actually an act of mercy during which he patiently puts up with a great deal of nonsense on our part. If God were hasty by human standards, he would wait for no one, and those of us today (or even in A.D. 96) would not have had any opportunity to respond to the gospel. In fact, his love for the elect is shown by the fact that God waited until 1953 to save me. When Peter says that God is "not wanting anyone to perish," he is simply confirming in different words what he heard Jesus say: "*All* that the Father gives me will come to me" (Jn 6:37). God is not willing that *any of us,* the beloved elect, should perish, but purposes that all of the elect from all times should come to repentance. Furthermore, in a Greek sentence such as this, an indefinite pronoun such as *any (tinas)* normally refers to the most immediate antecedent in the sentence. Thus *any* must mean "any of us" (the elect and beloved to whom the letter is addressed).

The burden of proof now reverts to Arminians to show why *any* must mean "any human being who ever existed." Unless this can be demonstrated, the verse is not "obviously Arminian" anymore. The reader must decide whose interpretation is forced and unnatural and whose presuppositions are most consistent with both the immediate and more distant contexts in these two Petrine epistles. There are many other highly Calvinistic verses in 1 and 2 Peter, but I will leave them to the reader to look up.

First Timothy 2:3-6 is another text that is often considered a problem passage for Calvinists:

This is good and acceptable in the sight of God our Saviour; who will have *all men* to be saved, and to come unto the knowledge of the truth. . . . Christ Jesus . . . gave himself a ransom for *all,* to be testified in due time. (KJV)

The Arminian assumes that "all men" and "all" must mean "all existing human beings," or "all without any distinction or exclusion." Unless these words do mean this, the Arminian force of the verse is lost. I will now demonstrate that this interpretation is not only exegetically unnecessary, but that it is also not even theologically possible.

All (pas) need not mean all examples of its class whatsoever. Proof of this is readily available without going outside 1 Timothy, which has many references to "all" in the KJV. (See 1:16; 2:1, 2, 11; 3:4, 11; 4:8, 9, 10, 15; 5:20; 6:10, 13, 17.) Second Timothy contains another fifteen occurrences. These books also have more occurrences that are rendered "every."

In order to disprove the Arminian presupposition that the occasions of *all* in 1 Timothy 2:4 and 6 must mean "all existing examples" of the class referred to, it is only necessary to show a handful of occasions where *all* cannot mean all existing cases of its referent. Then the verses in 1 Timothy 2 may reasonably have a more restricted meaning. If it can be shown in addition that the word *all* often means "all kinds of" instead of "all existing examples of" its referent, the verse is no longer an Arminian stronghold.

The following samples selected from over forty occurrences in 1 Timothy alone establish the point.

In 1 Timothy 1:16 "all longsuffering" (KJV) does not mean every existing case or example in which a person might show patience, but "all kinds of longsuffering" or "in every case of longsuffering God gives you."

In 2:1 "first of all" does not mean that this is the first thing said in the letter (it is in the second chapter), but that it is "most important for the present."

In 2:4 "all men" could not include Judas Iscariot. Therefore, it must have at least some restriction. The alternative ("all existing human beings whatsoever") would be universalism.

In 2:8 "everywhere" can hardly be meant to include "at the North Pole" or "in hell." It simply means "in the churches or prayer meetings."

In 4:4 "everything God created is good" does not include Satan. Arsenic-laced milk and the tuberculosis bacillus, while creations of God, are not to be accepted as good with thanksgiving. The "all" here simply means "all kinds of normal foods." In any case, verse 4 seems to be limited by verse 3 to a discussion of food and marriage.

In 6:10 it can hardly be true that "the love of money is the root of every existing evil." The origin of Satan's sin and the destruction of Pompeii in A.D. 76 were certainly evils, but neither had anything to do with the love of money. "All" here simply means "many kinds of evil."

In 6:17 "everything for our enjoyment" cannot include sin and traveling to the stars. It must mean only that God is the one who gives us the blessings we have.

These cases (and dozens more could be offered) show that *all* in fact usually means "many of" or "all kinds of" its referent class, and hardly any examples can be brought forward where it could only mean "every existing example" of the thing referred to.

We now come to the problem in 1 Timothy 2:1-6. Paul begins by saying that even when we live in a persecuting age (such as the Roman Empire under Nero) we should nevertheless pray for all kinds of people, even our rulers, who may actually be our persecutors. We are told that we should pray for them in order that we may "live peaceful and quiet lives in all godliness and holiness" (v. 2). Kings have a responsibility under God as his viceregents over society, and we should certainly at the very least pray that they will have wisdom to do what they ought to do.

Paul goes on to say that praying for rulers as well as other kinds or classes of people is good and acceptable in God's sight (v. 3). We are also told that God is "our Savior." This presumably must mean that he is the Savior of the Christians to whom the letter is addressed. Paul then says that as "our Savior," God "wants all men to be saved" (v. 4). This cannot include those already in hell, on whom his wrath already abides forever. Therefore it cannot mean "all existing human beings," even on an Arminian basis. Since the issue in verses 1-3 seems to be to include rulers and persecutors ("all classes of people"), the "all men" of verse 4 would most naturally mean "all kinds of people." This provides a perfectly sensible alternative to the Arminian use of the verse to establish a universal intention in the atonement. In fact, ever since Augustine this has been the preferred Calvinistic understanding of the verse.

"Who gave himself as a ransom for all" (v. 6) likewise may reasonably parallel the language of Matthew 20:28, where Jesus speaks of himself as "a ransom for many." In Isaiah 35:10 "the ransomed of the LORD" is a title of the victorious elect entering Zion at the second coming of the Messiah and quite certainly does not include all existing men. When the atonement is predicted in Isaiah 53, verse 11 says that Christ will "justify many" by his death. This chapter in Isaiah contains the Old Testament understanding that is behind the ransom expressions in the gospels and epistles.

Therefore there is simply no reason to assume that "ransom for all" can only mean that Christ intended to die substitutionally for "all existing human beings." It simply means "all of God's people" or "all kinds of people" (as in vv. 2, 4).

The burden of proof, then, reverts to Arminians to show that this reasonable alternative to their use of the passage is impossible and that "all men" can only mean "all existing human beings." But as long as the above exegesis stands as a reasonable alternative, they cannot claim any longer that the Calvinistic understanding of these verses is forced and unnatural. The passage is now, as I have put it, removed from the Arminian arsenal. There is simply nothing in 1 Timothy 2 to help the Arminian.

Not only is the Arminian understanding of these verses exegetically unnecessary, but it was long ago shown to be theologically impossible. In John Owen's great defense of particular redemption titled *The Death of Death in the Death of Christ* (1648), which the Arminians seem unconcerned to answer, the following argument appears:

> God imposed his wrath due unto, and Christ underwent the pains of hell for, either all the sins of all men, or all the sins of some men, or some sins of all men. If the last, some sins of all men, then have all men some sins to answer for, and so shall no man be saved. . . . If the second, that is it that we affirm, that Christ in their stead and room suffered for all the sins of all the elect in the world. If the first, why then are not all freed from the punishment of all their sins? [The Arminian] will say, "Because of their unbelief; they will not believe." But this unbelief, is it a sin or not? If not, why should they be punished for it? If it be [a sin], then Christ underwent the punishment due to it or [he did] not. If so, then why must that hinder

them more than their other sins for which he died, from partaking of the fruit of his death? If he did not [die for this sin], then he did not die for all their sins. Let them choose what part they will. (p. 61)

He later adds,

Is there any new shifts to be invented for this? That is, Christ did not die for their unbelief, or rather did not by his death remove their unbelief, because they would not believe, or because they would not themselves remove their unbelief; or he died for their unbelief conditionally, that they were not unbelievers. These do not seem to me to be sober assertions. (p. 137)

The Arminian responses to this argument usually fall into two categories. Either they complain that they are being pressured by an "unnatural logic" (as if an argument ought not to be believed if it is logical), or they simply ignore the argument as if it did not exist and refuse to read John Owen. Calvinists find these responses irresponsible, but we cannot do much about them. We can pray that our Arminian friends might take the subject more seriously. We can also point out that if Calvinists' arguments should be rejected because they are "too logical," then Arminians also fall under the same criticism, at least when they are logical. When not trying to be logical, they have no claim on the mind or conscience. Illogic quickly reduces to the unintelligible, and calling it a "mystery" does not solve the problem.

J. I. Packer wrote the introduction to the Banner of Truth edition of *The Death of Death* when it was republished in 1959. He adds the following comment:

Nobody has a right to dismiss the doctrine of the limitedness of the atonement as a monstrosity of Calvinistic logic until he has refuted Owen's proof that it is part of the uniform biblical presentation of redemption, clearly taught in plain text after plain text. And nobody has done that yet. (p. 13)

Conclusion

Enough said—the ball is once again in the court of the Arminians. One warning remains from history. In his disastrous attempt to provide a fresh theory of the atonement in *The Nature of the Atonement* (1856), John McLeod Campbell noted that if one accepts the penal substitutionary nature of the death of Christ, John Owen's conclusion concerning a limited atonement "seems unanswerable" (pp. 50-51). Campbell's solution was to abandon penal substitution and to offer a notion of God's acceptance of Christ's "repentance" on behalf of us. Are today's evangelical Arminians willing to do this?

Those churches that became Arminian in the seventeenth century drifted into Socinianism and Arianism in the eighteenth century and were mostly dead by the nineteenth century. Some became Unitarians and Universalists and have survived into our own time in this form. The atheist George Santayana was wiser than some evangelicals when he pointed out that those who ignore the lessons of history are doomed to repeat its errors. The Holy Spirit did not delay his teaching ministry until our own century, and it makes no sense at all for us to ignore the vast store of theological writings from the past, thereby dooming our own age to the useless reinvention of square wheels.

Revealed truth, then, is one and indivisible, a coherent and comprehensive vision of reality, reflecting at the infinite level the exhaustive consciousness that God himself has of his creation. The Arminian insistence on introducing into the biblical system the alien and unprovable assumption of human autonomism or the freewill theory will sooner or later make havoc of the whole. It is only a matter of time and the inevitable progression of human thought. Clark Pinnock and other "freewill theists" do not arrive at their Arminianism by the exegesis of Scripture, but by reconstructing an already established Reformation theology around the presupposition of an autonomously free will. And they do not come to the freewill theory as a necessary conclusion from the Bible. They *begin* with it as the necessary presupposition of their humanism.

The unavoidable conclusion is therefore that Arminianism is a humanistic deformation of Reformation theology, not merely a legitimate and harmless variation. It is far more accurate both historically and logically to call it a form of humanism than a form of evangelicalism.

Further Reading

I have already noted at the end of previous chapters the large numbers of "Arminian" verses explained by John Gill in *The Cause of God and Truth*. Gill spent fifty-one years in the same Baptist pulpit in London, and during this time he preached and published an exegetical commentary on the entire Bible verse by verse (New Testament in 1748, Old Testament in 1766; reprint Grand Rapids, Mich.: Baker, 1980). He is the only man in the history of the church to have accomplished this. Naturally, all the verses used by those on both sides of the Calvinist-Arminian controversy are treated carefully in these volumes.

The fourth and last part of John Owen's *The Death of Death in the Death of Christ* in volume 10 of the *Works of John Owen* (London: The Banner of Truth Trust, 1965-1967) consists mostly of Owen's treatment of difficult verses used by the Arminians.

10

The Problem of Evil: The Final Stronghold of Unbelief?

*T*here are three major objections to Christianity* that are raised sooner or later by all contemporary religious seekers. The first is, How do you know the Bible can be trusted? This is the epistemological question, which challenges the authority of Scripture. The second concerns science and the secular view of reality: What about Adam and Eve and the dinosaurs? This is the onto-logical question, which seeks the true viewpoint of the world. It challenges the Christian to make sense of secular science and come to terms with the modern scientist's version of the great chain of being. The third issue is the ethical question: If God is really good, why does he allow so much evil in the world?

There is a fourth question that is not, strictly speaking, an objection to the Christian faith at all, but it needs to be answered somewhere within the Christian worldview. It is the teleological issue: What is the meaning of life?

The Biggest Problem of All

Of the three objections above, the problem of evil is by far the most serious objection to the Christian view of God, often carrying a great deal of moral

and emotional freight along with it. Many philosophers regard it as the decisive disproof of the existence of the God of the Bible.

Several non-Christian religions (especially Eastern religions) have the problem of the origin of evil at their foundation. This was true of Gnosticism in
the second and third centuries of the early church, and is still true of many
branches of Buddhism today. Therefore, it must be taken very seriously by
the Christian apologist. I will first present the problem in its most traditional
form, which suggests the incompatibility of God's own attributes. Atheists
make use of this form in order to show that the idea of a God like that of
the Christians is flatly unintelligible. If this is really so, the central idea of the
Christian religion is rendered absurd, and atheism becomes more attractive.
Because of its usefulness to the skeptic, the problem of evil is often encountered as the final stronghold of unbelief. That it is indeed a stronghold may
not be doubted. But whether it is unbreachable, we shall see.

Three propositions are said to be involved in traditional theism, and it is
claimed that they cannot all be true at the same time:

1. God is omnipotent.

2. God is completely good.

3. Evil exists.

God is said to be omnipotent. This does not mean that he can do or be
anything conceivable, such as make a stone too heavy for him to lift, or create
a square circle. This kind of conundrum is based on a misunderstanding of
God's nature and is really nothing more than a grammatical error or a confusion of categories. *Omnipotence* merely means that God can do anything
he wants or wills to do. He does not will to do the irrational or the meaningless. He could, however, do anything that is logically compatible with his
own attributes.

Next, God is said to be completely good. This is taken to mean that God
is morally required by his own nature to do whatever good is in his power
and presumably always wills and does the good. Were he not always to will
and do the good, he would not be *completely* good.

But evil nevertheless exists. Where then does evil come from? Presumably
God is quite capable of preventing evils from coming into existence, or at the
very least of eliminating all the evils that do exist. But evils still exist. If God

is truly good, he would destroy evil. And if he is omnipotent, he certainly could. It seems that God may be either completely good or omnipotent, but he cannot be both if evil exists.

Possible False Solutions

To disprove a logically valid argument, it is only necessary to invalidate its assumptions, or in the case of a syllogism, one of the premises. So there are clearly at least three easy ways to solve this problem. One may deny God's omnipotence, his complete goodness or the existence of evil. But none of these paths are available to the orthodox Christian, for the following reasons.

We will consider the last of these three ideas first. We might question the reality of evil itself, but the reality of evil is a fundamental pillar of the Christian worldview. The Bible's statements about Satan, the Fall of our first parents, sin and its seriousness, and the reality of historical and eschatological judgments by God cannot be explained away as if they were not essential to the biblical picture. The Christian is therefore not at liberty to deny the reality of evil with Mary Baker Eddy's Christian Science Church as "an error of mortal mind." Nor may we reduce it to *maya* ("illusion") with the Hindu. The Bible's doctrine of hell, where unrepentant sinners will be lost forever, and the need for "a new heaven and a new earth" show that God has prepared for the future judgment and final demise of evil. So evil must be a real part of the Christian worldview. Nor is this affected by the common medieval theory derived from St. Augustine that evil is just privation of the Good. Even a privation must have some ontological status in the being it affects. It is at the very least an attribute or property of an existing thing or state of affairs. For the Bible writers, then, evil is real and deadly serious: "The soul who sins shall die" (Ezek 18:4 NASB).

Some writers within the more liberal Christian camp have tried to put evil in a better light by borrowing from Eastern religions. These views teach that evil is merely a "lesser good" or is somehow ontologically necessary to the formation of souls as we know them. From this viewpoint, evil is just a matter of perspective. Somehow evils are part of the higher unity. The world is "a vale of soul-making" in which evils are necessary and presumably un-avoidable.

The main problem with this approach is that the Bible presents God as holy. God himself takes evil seriously and rejects evils in history through both judicial and practical judgments. Evil even has its own eschatology, its own destiny. It is always treated as a real problem, to be resisted morally, judged by God and finally put away forever. But even if evils have their uses, this does not explain how God can allow so many, and most evil seems to have no redeeming value at all.

The Christian who takes the Bible in its most natural sense cannot deny either the existence or the horror of evil. Somehow we must reconcile its existence with a good and sovereign Lord, who says he will finally destroy it and wipe away every tear (Rev 21:4).

Similarly, to minimize the omnipotence of God is also to undermine the historical orthodoxy of all the mainline branches of Christianity: Catholic (both East and West branches), the Reformed, Lutheran, Baptist and other independents all hold this doctrine without compromise. Until their confessional stances were weakened by the unbelief involved in modern post-Enlightenment liberalism, all mainline churches taught it as a matter of course. Its denial was instantly recognized as a heresy of some magnitude because it is clearly a biblical doctrine, as the following evidence indicates.

From Genesis 1:1 to Revelation 19:6, the doctrine of divine omnipotence is both stated and implied in every imaginable situation. The doctrine of creation is a suitable place to start. God created ex nihilo (from no previously existing substance). This means that all existing entities derive their properties and relations from God. That is, all states of affairs that have followed the creative act owe their reality in turn to that initial act of creation, as well as to whatever additional providential acts God might perform to keep things on track as his program unfolds. The only way out of this highly predestinarian conclusion is to either allow that behind God there is a realm of eternal matter (or chance, or nonbeing) that he does not control, or that he somehow lost control of things after the creation itself.

These two moves are often made in one form or another in order to protect the presupposition of human autonomy. The first is contrary to such texts as John 1:1-3, which states flatly that nothing exists that God did not create. This excludes any background realms of preexisting matter or any void not controlled by God or any realm of mystery that God cannot penetrate. The second move involves the introduction after creation of an unpredictable factor such as free will. In this view, human freedom is as creatorially sovereign in its own realm as God himself, bringing states of affairs into existence without any divine control or rational predetermination. But people who take these positions rarely realize what the implications are for other biblical doctrines. In this second case, the result is a reduction of God to a finite deity who cannot cope with the mess he has created. He then resembles Jupiter or Marduk, but is quite unlike the Yahweh worshiped by the prophet Isaiah.

Consider the elements of the high monotheism of Isaiah 40—55. In 40—44, God's uniqueness, knowledge and power as Creator are emphasized in reation to his people Israel: "I, the LORD, am the maker of all things, stretching out the heavens *by Myself,* and spreading out the earth *all alone"* (44:24 NASB). In 45:6-7, he says, "I am the LORD, and there is no other, the One forming light and creating darkness, causing well-being and creating calamity; I am the LORD who does all these" (NASB). As elsewhere in Isaiah, these expressions incorporate the terms of the original Genesis story.

These chapters constitute an extended exposition of what monotheism really involves. For Isaiah, God's sovereignty is best expressed in creatorial terms. The New American Standard Bible quoted here is perhaps not quite as forceful as the King James Version. Not only does the verse in the Hebrew use the terms *made, caused* and *created* virtually as synonyms, but the word rendered "well-being" is the usual term *šālôm* for peace among human beings. The word rendered "calamity" is *ra',* the usual Hebrew word for evil, translated as such over 440 times in most translations. A glance down the concordance list soon shows that many sins are also included in this broad term, along with natural evils that have no immediate origin in human sin.

The translation given above is certainly possible, but the King James Version gives it more starkly: "I form the light, and create darkness: I make peace, and create evil." Of course, it does not say that evil was present at the original creation ex nihilo. But one cannot avoid the conclusion that whatever evil(s) may be contemplated here, they are ultimately the result of God's creatorial power and sovereignty, although many steps may have intervened between the good creation of Genesis 1 and the first appearance of these evils in history.

The only two alternatives are either that such evils come into existence through a creative power other than God or that God is merely a finite entity like us, only bigger; as such, he is eternally limited by a larger and more ultimate surrounding void of chaos, of which evil is a facet. This last view is one of the more repulsive elements of generic paganism and is instantly repudiated by the regenerate mind.

A finite god is an idol pure and simple. One of the key questions we are addressing is how far a professing Christian is willing to retreat into such a distorted view of God in order to defend a compromise with the fallen assumption of autonomy.

The attitude of Isaiah in regard to this question of finite godism is strongly repeated in Proverbs 16: "The plans of the heart belong to man, but the answer of the tongue is from the LORD. . . . The LORD has made everything for its own purpose, even the wicked for the day of evil" (vv. 1, 4 NASB). Furthermore, "the mind of man plans his way, but the LORD directs his steps" (v. 9 NASB). And finally, "The lot is cast into the lap, but its every decision is from the LORD" (v. 33 NASB). Clearly for this writer too, the human intentions cannot override the plans of God.

Isaiah continues in 46:9-11, "I am God, and there is no other. . . . I make known the end from the beginning, from ancient times, what is still to come. I say: My purpose will stand, and I will do all that I please. . . . What I have said, that will I bring about; what I have planned, that will I do." And we read in 55:8, 10-11 that

"My thoughts are not your thoughts,
   neither are your ways my ways," declares the LORD. . . .
As the rain and the snow
   come down from heaven,
and do not return to it
   without watering the earth, . . .
so is my word that goes out from my mouth:
   It will not return to me empty,
but will accomplish what I desire
   and achieve the purpose for which I sent it.

This is a clear statement that God never fails to successfully adapt his means to achieve his ends. The God of the Bible never fails to rationally relate his acts to his intentions. Isaiah regards this as one of the distinctive features of his monotheism.

A popular modern grappler with the problem of evil is Rabbi Harrold S. Kushner. In his popular book *When Bad Things Happen to Good People,* Kushner tells us that these bad things happen because there are just some things God cannot cope with. This causes us to wonder what authority Isaiah holds for him. A finite God is a figment of the would-be autonomous mind. It is an idol, and John warns us to stay away from idols (1 Jn 5:19-21). To postulate a finite God is to reject monotheism, for only another being of infinite potential could limit God.

The God of the Bible, then, is omnipotent, despite the difficulties whether real or imagined. We know he is omnipotent because he says so, and he is the truth by his own definition.

If we may not have a finite God or dismiss evil as just a bad perspective, then perhaps there is a solution in the idea that God is not completely good. We will not reiterate here the hundreds of Bible verses that prove God to be intrinsically good, righteous, holy and just. Once more, Scripture is abundantly clear on this issue. Even the atheist Antony Flew says in his *God and Philosophy* that the assertion of the Hebrew prophets that the Lord their God is a righteous God is "magnificent" and then uses the same term to characterize the view of Descartes (pp. 77 and 109). What this could mean to one who does not believe this God exists is none too clear. The problem, however, does not lie in God's character, but in those human perspectives about God that seek to limit him in the interests of human autonomy. To begin with, why should anyone assume that God is under any obligation to either prevent evils or eliminate them as soon as they arise? God's goodness is correlative with his wisdom as well as with his omnipotence. He may simply have plans that make perfect sense to him and that include his own long-term response to evil. There seems to be no reason provable from the Bible why God should not have designed a universe in which evils of various kinds were inevitable. This does not logically entail his expressing approval of my personal sin.

God is said to be good in two senses, and both are equally important for the resolution of the problem of evil. First, God is good in the sense that he

does good things like showing mercy and justice, preserving sinners who actually deserve to go to hell and faithfully fulfilling his promises and predictions. He promises that he will indeed eventually destroy all evils, but not yet.
Second, God is good in the sense that his will is the origin of the good in its
totality. When Socrates asks (in Plato's *Euthyphro*) whether the gods approve of the good because it is good or whether goodness is good because the
gods approve of it, he raises the question of the location of ultimacy, which
we will examine in the next chapter. For our present purposes, Socrates
wanted it understood that the good is itself ultimate and that it is knowable
to us directly as an intelligible standard. For Socrates, the wise person has an
innate certainty, a self-referential instinct about what good is. The "gods" are
just finite aspects of being-itself and therefore not themselves the origin of the
good. Thus the Greek gods looked up to a standard above themselves.

For the Christian, the good is not an entity or value independent of Yahweh
as Creator. We must insist with the Bible that the good is good because it is
approved of by God as the ultimate reference point in himself for evaluating
everything. The first reference to goodness in the Bible (Gen 1:4) is the statement that the newly created light was good simply because it was the work
of God. Good is good because it is God who does it. What God does is good
by his own definition. Our God does not look up to a standard above himself.
In particular, there is no realm of mysterious chaos behind him to which he
must in any sense defer. Our God is himself the standard of the evaluation
of everything, including the intelligibility of the question in the first place.

This view is not "a pretentious tautology," as Flew would have it. It does
not mean that Christians merely worship "infinite power as such" (*God and
Philosophy,* para. 5.21, p. 110), for no such thing could exist in our worldview.
The God of the Bible exists with coherent attributes that do not function or
mean anything in isolation. They could have no meaning independent of
God's character as a whole. The whole point of Christian worship of God as
Creator is that he is the origin and standard of the good in all its phases and
applications to life and society, whether individual private holiness or social
justice in the public courts of law. Flew argues that on the Christian basis
"there can be no inherent moral reason why this rather than that ought to be
thus commanded" (5.20, p. 109). In this he reveals his resentment of God's

telling him what to believe. His attitude contrasts unfavorably with that of Abraham, who, when told to do so by God, prepared to offer up his only son as a sacrifice. Of course, God did not let Abraham actually carry out this order.

The problem of self-referential objectivity versus relativistic subjectivity is a case of the one-and-many dilemma of the fallen mind and cannot be discussed in detail here. We may note that Flew seems to want to control the high ground of objective values while claiming that the theist appeals to subjective values. But life is never that simple, especially when axioms are being chosen. Flew says that allowing "standards of right and wrong which are, at least logically, independent of God's will," invites "moral criteria which are in no way subjective" (5.20, p. 109). But how can we take him seriously at this point? Does he really think that if a judgment is made independent of God's will, it will be somehow naturally objective?

Before he can carry this argument through, he is obliged to first show that objective moral standards actually exist. Then he must show that they can be known to us apart from a revelation whose truth and reliability depends on God's inspiration and preservation of it in history. Then he must show that his understanding of it is not "subjective" but is universally applicable to other human minds. Then he must show that it applies to the case at hand.

For a finite mind, the problems involved here are insuperable. In any case, Flew cuts off this route for himself. He correctly warns us that "we cannot deduce any normative conclusions from premises which are all neutrally descriptive, [or] infer what actually is the case purely from considerations of what ideally ought to be" (p. 107). This well-stated consideration alone puts to rest any hope of finite independent objectivity.

Flew complains that when Christians state that "God is good . . . means God does what God wants," this is "a truth no doubt, on a Christian view, but not, surely, quite the particular truth originally intended" (p. 51). But exactly why is this a puzzle to him? Anyone who believes that God is the ontological and moral reference point for all valid statements about the moral world certainly intends "originally" to make God's will the determiner of all good. Flew's assumption seems to be that a Christian would "originally" intend to have God submit to standards outside of himself, and he wants to sound surprised that one should appear on the scene of this age-old debate who does not suffer this gladly.

Does he not know what a reference point is? Does he think he has no reference point himself? Presumably not, for he has made his own starting assumption clear (para. 3.20, p. 69). His reference point is the Stratonician presumption, which states that the principles of the world are found within the world. In other words, his starting point is that the world is intelligible in terms of itself alone, without referring to the God of the Bible. The Christian's authority and presumption at this point comes from Moses, not Strato.

God Versus Syncretism

The prophet Isaiah settles God's attitude toward any form of compromise with heathen idols, intellectual or physical: "I am the LORD; that is my name! I will not give my glory to another or my praise to idols" (42:8). He particularly repudiates deference to divinities such as chance and fate, and the gods called "Fortune" and "Destiny" in Is 65:11 were apparently personifications of the Babylonian version of the one-and-many problem. To the technical question of whether God created also the "deep" of Genesis, the answer is found in such passages as Job 28:12-14 and Proverbs 8:24, where the deep pleads ignorance because it did not exist before wisdom. Apparently the deep cannot interpret itself without a prior word from its Creator. In the New Testament, Paul observes: "Has not God made foolish the wisdom of the world? For since in the wisdom of God the world through its wisdom did not come to know God, God was well-pleased through the foolishness of the message preached to save those who believe" (1 Cor 1:20-21 NASB) and "What fellowship can light have with darkness?" (2 Cor 6:14).

So naturally Antony Flew is particularly uncomfortable with believers who insist on letting God be the standard of meaningfulness in his own creation. For example, when we say with historic Christian orthodoxy that God's will is the standard of goodness, we are simply extending the idea that God is the Creator to the moral realm. That is, God created goodness *simply by creating per se,* and then pronouncing what he had done good by definition (Gen 1:4, 10, 12, 18, 21, 25, 31), Socrates or no Socrates. If God exists, this view is unavoidable, for his being the Creator involves his creating ethical relations also. The good is good because God pronounces his own works to be so, without asking for the approval of Socrates' daemon.

Flew perhaps prefers to deal with Christians who side with the traditional Socratean-Aristotelian-Arminian-Butlerian idea that the good is somehow objectively independent of God, because he knows that this is an internally incoherent position that he can destroy logically. He can easily make those Christians look silly who want to base their apologetics on a syncretism with the non-Christian presupposition of the autonomy of the human mind. He does this with meticulous effectiveness in *God and Philosophy* (see 4.15 on p. 81) and is quite right to do so. The tragedy is that when he had this book reprinted in the late eighties, he pointed out in the new preface that no serious refutation had been published since it first came out in 1966. This is a pitiful testimony to the powerlessness of syncretistic traditionalist apologetics to deal with such an attack on Christianity. The strength of Flew's testimony against the traditional arguments lies entirely in the internal inconsistencies created by the age-old compromise with autonomism that traditionalist apologetics displays.

Frederic Platt's article in James Hastings's *Encyclopaedia* is a classic case in point. He says that in order to appreciate the philosophical influence of Arminianism, its "two great principles" must be recognized. These are "its ethical recognition of justice, and the emphasis it lays upon the human" (p. 809). By the first, he means that Calvinism is "ethically unfair" in not recognizing "equity in the divine procedure," because it refuses to hold that "the rights of man" are equal to the rights of God. That is, the Creator "owed something" (that is, is obligated to) the creature. Platt calls the second principle "the innate liberty of the human will." So Platt's Arminianism begins with the principles that justice is an objective standard outside of God and that the human will is autonomous. In this way, the Christian idea of God and his attributes must bow to a pair of presuppositions smuggled in from Greek philosophy.

Platt is quite clear concerning whose side he is on in this matter of rights and fairness. He says that the kind of justice assumed by the Arminian is one that is "common to God and man." That is, justice is a value independent of both God and human beings to which *both* are by equity obligated to submit.

For Platt, God approves of a particular good because it is independently good.

He next makes the revealing statement that "Arminianism was always most successful when its argument proceeded upon principles supplied by the moral consciousness of man" (p. 812). That this startling admission is no accidental utterance is shown when he says that "the true ethics . . . must be based on the inward compulsion of conscience, not upon any external authority." "Thus the free will of man [is] regarded as conditioning the absolute will of God." This means that God's will is not absolute (or ultimate) at all. There are no ultimates, just big and small wills, and if any standards are common to both God and humanity, both are equally answerable to them.

This is what Platt means by "equity," and it necessarily involves abandoning the fundamental principle of the Reformation: "My conscience is captive to the Word of God. I can do no other." The Arminian says that his or her conscience may quite possibly allow itself to be influenced by the Word of God, but never allows itself to be its captive—one might just as easily decide to do something else.

Platt sees clearly that historically when these two ideas were accepted (that God owes the creature equal deference and that the human will is autonomous), "the old absolute unconditionalism became untenable" (p. 812). For the Arminian, God is obligated to standards outside of himself, identified in the nature of being by an autonomous human instinct. For the Calvinist, however, God is himself the ultimate origin of moral meaning. We are faced here with the issue of the location of ultimacy, for we must locate our ultimate reference point somewhere. These two positions are incompatible—we must choose, and cannot avoid choosing, between them. The only alternative is an unstable compromise followed by a relentless historical drift toward a more consistent humanism, as Platt so vividly documents in his article.

The Freewill Defense

The most popular solution to the problem of evil is the freewill defense. The most common explanation offered is that because God made us with a free will, sin and its subsequent evils are not God's fault but ours. His gift of free will was an act of supreme love, and was in any case necessary to his being worshiped and loved freely in return. In this view, free will guarantees responsibility, which gets God off the hook. God is not responsible for evil. In fact, the desire to have God freed from responsibility for evil is probably the strongest motivation for assuming free will. So Platt speaks for all Arminians when he links free will with responsibility, simply assuming that it thereby shifts responsibility from God to humankind. He repeatedly pleads for Arminian "moderation" and "conditionalism" against Calvinist "absolutism" and "determinism."

The word *determinism* is one of those things used to frighten the inquirer away from seriously considering the Reformation denial of free will. The word means that all states of affairs in a created cosmos are caused by previous states of affairs—that there are no uncaused or chance events. The causes may be physical, moral, mental, spiritual or from God directly or indirectly, but nothing happens without a sufficient cause. The important thing however, is to realize that *the only possible alternative to determinism is indeterminism, either complete or partial.* Platt, for example, speaks of determinism in the physical realm but insists on free will interrupting the "causal chain" in the mental or spiritual realm.

If the events of the world are not wholly determined, they must be at least partially indeterminate. This is what the presumption of free will requires. Acts of the will are not determined by previous states of affairs either from within human nature (the bondage of the will to the sin nature) or from without (for example, God does not override the will's freedom).

We will now look at a few implications of this position. Since no one (except the more extreme followers of David Hume) thinks our experience of the world is wholly indeterminate, we will not consider that position here. Meanwhile, the traditional freewill defense tries to free God from responsibility for the glitches in his creation by relieving him of sovereign control through a partial indeterminism. But does it work?

Indeterminism?

Let every Christian consider what would follow if Arminian indeterminism were really true.

1. Partial indeterminism has one obvious problem that cannot be easily answered. Which events are determined and which are not? More particularly,

which causes are really just influences that are easily resistible by the will? At first it looks as though Arminians only want to exclude acts of the will from divine determination. But we have already shown that according to the Bible, there are at least some influences on the will. This would mean that the will must always overcome these influences in order to be completely free to do what it wants. But this in turn means that the will is influenced by desires and inclinations that are presumably not always wholly neutralized. How could we ever know enough to be sure to choose against every influence? It turns out that it is virtually never clear exactly when the will would be truly free. The problem of what to disallow from influencing the will is itself problematic. It is hard to see when one could ever be satisfied in any particular case that the will was really acting with complete autonomy. Complete free will would virtually require human omniscience.

2. Is the reasoned argument to be excluded from being allowed to move the will? It is often insisted even by Arminians that at least ideally the will should act in harmony with the intellect. But we are all familiar with the person who is offended by the necessity of the conclusion to a valid argument, countering it with "But you're being too logical!" One gets the impression that some Arminians feel that if the conclusions follow correctly from the premises, they must be rejected! Nevertheless, if the will bows to the logic of a valid argument, has it not given up its autonomy? In such a case, it has certainly accepted the control of an outside authority. If it is objected that the choice may be a willing decision to bow to logic, what causes the will to bow this time but not always? Is it just chance?

When a visiting Arminian at a local seminary told the students, "I don't like syllogisms because they back me into a corner!" I responded, "I *love* syllogisms precisely *because* they back me into a corner. I need the discipline of consistent reasoning because I am a sinner who needs the laws of logic to force me to face the implications of my errors. How else can I make any progress in understanding the Bible and so develop a fully coherent and faithful worldview?"

We also must not forget that one of the main arguments that theological liberals have used against the Bible's claim to be a direct propositional revelation has been that if God revealed himself directly like this, the revelation would be infallible and we would no longer be free to reject it. In other words, the idea of an infallible revelation must be denied because it is a threat to human autonomy. (This type of reasoning is documented in such discussions as H. D. McDonald's *Theories of Revelation* [London: G. Allen & Unwin, 1963], pp. 77ff, 332, and Cornelius Van Til's *The New Modernism* [Philadelphia: Presbyterian & Reformed, 1946], especially, chapter three, "Dialecticism.")

3. The reason we call an event a *chance* event is because it does not appear to be controlled or caused according to any definable pattern or law. But this means that it is in principle unpredictable. That is, we cannot know when it will go one way rather than another. Our belief in chance is therefore a function of our ignorance of causation.

At the same time, recent developments in chaos theory are lending weight to the view that there may in fact be no strictly chance events in the world at all. Even things like the upward curl of smoke from a cigarette, the branching of capillary tubes in our blood vessels or the fall of leaves from a tree, which we previously assumed to have a large element of chance in their structures, turn out now to develop according to mathematical formulas. The same seems to be true for social events like the movements of large crowds and other events made up of large numbers of human choices. Perhaps the ignorance gap can be closed, if only in the abstract world of statistics. This should give the freewillers pause.

4. I will not repeat here the difficulties facing a believer in free will who contemplates what would have happened if Joseph had decided to leave Mary with Elizabeth and go on to Bethlehem alone with the required information for the census. In this example, free will becomes the Grinch that stole Christmas from Bethlehem.

5. All Arminians consider it reasonable to tell the unbeliever that "God has a wonderful plan for your life." But what could this mean if a person by uncaused (indeterminate) events eventually goes to hell? How can Arminians honestly tell unbelievers that God loves them if God is not willing to do what is needed to save them? Strictly speaking, does he ultimately leave it up to them (or worse, to a randomly acting free will) whether they will finally do enough to save themselves? What kind of love is so vague and undiscriminat-

ing that it leaves the eternal salvation of its beloved in the hands of an autonomous mechanism in their heads, rather than acting to *secure* that salvation? How can God love us if he is incompetent?

6. Arminians can never have full assurance of salvation in this life, but the
situation in the afterlife is even worse—believers can still be lost finally. How
then, can Arminians be certain that they will not sin in the distant future of
heaven? If it is objected that we have free will now, but will not have it in
eternity, it would seem that a free will is not really necessary to the image of
God after all. But this was supposed to be one of the main arguments in its
favor. If God does not want us to have a free will in heaven, why would he
frustrate his own purposes by giving it to us now?

7. When God decided to give us free will, he must have known that at least
statistically some humans and angels would eventually decide to disobey him,
even if Adam and Eve remained sinless. In fact, if he had even the foreknowledge implied in the ability to make a lucky guess, he must have known that
sin and its attendant evils were inevitable, once autonomous wills were allowed. But this means he was indeed "responsible" for evil in the sense that
it happened because he did not do what was necessary to stop it.

Consider the events in the Garden of Eden. If God wanted to save Adam
and Eve from sinning, he could have prevented the serpent from being effective in the first place by simply arriving on the scene of the temptation and
arguing them out of it, a form of what Arminians call *moral suasion.* He could
have shown them a preview of the BBC series *The World at War* (apparently
God has no trouble getting previews!) and warned them that this is the kind
of thing that will inevitably happen if they follow Satan's worldview. Can
anyone imagine that God would not have been able to *convince* this couple
not to listen to Satan? If a sinner can be convinced of the truth of the gospel
today, why could God not couple moral suasion with reasoned arguments to
convince Adam and Eve of the error of the satanic way, thus showing them
the error of the demonic *theoria*?

If a lifeguard on duty simply watches passively as a boy struggles in the
waves until he drowns, we would certainly not absolve her of responsibility,
because she had the opportunity and physical ability to save him. Does God
not have an analogous ability to save any sinner? Could he not have saved

Eve from the serpent's blandishments? Postulating free will is not much help in these cases.

8. As a final problem for Arminians, consider the matter of prayer. All evangelicals pray for the salvation of individuals, fully expecting that the effective prayers of the righteous can accomplish much (Jas 5:16). But how can Arminians pray for the conversion of an individual person if God would have to override the free will to convert that person? The most Arminians could pray for would be neutral, nonthreatening things that do not infringe upon the "rights" of the sinner.

Calvinists can happily pray for specific people to be converted, because they know quite well that if God does not in mercy intervene to free sinners from spiritual death, they will never be saved at all. God may have willed that particular prayers will be part of the chain leading to a person's salvation. Prayer is both reasonable and effective, precisely because God is in control and can override the human will to answer them.

Postulating free will is no help with the problem of evil. God could certainly create beings with wills that always gladly choose the right. We know from the Bible itself that God is quite capable of creating sinless beings who always willingly do the right thing. Adam and Eve before the Fall were such people, at least for a while. So is the incarnate Christ. So are the elect angels of 1 Timothy 5:21. So are the resurrected and glorified saints in heaven. If it is claimed that these all have free will and that at the same time this is quite compatible with their being fixed in immutable righteousness forever, how does free will get God off the hook with the problem of evil? It merely underscores the fact that he is quite capable of producing a world in which beings with free will always do the right thing and make the right choices, yet he chose to create the world we see now.

Perhaps the assumption of free will places a burden on the shoulders of Christians that they are unable to bear. The freewill theory simply postulates free wills as a hypothesis or assumption. But if we cannot first prove that free will exists in the required sense, it cannot be used as an explanation for *anything*. We must first establish the major premise. Only then can it function as an explanation for something else. The disturbing fact remains, however, that the Bible never uses the idea of free will as an explanatory category. It is an extrabiblical intruder from the world of unbelief, a rogue virus from another galaxy.

Luther used to say that all the major types of heresy seem to have different heads, but they are all tied together by their tails. The same is true of the various humanisms. Strato's assumption that the world is innately intelligible to itself, Flew's denial of any divine determination, Socrates' insistence on the good being independent of the gods' opinion of it, humanism's assertion of the autonomy of human thought and the modern evangelical's efforts to mod- ify the doctrines of the Reformation to conform to the freewill theory all share a common denominator: apostate autonomism. They are all examples of what it means to locate ultimacy in the world rather than in God. But the believer should first consider the material in the Bible on God's exhaustive determi- nation of the direction of his own creation.

Biblical Determinism

The doctrine of creation itself requires a high degree of determinism. The Bible consistently supports this with abundant precepts and examples. We have already noted that God claims to control human decisions, from the choices of a king to the throw of a die. A case of this from the New Testament is found in John 19. The psalmist had said ten centuries before that the Messiah would experience his garments being gambled for in connection with his death (Ps 22:18). The soldiers responsible for executing Jesus noticed that one of his garments was seamless, being woven from top to bottom, making it a rather expensive piece and best left intact. So they decided to cast lots for it, rather than tearing it up to divide among themselves, "that the scripture might be fulfilled which said, 'They divided my garments among them and cast lots for my clothing' " (v. 24).

Numerous freewill decisions contributed to this fulfillment, from somebody lovingly providing the garment for Jesus' use in the first place to Jesus decid- ing to wear it that day and the soldiers deciding to gamble for it. A dozen other human choices were needed to bring all the details together. The prediction also contains many other distinguishable elements. As a prediction, it required detailed prior knowledge of a single historical moment in the distant future. Either God saw a sneak preview of the film, or his detailed knowledge was actually knowledge of his own plans, necessarily including all the freewill decisions that made up the event. Had any one of those many human choices gone the other way that day, the prediction would have been invalidated and all the angels looking over the edge of the clouds would have been disappointed (1 Pet 1:12).

Arminianism seems to be stuck with God's predictions being nothing but lucky guesses that somehow always turn out right in the Bible. But this is either pure chance or predetermination without the word *determinism*. No one escapes some kind of determinism, and postulating free will is no help.

To close out this consideration of the humanistic denial of divine determination, we will turn to two accounts of Jesus' death in Acts 2:22-36 and 4:27-28. In the first passage, Peter says, "This man was handed over to you by God's set purpose and foreknowledge" (v. 23). In fact, "it was impossible for death to keep its hold on him" (v. 24), because God predicted that he would rise from the dead in the Psalms. In other words, because it was predicted, it was not possible for it to be otherwise. In the second passage, Peter and John state in a prayer that Jesus' enemies "were gathered together against Thy holy servant Jesus, . . . to do whatever Thy hand and Thy purpose predestined to occur" (NASB).

The Bible teaches that far from being some sort of chance event dependent on the free wills of sinners, the crucifixion, the most disgusting and unjust judicial murder in history, was expressly planned and carried out according to God's explicit predestination of all the microscopic details involved (don't forget that seamless robe) and achieved exactly what he wanted. We must remember that Isaiah 53, as part of the great argument for monotheism in Isaiah 40—55, states that "the LORD was pleased to crush Him, putting Him to grief" (v. 10 NASB). But if this, the greatest of all evils, was predestined, what are we to say of numerous serious but lesser evils?

Job says that God can do anything he wants to do, Isaiah says that God actually does everything he intends to do, and Paul says in Ephesians 1:11 that he "works out everything in conformity with the purpose of his will." We can only conclude that "the mind of the Spirit" is totally uniform throughout the Bible on this issue (see 1 Cor 2:6-16).

When Jesus wanted to emphasize that God's control of the details is total, he chose illustrations drawn from trivially small facts in our common experience. He said that God numbers all the hairs of our heads (Mt 10:30) and that not even a sparrow falls out of the sky without God's being involved (Lk 12:6-7). Had the Lord lived in the twentieth century, he might have said, "God's exhaustive sovereignty extends to both the position and the velocity of every subatomic particle from the last electron in your fingernail, to the least particle of cosmic dust on the farthest edge of the most distant galaxy; 'I, the LORD, do all these things' (Is 45:7). But you are worth more to me than any number of subatomic particles."

The Bible goes out of its way to include in God's control the decision-making functions of the human mind. In 2 Thessalonians 2:11 Paul says that God will send the wicked "a powerful delusion" in order to prepare them for judgment. In 1 Samuel 16, God sends an evil spirit to torment the wicked Saul and bring him to the brink of insanity. In 1 Kings 22, God invites an evil spirit (or is it just a perfectly good angelic being who agrees to obey God?) to deceive King Ahab by lying to him through his prophets. The result of this deception is Ahab's mortal wounding at Ramoth Gilead. The writer notes laconically that some unknown soldier let off a bowshot "at random," and the arrow found a chink in Ahab's armor. The soldier was not even aiming straight, but Ahab bled to death that evening, as predicted. His last political act had been to take the time to persecute Micaiah, God's prophet. The wicked, it seems, die the way they live.

More positively, Paul tells us that as the believer grows in grace, God both induces the right decisions and causes them to be done, once they are induced (Phil 2:13). Without this degree of control and interference, we would never manage to get sanctified.

Paul also says that the absence of revelation can produce certain effects God wants (1 Cor 2:6-8). He says here that if the people who arranged the execution of Christ had had any knowledge of the revelations made to Paul, "they would not have crucified the Lord of glory." That is, God could have prevented many evils simply by making further direct revelations, just as Jesus himself said in Matthew 11:21 about the cities of Tyre and Sidon.

Our conclusion from even so small a selection of the evidence is that there is no physical or mental event in the creation that is not controlled by God.

Further verses for consideration include Daniel 4:35, Psalm 147:5, Ecclesiastes 3:11, John 6:64, Ephesians 3:9 and Revelation 1:18.

The Real Solution

Let it be stated plainly here that the problem of evil can be solved in a straightforward manner by proposing that if God decides to predestine or decree any particular evils for any purpose he may intend, who are we to answer back to God (Rom 9:19-24)? However galling it may seem to the fleshly mind, God is the final reference point for what counts as the good, not me, the sinner. If ever there was a practical application of Jesus' prayer "not my will but yours be done" (Lk 22:42), this would be it. The good is good because God determines it as such, not because it conforms to my irrelevant innate conception of how things ought to be. It is wholly beside the point that I might personally prefer things to be otherwise. Sufferings may be persuasive, but they are not in themselves arguments that can be valid or invalid. Human suffering is a body of data that must be interpreted according to presuppositions before it can be understood in any sense. It does not mean anything by itself, however horrible we may find it.

Antony Flew in *God and Philosophy* claims that to "define goodness in terms of God's will" is "to break totally with all ordinary standards both of meaning and morality." It is also "to reduce your religion to the worship of infinite power as such" (para. 2.46, p. 50). He reluctantly admits that "to the extent, of course, that you are prepared to do this, there can for you be no Problem of Evil" (para. 2.47, p. 51).

But "ordinary standards" of good and evil are precisely what is being questioned by the Christian who wants the unbeliever to give himself up as the final standard and to call upon God for righteousness. This is not a problem for the Christian, but rather the whole point of the gospel's call for repentance. A repentance that does not touch one's controlling assumptions is too superficial to be worthwhile. As for our "[worshiping] infinite power as such," this is an oddly reductionist misrepresentation of our position, which in the same chapter he has been anxious to show has important internal relations and implications far beyond creatorial sovereignty per se.

Flew can hardly hide his anger (or is it disgust?) with those of us who hold this position, but he is determined to be straightforward about what it amounts to. He admits again that if God is his own reference point for the good, *this offers a decisive solution to the problem of evil* (para. 5.21, p. 109). But he cannot leave it there. He must make this admission seem too frightfully dubious to be attractive. He implies that it is not "decent" (p. 50), and shortly thereafter "uncomfortable" and the "last resort" of apologetics (p. 51). He even invokes the authority of Piaget to call it "infantile" (p. 114). Earlier he calls it "Gordian," a reference to the Greek story about Alexander, who solved the problem of how to untie a mysterious knot by arbitrarily cutting the rope (p. 110).

But my arguments have cut no rope. I merely disagree with the humanist dogma of the autonomy of human thought, on which all the objections to God are based. There is no need for believers to accept the tying of the knot in the first place. It is only autonomism that makes the knot appear necessary.

Flew's treatment of the Bible's solution to the problem of evil is very re-vealing of his attitude toward Christianity. He treats those who want to start with the Stratonician presumption of a self-interpreting cosmos as if they were basically sensible and honest, while those of us who want to start with the Creator as the ultimate reference point are obscurantist and arbitrary. But this is often how dogmatisms work: I am objective, but you are just arbitrary. That he really does think this way is revealed in such odd admissions as the one about Strato's assumption being "defeasable, of course, by adverse argument" (p. 69).

But if the question of one's ultimate reference point is really a presumption, how can it be proved or disproved by arguments? If it is chosen or rejected as the result of argument, it is no longer a presupposition, but a conclusion from previous presuppositions. If Flew says that presuppositions cannot be proved, but they may be *dis*proved by arguments, this prevents him from even starting those arguments, for even a disproof is itself based on axioms treated as ultimates.

The only sense in which a presupposition can be proved is to the degree that it can be confirmed by whatever facts and coherence may follow intelligibly from it. If an assumption makes nonsense of reality, it cannot be thought of as an explanation of that reality, because if reality is nonsense, nothing can count as an explanation for anything. This is the main reason why non-Christian answers to the one-and-many problem are unacceptable: they only appear to work if we are willing to hold contradictions in tension and appeal to mystery.

Job's Answer to the Problem

Even an atheist like Antony Flew can see that the problem of evil is not a problem for one who simply trusts God. This was Job's answer against his "comforters," who insisted that he must have done something dreadful to be treated that way. God answered him out of the whirlwind by simply asking, "Where were you when I laid the earth's foundations?" (38:4). This was also Paul's answer in Romans 9:19-20.

God never questioned that Job was in fact an unusually righteous man, although by God's standards all are sinners to whom by justice alone only death is due. And Job agreed; earlier he had pointed out to his doubting wife that if it is good enough for us to accept good things from God, we ought to be willing to receive adversity also. The good gifts God had given him were God's both to give and to take away as he willed (1:21). Job maintained the correct position on the question of sovereignty: "I know that you can do all things; no plan of yours can be thwarted" (42:2). It seems that Job was no Arminian.

Who Then Is the Author of Sin?

The Westminster Confession states that "God from all eternity did by the most wise and holy counsel of his own will, freely and unchangeably ordain whatsoever comes to pass: yet so, as thereby God is neither the author of sin, nor is violence offered to the will of the creatures, nor is the liberty or contingency of second causes taken away, but rather established" (3.1). This careful statement says that

1. Everything that happens is ordained by the will of God.
2. God is not the *author* of sin.
3. No *violence* is done to the creature's will.
4. The contingency of secondary causes is *established* by this divine foreordination.

These statements imply a specific view of the relationship that God has to sin and other evils. They are all included in God's free and unchangeable ordination, while yet God is not the author of sin. This is because first, God does not violate the human will, forcing people to sin against it, and second, because the secondary causes that give rise to sin are secured in their operation by the same "wise and holy counsel" to so ordain. God is the first cause of everything that happens (including all evils), because as the Creator he causes "whatsoever comes to pass." "Second causes" are the later things in the sequence of events (like Satan, Adam or me), from whom sins directly proceed. These secondary causes are the author(s) of sin, because they are the direct causes of it. According to the Westminster Confession, God is holy and separated from my sin by not being the direct cause (or author) of it. A cause may be ultimate (of which God is the original cause) or it may be proximate, such as the sinner. Therefore the sinner, not God, is the author of sin for the same reason that a father is not the author of his son's book.

The confession's view of the matter essentially summarizes the view of John Calvin himself in his *Concerning the Eternal Predestination of God* (1552). "First, it must be observed that the will of God is the cause of all things that happen in the world: and yet God is not the author of evil" (p. 169), for "the proximate cause is one thing, the remote cause another" (p. 181). Nevertheless, "Certain shameless and illiberal people charge us with calumny by maintaining that God is the author of sin, if his will is made first cause of all that happens." Calvin specifically rejects the shift "that evils come to be, not by his will, but merely by his permission" (p. 176). On the contrary,

> the will of God is the chief and principal cause of all things. . . . But the higher remote causes He hides in Himself, so that out of them what He makes possible by them is necessary. . . . God does nothing without the best of reasons. But since the most certain rule of righteousness is his will, it ought, as I may say, to be the principal reason of all our reasonings.

The reader is referred to section ten, titled "Providence" (pp. 162-85), where the great Reformer summarizes his position.

Responsibility Again

I have already noted that the word *responsible* is simply a synonym for *answerable* and that the Bible bases human responsibility on three things:

First, there is the right of the Creator to do what he wills with his creation (Mt 20:15; Rom 9:18-23). Therefore the creature is obligated to give an account to God if called upon to do so. In this most fundamental sense, God cannot be responsible for anything he does, because there is no one for him to be answerable to. The alternative offered by Arminianism is that I call God to account simply because I appeal over his head to my own instinctual awareness of a good more ultimate than God himself. This is simply not a Christian response to the situation. It is just humanism hiding behind the language of a traditional piety.

Second, we are responsible in the sense that a cook is responsible for the meal he cooks; that is, *he did it.* Therefore sinners sin, and having done so, are answerable for what *they* have done. In the same way God is responsible for evil in three senses:

1. He created a world in which evil was inevitable, given the starting conditions in the Fall.

2. He allows many evils he could easily prevent or mitigate.

3. He continues to uphold the existence of the world in such a way that evils continue. For the Christian, this is God's world. It is not owned by Satan, nor is it made of a mysteriously evil matter emerging from primeval chaos (compare with Flew, *God and Philosophy,* paras. 2.34—2.39, pp. 43-47).

Nevertheless, God is not responsible for evil in the sense that he is not answerable to anyone. On the contrary, the sinner is answerable to God. This is clearly Paul's perspective in Romans 9—11.

Third, there are degrees of responsibility involved in the degrees of knowledge we have. Those who sin against more light will be punished more severely. While God has exhaustive knowledge of all beings past and future, again there is no one for him to sin against, for his will is the standard of the good, says Calvin, contra Socrates.

If we have this clear basis in the Bible for our concept of responsibility, what need have we for an extrabiblical theory that actually undermines the connection between person and act, handing over a vast realm of reality to chaos and old night without undergirding responsibility?

We need to come to terms with all the data in the Bible on the high degree of divine control of both physical and mental events. If my idea of God cannot cope with this data of revelation, so much the worse for "my idea" of God. The more of the Bible we omit in our teaching to this generation, the more the next generation will feel free to move even further away than we have from the fullness and coherence of the Christian worldview.

When Paul said farewell to the Ephesian elders (Acts 20:17-35), he made two points that are relevant here. He warned about false teachers arising from within the fellowship of the body, and he told them that they must teach "the whole counsel of God," not just the bits people want to hear. In his very last letter, he said that the time will come when sound doctrine will become almost universally unpopular and that when this comes upon the churches, the correct response is to go on teaching the *whole* body of revealed truth anyway (2 Tim 4:1-5).

The question of responsibility is therefore the reflection in the moral realm of the relation of the creature to the Creator, of the ontology of createdness itself. It is severely damaged by introducing the self-replicating virus of apostate autonomism into an otherwise coherent program.

Further Reading

All standard introductions to the main topics of philosophy have chapters on free will and responsibility. Gordon Clark's *Religion, Reason, and Revelation* (Nutley, N.J.: Presbyterian & Reformed, 1969) deals with God and evil in its last chapter.

Those who wonder what Augustus Toplady thought about God's predetermination of things should look at his essay titled "The Scheme of Christian and Philosophical Necessity Asserted," in *Works* (London: J. Cornish, 1861), an answer to Wesley's position. He also produced an account called *Historic Proof of the Doctrinal Calvinism of the Church of England.*

For a thorough refutation of the traditionalist apologetic answers to the problem of evil, see Antony Flew's *God and Philosophy* (New York: Harcourt, 1966).

John Calvin answered the use made of the question of evil by Pighius and Georgius to undermine God's sovereignty in his *Concerning the Eternal Predestination of God* (reprint London: James Clark, 1961). His answer is the same as Gordon Clark's: what God does is right because God's will is the standard of what is right, and sinners have no rational basis for mounting an objection against their Creator. The excellent James Clark edition was translated and edited by J. K. S. Reid, who wrote a very helpful (but somewhat Barthian) introduction.

11
The Location of Ultimacy & the Attributes of God: A Current Debate

*T**he preceding chapters have sought* to show that the historic alliances of Christianity with the humanist presupposition of human autonomy have involved a progressive syncretism with non-Christian thought. It is essentially what Paul calls conformity to the course of this world (Rom 12:1-2). It is mere obedience to the Zeitgeist, submission to the spirit of the present age. I have shown directly from Scripture that it is incompatible with the particularism of the Bible and have observed from history that when the Arminian Remonstrants allowed this assumption free rein, it caused a progressive disintegration of the Reformation theology of salvation and had to be refuted at Dort. I have also noted what Arminian scholars have said happened to those churches that fell under the spell of an increasingly liberalizing Arminianism.

Historically, the present alliance of evangelicalism with Arminian thinking dates mainly from the age of Wesley. It was then that evangelical theology developed the habit of limiting the debate to the subject of salvation only, despite the efforts of Augustus Toplady to show that if it exists at all, a full-scale divine sovereignty must be a universal principle.

After about 1960, modern evangelicalism began to throw off the narrowness of the fundamentalist era. It began to learn from the Dutch tradition that Christianity is not just another "religion" but must be a totally comprehensive worldview.

The Dutch part of the Reformation church has pointed the way to a larger view, starting with Calvin himself and blossoming in such persons as Abraham Kuyper, Herman Bavinck and Cornelius Van Til, and now in a hundred others. More recently, in the prophetic call of Francis Schaeffer, Western evangelical churches have been introduced to a more exciting and comprehensive vision of how to defend the gospel. We were all encouraged by Schaeffer's ministry to aggressively challenge the autonomist intellectual pretensions of a lost world. Many modern evangelical apologists at last have the conviction that worldview apologetics is the way into the future. It is now widely realized that the gospel must be presented to the world of fallen thought as a total challenge, as a comprehensive vision of reality, not just as an alternative privatized religion within a religiously multicultural scene.

The Greek presupposition of metaphysical autonomy, under the term *free will,* continues to act much like a computer virus, progressively disintegrating the whole program unless it is confronted and destroyed. If Christians do not confront it but continue to wed their gospel to it in each generation, they will continue to find widening gaps in their theological foundations and undermine their apologetic efforts in defense of a reduced and compromised theology. Friendship with the world is still enmity with God, whatever *pragmatism demands.

The Unanswered Question
The question therefore remains unanswered on the current evangelical scene concerning the theological basis for apologetics—is it possible, let alone necessary, to base Christian apologetic methods on purely biblical presuppositions? Or must we join the queue behind Aristotle, the pseudo-Dionysius, Thomas Aquinas, Butler's *Analogy* and the Arminian-humanist synthesis to develop some fresh form of the great syncretism of Greek and Christian think-

ing and base our apologetics on that?

There are several reasons that this question is not adequately faced today. The first is the underlying anti-intellectualism of so many, together with a loss of confidence in doctrinal formulations. Modern evangelical pragmatists behave as if we can get along without clear doctrinal foundations. Second, many evangelicals have no knowledge of the history of the perennial syncretism with humanism down through the years and simply trust that theology will somehow keep itself pure from the world by limiting itself to a handful of key fundamentals. But history says otherwise. It did not work in the early church, when these fundamentals were the Apostles' Creed. It did not work in the Puritan era, when John Owen argued with Richard Baxter about the minimum requirements for a reasonably comprehensive state church. Nor did it work in the 1920s, when the fundamentalists drew up short lists of five, seven or ten fundamentals to form the last wall of defense against modernism. The result was that they lost control of almost all the major denominations.

The Case of Clark Pinnock

The most important reason for our unwillingness to face the syncretism issue is the declining status of the theology of the Reformation among many evangelicals today. This in turn means that the relation of apologetics to systematic theology, and therefore to the methods of Calvinism and Arminianism, is equally unsettled. I have chosen the case of Clark Pinnock to illustrate this because of his undoubted credentials and continuing influence as an evangelical. His own reaction away from Reformational thinking is relatively easy to trace in his various publications, and he speaks plainly.

Pinnock completed his doctorate in Manchester under F. F. Bruce, a highly effective New Testament scholar who emphasized the facts but had little confidence in systematic theology. In England, Pinnock gave a lecture later published with the title *In Defense of Biblical Infallibility,* which earned him a name as a real conservative. In those days he seems to have been a mildly Calvinistic Baptist.

Pinnock, like so many of us at the time, was encouraged toward apologetics by Francis Schaeffer in the mid-sixties. After a stay at L'Abri, he taught in America and soon brought out a little summary of what he had learned from

Schaeffer in a book called *Set Forth Your Case*. This appeared to commit him to an approximately Schaefferian apologetic. By the time I met him at Trinity Evangelical Divinity School in 1970, however, something else had happened. Pinnock had begun to ask the big question about the theological and philosophic basis of Schaeffer's apologetic methods, and he did not like what he found. Like others, he had discovered that much to his dismay, the whole thing depended on how consistently you were willing to attack the fallen sinner's autonomy. Autonomy turned out to be nothing but the freewill theory! In order to be an effective Schaefferian, it seemed that one needed to study people like Van Til and Herman Dooyeweerd and become a serious Calvinist. Calvinistic apologetics meant some form of *presuppositionalism. This seems to have been the straw that broke the back of Pinnock's camel.

That year (1970), the Van Til Festschrift *Jerusalem and Athens* came out. It contained a rather negative and trivializing essay by Pinnock that criticized Van Til's dependence on presuppositions, as if Pinnock were not bound to them himself (p. 420). In his polite response to this attack, Van Til characteristically combined patience with precision:

> I agree with you that Scripture should speak for itself. In fact, I want it to tell us what God is, what the world is, and what we as men are, not *after,* but *before* we start speaking of metaphysics, epistemology, and ethics. To think that I conceive of "the Christian Faith" as an "abstract metaphysical system supported by presuppositionalism" is to misunderstand completely the whole thrust of Reformed thinking. I observe, rather, that as Christians we must look at the world as Christ himself looked at it, and insofar as any man does not, he views it falsely. Consequently, the attempt to find God in the world without looking through the eyes of Christ is fruitless, not because the world does not reveal God (it continually shouts of the existence of God to men) but because *men need new eyes!* (p. 426, my emphasis)

Here we have the presuppositionalist apologetic in a nutshell. All apologetic argument is dependent on ideas of ontology, epistemology and ethics. But the unregenerate mind rejects what God says about these things as a threat to its autonomy. The only god it is willing to admit is not the God of the Bible. Therefore, all the facts of experience reveal only an idol, since the fallen mind is controlled by fallen presuppositions. Even Pinnock's presuppositions determine and limit his results. When Van Til says that "men need new eyes," he is merely repeating what Paul says in 1 Corinthians 2:14, that the "natural man" (NASB) is incapable of receiving the facts as interpreted by the Spirit, because they can only be "spiritually discerned." That person is "sensual, having not the Spirit" (KJV), as Jude 19 explains the term *natural,* needing regeneration "in knowledge" (Col 3:10). But this is to be a Calvinist on the topic of depravity, and Pinnock has abandoned Calvinism for Arminianism.

The New Apologetic

After publishing incidental evidence in the seventies that he had indeed given up all five points of Calvinism, Pinnock also produced *Reason Enough: A Case for the Christian Faith* (1980), in which he repudiated much of what he had learned from Schaeffer about apologetic methodology. In this book, unregenerate claims to intellectual and moral autonomy are defended, not challenged. Now instead of being converted to Christianity from heathen darkness, our cultured despisers are, in effect, invited to convert from Arminianism to Arminianism and to add the words "Jesus is Lord" en route, as the result of the pragmatic acceptance of a cumulative probability.

While Pinnock's apologetic in *Reason Enough* cannot be analyzed in detail here, one or two observations must be made to make clear his method. He begins by selecting what he considers to be the five most important areas of evidence for Christianity. They are the pragmatic test, the evidence of religious experience, the rationality of the cosmos, historical evidence (especially about Jesus) and the evidence from the life of the church. Of these, the second and fourth are really the same empirical test, being merely different factual areas, while the first and fifth are really the same argument from pragmatic usefulness. "The rationality of the cosmos" repeats the usual Arminian confusion between natural theology and general revelation. From this Pinnock tries to salvage an argument from design and a vague impression from what was originally the cosmological argument, based partly on an argument from the evidence for a sudden creation.

The method is simple enough: discuss a variety of traditional arguments and try to salvage a general impression from them without actually claiming that any of them are conclusively valid. As with a pointillist painting, if you step back far enough and have a normal imagination, it will look like a picture; up close, it is just patches of dots. This may also be called the "leaky bucket method" of apologetics. If one leaky bucket will not carry enough water to the fire, perhaps ten leaky buckets might do it by creating some kind of cumulative effect.

Pinnock modestly claims to have done much like Paul at Lystra, merely laying a steppingstone, a preparatory step encouraging the unbeliever to take the message of the Incarnation seriously. He does mention the problem of evil but declines to tell us what the answer would be, except to claim that the answer is "the gospel itself." This is no doubt correct, but in what sense? In his last chapter he does offer an answer to this dilemma, but we shall see that, unfortunately, his answer is worse by far than the original problem.

The Location of Ultimacy

Sociologists invented the phrase "the location of ultimacy" many years ago and used it to identify the way certain cultures and communities refer to their ultimate standards or sources of religious meaning. They had thereby identified the importance of the philosophic issue of locating an ultimate origin of meaning for building a stable culture. Analyzing the way cultures develop out of the decision to locate ultimacy somewhere (in this world or the next, in the state, in a revelation, in a mystical experience, etc.) became a major sociological industry, and some very important discoveries were made. For example, philosophers had been saying for centuries that the ultimate reference point in a worldview or philosophy has important effects on how the culture flowing from that worldview thinks of God and the progress of the world. Finally, it influences how that culture treats human beings under its power.

Sociological studies have now abundantly verified this insight. In an important study of religious cultures, Donald E. Brown's *Hierarchy, History and Human Nature* shows that the degree of rigidity in hierarchical views of the world seems to explain why some cultures have generated virtually no real histories, but only mythologies. The study combines sociological methods with those of anthropology and the problem of historiography to analyze the types of history generated by a wide variety of religious cultures. It has become clear that one's cosmic ontology determines what history will look like and even whether historical thinking will be possible.

The Christian Ultimate

I have noted Pinnock's drift into Arminianism. His own account of it can be read in the first chapter of *The Grace of God, the Will of Man.* Let's consider what the problem of the location of ultimacy means for the Christian and then see what Pinnock has done with it.

When such passages as Genesis 1—2, Isaiah 40—55, Romans 1, John's prologue and Paul's critique of the Colossian heresy refer to the creation, they are all taking sides on the question of where to locate ultimacy. The issue is this: What will be the ultimate fallback position for ontology (statements about being or what exists), epistemology (what counts as reliable knowledge), ethics (how we get standards for moral decisions) and teleology (where it is all going, or where purpose comes from)?

No one escapes this type of question, not even those who refuse to take it seriously as determining everything else; they simply follow the world's lead by default. This issue is nothing less than how we arrive at the ultimate reference point or presupposition in terms of which everything else is intelligible. The four areas listed above together make up the basic structure of our worldview, our basic *theoria* about what reality is. By *ultimacy* is meant that mysterious thing behind everything else, in terms of which everything is orderly and meaningful. By its *location* is meant that a decision has to be made (and is inevitably made) about whether the ultimate is to be the God of the Bible or something else. When I say that this decision is *inevitably* made, I mean that if anything intended to be truth is uttered about reality, that proposition presupposes a principle of ultimacy in order to be intelligible.

To say that the Christian locates ultimacy in the God of the Bible is simply to agree that the God referred to in Genesis 1:1 is the origin of being and meaning and goodness and the director of his own creation. It follows necessarily that all other conceptions of ultimacy are forms of idolatry, for there can only be one ultimate and that is either God himself or something in his creation. There are no other alternatives, as Isaiah is at pains to make clear.

That is, if Yahweh is not your ultimate, you are an idolater. But what *kind* of ultimate will meet our philosophic needs?

John 1:1-3 is decisive here. It is a self-conscious exposition of the opening verse of Genesis, starting with the very same verbal form as the Septuagint *(en archē)*, which was the widely used Greek version familiar in the first-century world. John's first verse states that "in the beginning" the Logos existed already within the being of God. That is, just as God is eternal, the Logos is eternal. To unpack this claim, John then states that *everything* came into existence because the Logos made it, and nothing came into existence without the Logos. The key point is that in the beginning God existed alone with his Logos, and then he created, bringing into existence everything that "becomes." This can only be denied by agreeing with generic paganism that being-in-general exists over against God and has existed eternally alongside him as a secondary and perhaps competing source of being. John wants to make explicit the creation ex nihilo (out of nothing) that he recognized in the Old Testament. He distinguishes his Logos from the Greek Logos, which was the impersonal rational structure of being-in-general, usually functioning as the Greek principle of unification.

The climax of John's case for distinguishing his own vision of the Logos from the Greek abstraction is "the Word became flesh and made his dwelling among us" (v. 14). John's religious purpose is to force the reader to confront the life-giving power of the Logos incarnate in Jesus and to demand a choice between this and any alternative pagan concept of God. The rest of John's Gospel may be thought of as a commentary on the prologue (1:1-18), and particularly on the fourteenth verse. The whole point of John's prologue is to encourage the reader to consider the Logos as having become historically incarnate in Jesus and to recognize him alone as the only alternative to the darkness of Greek paganism in both its pantheistic and polytheistic forms (v. 5). It is inconceivable that John would want us to conclude that his Logos is just one of several probable religious possibilities that all have an equal right to be considered as the final truth.

Since the difference between Strato and the Bible is really the question of whether there is only one kind of being (the world of finite empirical experience) or two (the God of the Bible also exists, related to the finite world as its Creator), the question of where to locate ultimacy is the same issue. Strato said that the principles for interpreting the world are to be found themselves within the world; that is, the world contains its own ultimate meaning. In contrast, the Christian locates the principles for interpreting the world in God. They are only accessible to us by his telling us what they are in a verbal revelation in history. That is why the propositional element is so essential to the doctrine of inspiration.

Since all Christians believe in God over against Strato's atheism, we can move on to the next two implied issues.

First, if whatever exists consists of two kinds of being and two only (the infinite-personal, self-contained God of the Bible and his finite, dependent creation), it should be obvious that the Christian must locate ultimacy in God and not in the world or in any aspect of it. That is, by *God* I must intend to mean that God's very nature includes that he is the ultimate reference point for understanding reality. God first tells me what he is like, and then he tells me that he made the cosmos for his own glory. God is therefore the determining origin of being, knowing, choosing and purpose throughout all realms of experience. Truth for the believer must be simply God's interpretation of reality. Only in terms of God's prior plan is anything whatsoever made intelligible, including also the relation between any question and its answer.

Second, the Christian, having heard God describe himself, believes the Bible when it says that God is omnipotent, omniscient and a Trinity antecedently in himself prior to creation. Although the Bible does not use these technical terms, it contains statements that require them. When Christians claim to locate ultimacy in God, we do not merely believe that a god of some kind exists, but that the particular God revealing himself in the Bible exists, the infinite-personal ontological Trinity identified in the mind of Jesus and declared in John's Gospel (1:18). Everything else exists within the temporal flow of his creation, and being created by God is to be made intelligible in terms of God as its origin of meaning.

Tiamat Lives Again

Clark Pinnock addresses the problem of evil in his last chapter, titled "Real Difficulties" (*Reason Enough,* pp. 114-17). He first moves to use the standard freewill defense, saying, "I suppose the great bulk of the problem can be placed on mankind's shoulders, who has misused his creaturely freedom, and the reason God allowed this to happen relates to his respect for man's relative autonomy." This is perfectly appropriate for an Arminian. But what of the vast mass of evil that cannot be blamed in any direct sense on us? Pinnock then says that the Bible also "recognizes a mysterious dimension . . . *a dark power of chaos that was there from the beginning"* (p. 115, my emphasis).

In order to make this ultimate dualism seem Christian, he appeals to "the first few verses of the Bible according to the best translations." In claiming that Genesis 1:1-2 teaches an original "chaos," Pinnock is siding with those who claim that Genesis 1 is originally a polytheistic document, reflecting the Babylonian mythology of Tiamat, the female principle of primeval chaos, being attacked by Marduk, the male principle of order. Out of this battle (yet another pagan version of the old one-and-many problem) came the relative degree of order we experience as the cosmos. Although there is no ground for believing it, the liberals have often claimed that the Hebrew word for "the deep" *(t^ehôm)* is really the Babylonian word for Tiamat. It is sometimes sagely noted that the two words have two letters in common. The "deep" was therefore "formless and void" or "waste and empty" in the sense that it was a realm of nonbeing or chaos equally ultimate with God and presumably coeternal with him. This is the "chaos" to which Dr. Pinnock is appealing in his reference to "the best translations."

The inevitable result of this type of exegesis is that the Creator is now a finite deity surrounded by *being per se*. We do not even know whether this god is bigger or more powerful than the primeval chaos itself. If Genesis 1:2 teaches an original primeval chaos "according to the best translations," the Christian cannot be sure that the God of the Bible is even the biggest gorilla in the jungle anymore. We do, however, note that he resembles nothing so much as Plato's ignorant Demiurge, struggling to bring order out of the "mysterious dimension" of chaos. Both God and humankind are finally in the same boat, afloat momentarily on the vast and trackless sea of being. The monster chaos threatens from the depths, and the only flicker of light comes from what we are autonomously willing to put up with of God's meager efforts to influence those in the boat.

To test whether the liberal higher-critical exegesis of Genesis 1:1 is supported by scriptural usage, look up the occurrences of *t^{c}hôm* in such a source as Young's or Strong's concordance. There it is clear that the word is almost always translated as "deep" or "depth" and usually refers to the oceans. In no verse is the translation "chaos" required, much less "Tiamat." R. Laird Harris calls the "chaos" translation "tendential" and says that "*t^{c}hôm* cannot be derived from Tiamat" (R. Laird Harris et al., *Theological Wordbook of the Old Testament,* vol. 2 [Chicago: Moody, 1980], p. 966).

Finite Godism

One of the distinctives of historical Christianity and a key element in its view of reality is the continuity of the New Testament idea of God with the God of the Old Testament. The very doctrine of the Trinity itself was formulated out of the biblical data in order to preserve the central fact that the Jesus of the New Covenant is really the Yahweh of the Old Covenant incarnate in time and space, continually bringing his church out of heathenism by the ongoing sovereign power of his Holy Spirit. In careful harmony with the doctrine of creation, the divine attributes were described by such terms as *omniscience* to point to the historical evidences of predictive messianism and to signal a final judgment on sin. The word *omnipotence* was then intended to preserve the doctrine of an active, personal, immanent providence in the present. A finite God can cope neither with future prediction nor with present evils, much less with the vast, occult dimensions of the problem of evil in its more systematic forms as they come to flower in Gnosticism, Hinduism or today's trendy New Age philosophies.

We have seen how full the Bible's testimony is concerning the attributes of omnipotence, omnipresence and omniscience. They are called *incommunicable attributes* by Reformed theologians because they are the essential qualities distinguishing the creature from the Creator, and therefore cannot in the nature of the case be held in common with the creation. A created entity can no more be omnipotent, omniscient or omnipresent than it can be infinite or eternal.

The reader should pause here to reread chapter two on God in the Westminster Confession. It's a good idea to play Bach's *Brandenburg Concertos* (or his *Christmas Oratorio,* or Handel's *Messiah*) in the background while perusing this material. The greatest theology should always be accompanied by the greatest art.

What Is Idolatry?

The battle with idolatry running through both testaments is also a fundamental structural theme of biblical revelation. An idol may be variously defined or identified. An idol may be simply the alternative god of another religion, like Jupiter or Diana of the Ephesians. It may be the creature-worship described by Paul in Romans 1 or the ghastly old political deities of the Assyrians, Egyptians, Babylonians or Canaanites. Idols also may include the many material distractions we confront in the world of fallen culture, from one's job to the football season, or an Alfa-Romeo sports car.

In Isaiah 40—66 there is a more general and all-encompassing concept of an idol that is implied in the prophet's extended diatribe against idolatry. In its most general form, an idol is anything erected by the sinner to stand alongside the God of the Bible to keep him at bay, to limit him in some way within his own creation, to keep him in his place. This place is always a place of convenience designed by his compromised worshipers from which God can be recalled into action at their philosophical or political whim, without threatening their basic presumption of autonomy. It functions as a humanly chosen reference point, a competing origin of meaning and integration, so that human freedom to oscillate between preferred "relative absolutes" is preserved. In this way claims can continue to be made on a history that is forgotten, and a theological tradition can be appealed to while its content is being progressively abandoned. In this way Christian terminology can be used just as it was in the old days, with the words now given new meanings in conformity with the latest syncretism. The search for a workable syncretism between Christianity and heathenism would itself make a fine idol for an enterprising thinker. Historically, it often has.

Theological Crossfire

After brief introductions by each author, dealing mostly with attitudes and conditions for the discussion, a 1990 book by Clark Pinnock and Delwin

Brown, *Theological Crossfire,* wisely opens with a discussion of theological method. Like Platt, Pinnock wants to develop a mediating position, speaking hopefully of being some sort of liberal while retaining his evangelical stance, avoiding both heresy and idolatry at the same time. He characterizes the liberals as people who "seriously doubt that human beings are capable of possessing divine truth in such a way as to make them able correctly to label other people's convictions as false or damnable. They think that it is idolatrous to equate what we believe with absolute truth in this manner" (p. 13). Of course, this *skepticism both makes it automatically impossible to identify a heresy and reduces all claims to truth to a dead level of opinion. The question of whether the presupposition of autonomism by the liberals is not itself an example of idolatry is not raised by Pinnock.

Delwin Brown's introduction is also highly irenic. He hopefully admits that "we [liberals] have been blind to the full implications of our presuppositions," while the conservatives have been guilty of "a failure in our churches to love God with the mind" (p. 17). So far so good; what, then, of methodology?

Brown rightly roots his liberalism in the Enlightenment. He says that the real difference between liberal and conservative stances has nothing to do with the supposed battle between faith and reason, but is based on the conservative preference for authorities rooted in the past, while liberals opt for authorities rooted in modernity. He states flatly that while higher criticism and evolutionary theory have made the old belief in the Bible "simply not true," the conservatives still think that "everything the contemporary world might say must be judged by its conformity to biblical revelation." The liberal conviction is rather that "finally we must live by our best modern conclusions . . . the best criteria available in the present" (pp. 22-24).

When attempting to define his method over against orthodoxy, Brown the liberal Christian is in the same position as Flew the Stratonician atheist. The seeker must be "guided by the criteria of knowledge defensible and defended in the arenas of our contemporary discourse." That is, the principles of the world are to be found in the world itself—especially in the modern world. He speaks of "honoring" and "appreciating" the Bible, but immediately evacuates this of any sense that might restrict him, saying that it contains nothing unique and is neither coherent nor consistent in itself. So naturally for Brown, "the

Bible is not the criterion of truth." He is merely willing to allow it "importance" in "authoring our identities" (p. 28). That is, it remains one of the factors that helps us form our view of ourselves.

Pinnock then responds by saying that "method . . . surely comes first . . . in the order of theorizing" (p. 37), because there the question of controlling presuppositions is dealt with, affecting everything we do subsequently. He then identifies the main presupposition of past orthodox theologians: "The Scriptures were cited continually . . . on the assumption that they, being inspired by God, comprised divinely revealed and inspired propositions." Then in his "Positive Orientation" that follows, he begins by framing the discussion with the Wesleyan Quadrilateral of "Scripture, tradition, experience and reason" (p. 40). Then he states that because "experience played a role in God's giving of revelation in ancient times," that revelation "was not the communication of inerrant propositions dictated to scribes" (p. 43).

This, of course, bears marked similarities to the standard liberal argument against the authority of the Bible, which involves several assumptions, all equally important and all equally false. First, it is commonly assumed in this type of argument that because we are autonomous, revelation cannot be direct, since "experience played a role." This was Karl Barth's main argument against direct verbal revelation. Second, it is assumed that because we are autonomous, revelation cannot be propositional. Third, it is assumed that because we are sinners and therefore fallible ourselves, revelation must also be fallible, since it is mediated through a human mind. Fourth, it is assumed that if a revelation consisted of verbally inspired propositions, it would be nothing but a "dictation." Dictation, of course, is ruled out because it reduces the autonomy of the one receiving the revelation.

The importance of this view of Scripture for our present purpose is that it shows with great clarity Pinnock's firm commitment to the presupposition of autonomy. He allows it to determine in advance what the nature and content of divine revelation can be. But there is a price to be paid for this rigorous conformity to the liberal agenda, and Brown has no difficulty asking that it be paid right away. While Pinnock keeps referring to such evangelical concepts as "the faith once delivered to the saints" and "the authority of the Bible" and "the biblical content" and the New Testament proclamation being "binding" within "the grammar of faith," Brown simply zeroes in on the real problem that Pinnock has created for himself. He asks, "You speak of the basic grammar of Christian faith. What belongs to that grammar, and . . . how does the conservative theologian determine what in the Bible belongs to it?" (p. 49).

In these questions, Brown has exposed the fact that Pinnock has delivered himself into the hands of the liberal. Brown knows quite well that if revelation is not propositional and therefore contains no infallible information, the only question remaining is how consistent a humanist Pinnock is willing to be. When Brown asks quite reasonably, "Is reason not indispensable in the determination of that within the Bible that you think represents the basic grammar of faith?" (p. 51), he has identified for Pinnock's consideration the very question that the inerrantists have always demanded that liberal evangelicals answer. That is, if you do not believe the Bible to be inerrantly infallible in all that it says, you must have an authority outside the Bible to tell you what is reliable and what is not. Pinnock has wandered so far into the jungle of liberalism that he even asserts that "professing the authority of the Bible . . . does not . . . tell us where the locus of authority rests" (p. 53). But the term "locus of authority" is simply the term *location of ultimacy* as applied to the epistemological aspect of God's revelation. For an orthodox evangelical, the text of the Bible *is* the locus of authority, precisely because it is a direct propositional revelation.

Having excluded this propositionalism from the answer he wants to give to Brown, from now on Pinnock can never extricate himself from the same uncertainty that Brown expresses. In his own attempt to express what the Bible means for him as a liberal, he can only suggest that "the Bible does *author* our Christian identity, . . . that in our continual wrestling with it, it continuously authors who we are and what we are for" (p. 30).

That a particular community's holy books "author the identity" of individuals in that community could be said of the Qur'an in the Islamic community. It can also be said of what happens to a person who is already of the opinion that life is meaningless when reading the novels of Albert Camus or Jean-Paul Sartre, or to a person with a sadistic streak while immersed in reading the Marquis de Sade, or to a racist encountering Hitler's *Mein Kampf.* These literary sources are not revelations in the Christian sense, but they are all quite capable of "authoring" the reader's identity.

Powerful art, whether musical or literary, modifies the human spirit as we participate in its power to communicate meaning and to imply a worldview. This is why modern dictatorships (Stalin's and Hitler's most notably) have always restricted their artists, and why Counter-Reformational Catholicism created an index of prohibited books. Adolf Hitler used to lie on the carpet in tears while listening to recordings of Wagner's operas. His occult paganism was in the process of being "authored" by the sheer power of great music.

This is, of course, a purely natural phenomenon and is quite distinct from Paul's idea that the Holy Spirit empowers the Word to regenerate and sanctify the soul when the Christian is immersed in Bible study.

Pinnock on God and Man

In the section on the doctrine of God starting on page 61, Pinnock tells us that he wants to "maintain biblical theism." He then repeats what I have noted in his earlier writings: God created us with "relative autonomy" (p. 65). This means that God "limits himself" so that he has a "dynamic relationship" with us in which he experiences "change," so that "God's knowledge changes . . . through our decisions" (p. 66). The logic of this position requires that God be finite in his consciousness of the world, which leads directly to finite godism.

Pinnock, however, decides to have his cake and eat it too: "I believe that God could at any time exercise his power. . . . A finite god would not be able to do this, but the God of the Bible can do so" (p. 75). But the God of the Bible not only can but does "do so" in order to achieve his own coherent and eternal ends (Is 43:10-13; 46:8-11).

This movement back and forth between qualities of finitude while continuing to use the language of orthodoxy is one of the things that irritates Christians who encounter Mormonism. The Mormons want to describe God as Creator of *this* world only, allowing innumerable other creating gods all in process with their own worlds toward higher godhood. Then they turn around and try to sound orthodox by also claiming that God is "infinite." We must insist that this is a self-contradiction. Pinnock too cannot hope to save himself from finite godism by claiming that God is really all-powerful but chose to limit himself voluntarily. The same cannot be said of the God of orthodoxy. The God of Genesis may limit himself voluntarily to eight-legged spiders and four-legged elephants by deciding to create them that way, but this is only a limitation on the nature of the creation, not on God. Pinnock is actually saying that *God is really ignorant of future contingencies, when they depend on our autonomous choices* (pp. 66, 75).

But unlike our consciousness, God's consciousness is identically coextensive with his being. That is, God is exhaustively intelligible to himself (Mt 11:27; 1 Cor 2:10-11). If God is ignorant, he is also necessarily ontologically finite. He is also no longer omnipotent even in principle, for he cannot act in a realm of which he has no knowledge, having no control of an indeterminate future. Pinnock seems to have taken Eve's side in the Garden. Once she had limited God by her presupposition of autonomy, she correctly concluded that a finite God could not predict with any confidence that she would surely die. She had deprived him of exhaustive control of the future by embracing the theory of her own free will.

Further, has Pinnock forgotten the solution to the problem of evil that he published in *Reason Enough* in 1980? In this book on apologetics, he said that there was a realm of chaotic mystery in existence alongside God from the beginning, which may in some way (not spelled out) help us with the problem of evil. Strangely, he makes no appeal to this when answering Brown (pp. 75-76). Brown is not convinced by Pinnock's treatment, either: "I see how your freewill theism escapes some of the problems of classical theism, but I cannot understand how it addresses the theodicy issue" (p. 74).

Brown asks plaintively, "What is the alternative?" in response to Pinnock's methodological assumption that "the best that is known about the rest of the world" through "modern knowledge" must be the final test for truth in religion. But neither he nor Pinnock is in any position to really let a God who speaks in an infallible Bible be the ultimate standard for truth. Both have denied that such a Bible exists: Brown by his rejection of "ancient sources" and Pinnock by his rejection of the needed propositional element in Scripture controlled by God. Both are Stratonicians on the question of the location of ultimacy: Brown by choice and Pinnock by default. Brown admits that there are "pre-theological issues which can be productively discussed only on a neutral turf where everyone's assumptions are subject to the same scrutiny" (p. 82). But Pinnock is in no position to do this, because he has already conceded to Brown the basic humanist dogma of the autonomy of the human will. Neither of them questions this. Their own fundamental presupposition is not really "subject to scrutiny."

Brown wants to blame the influence of Greek thought for the orthodox idea of God. He refers to the abstract staticism of the Greek concept of perfection and quite reasonably moves to a Whiteheadian process vision of God to articulate his alternative. Pinnock, however, cannot challenge this odd reading of historical theology, since he admits that "we both criticize classical theism in much the same ways," an admission at least as damaging as any Frederic Platt could have made. Brown wants to seem open on the issue of ultimates, but it is not possible to imagine him really entertaining the idea that the independent, sovereign triune God of the Bible could provide such an ultimate in all four areas of being, knowing, choosing and purpose. His fundamental humanist assumption, the dogma of human autonomism, precludes it as a condition of the dialogue.

On the topic of human nature, Brown says repeatedly that we must not believe even the true insights found in Scripture "because it is in the Bible," but only because modern thought happens to validate them in some sense. He then adopts the Greek idea that we are both bodily and spiritual beings in that we are partly determined (over against "the illusion that we are absolutely free") and partly indeterminate (over against "the illusion that we are absolutely bound"). The standard humanist balancing act between the Parmenidean one and the Heraclitean many could not be better described (pp. 103-104). It is a picture-perfect illustration of where Van Til said the finite mind can be expected to finish up on the assumption of human autonomy. Pinnock's capitulation to the liberal agenda is startlingly illustrated when he tells Brown, "Make no mistake, I am happy that your analysis agrees with the Bible" (p. 115).

Pinnock starts off well on human nature but quickly makes the traditional moves of Arminianism. He begins his discussion by cutting himself off from the Bible with the claim that the first thing he wants to say about the "image of God" is that "first . . . we are personal agents as God is, . . . made free" (pp. 119-20). As we have seen above, no Scripture can be quoted for this. It is Greek mythology, not biblical exegesis. He then steps into conformity with Brown's paradox paradigm: "Thus we are both destined and free" (p. 121). He even equates sin with the denial of the freewill theory (p. 125) and takes a swipe at the Reformed view that the Fall was part of God's plan by saying that this would mean that humanity is "manipulated" by God. Here "manipulated" is used pejoratively, making God look bad if he dares to act in the human soul to implement his own purposes.

Pinnock thinks to save God from responsibility for evil again by saying that "creating human beings with freedom was a risky undertaking on God's part." Does this really mean that God could not muster the wisdom (or would it be imagination?) to see that he had actually made sin inevitable by creating autonomous wills and thus, in his divine ignorance of the future, held on to the vain hope that people might not sin after all, although he did nothing to prevent it? It would appear that on Pinnock's basis, the title "the Lamb slain from the foundation of the world" really only means "we will *try* to fix it if it should go wrong, but it will still be up to your free will."

Brown immediately nails Pinnock at the obvious point by asking how he can avoid the ontological problem of God's becoming dependent on us for key elements of his plan (p. 128). If we are "coworkers with God in the making of history . . . does this not imply that the human contribution is crucial to the achievement of God's aims? . . . If so, could God's effort in history fail without human cooperation?" Brown is gently pushing him to see if his view is really an unarticulated version of process theism, but Pinnock's immediate reflex is just to reaffirm the notion that free will is part of the image of God. Then he contradicts himself by claiming that because we are responsible, we are "not autonomous." But this is simply to give a privatized meaning to the word *autonomous* that it did not have before. *Autonomy* does not mean refusing "the directing hand of divine providence" (p. 129). Nor does it mean being unlimited. It means "acting according to one's own rules without outside interference." It is just a synonym for *free will.*

Perhaps Pinnock should respond to the relevant arguments of a truly systematic antagonist like Antony Flew. A careful reading of the crystal-clear argument in *God and Philosophy* (paras. 2.34-39, pp. 43-47) leads to a forceful conclusion: "In short: if creation is in, autonomy is out." If Pinnock tried to tell Flew that free will and autonomy are two different things, Flew would simply laugh. But having flatly admitted that "God's purposes for individual people can fail if they repudiate those purposes for themselves" (p. 129), Pinnock strangely contradicts his whole position again in his last sentence: "Nothing can happen that God is not prepared for and . . . in his wisdom cannot handle. *His anticipation of future contingencies is perfect"* (my emphasis).

Of this astounding utterance the following must be said. Either God's "anticipation" is a form of knowledge, or it is not. If not, God cannot know that which he anticipates. But if so, this is to admit the Calvinist doctrine that God has accurate knowledge ("perfect anticipation") of future contingencies, whether involving human choices or not. If God's anticipation is not certain, it can hardly be perfect knowledge. It cannot be both accurate and uncertain. But if it is certain, the events' future occurrence must be certain. Even God cannot have certain knowledge of uncertain events, whatever their cause. It seems, then, that Pinnock cannot sustain his claim that "God is not surprised by what any of his creatures decide to do. He can take actions that are appropriate to every such circumstance."

This logically requires two things, both rather difficult for an Arminian to accept. First, it demands that God must have exhaustive knowledge of all future possibilities (surely a form of omniscience), at least at the time of the creation. But Pinnock has explicitly denied this. It also seems to involve God's continually adjusting his plans to whatever I might do in such a way that he could have no "plan A" at all, only an infinitude of continuously variable "plan Bs." And all of his "plan Bs" are wrong too, except the last, which he has not invented yet. Only an arbitrary refusal to step into Heraclitus' river can save Pinnock from some form of process theology.

In Brown's final response to Pinnock on the topic of human nature, he pinpoints the very contradiction that I have noted earlier in the Arminian attempt to escape the double predestination implied in God's choice of Jacob over Esau before they were born (Rom 9). "I am unsure why God can so effectively manage the collective process, but not the personal processes that we are as individuals" (p. 134). The point is that if God's anticipations of future events are perfect, how can he have such an accurate awareness of universals (the collective process) without having the same degree of consciousness of the particulars that make up each class (the personal processes) at each step in the historical development? After all, it is the contents of the class that define its limits and distinguish it from a similar group. Unlike the case with you and me, it is logically impossible for God to have knowledge of a class with examples in it without also knowing those examples as well.

It just does not seem to be enough that God is only finitely smarter than we are. Is it really conceivable that when Isaiah's Yahweh affirms, "As the heavens are higher than the earth, so are . . . my thoughts than your thoughts" (Is 55:9), he only meant to imply a large but finite difference? Or, more to the point, when he says, " 'My purpose will be established, and I will accomplish all My good pleasure.' . . . Truly I have spoken; truly I will bring it to pass. I have planned it, surely I will do it" (Is 46:10-11 NASB), does he really only mean that he will be smart enough to invent a new plan when our free will frustrates the old one, as it must, statistically?

I will not reiterate in detail what such a notion does to the Bible's longer-range predictive prophecies. Remember the particularity of Bethlehem, foretold nearly six hundred years before it came to pass. Of course the freewill theist could always decide to do what the liberals have already done with Isaiah 40—66 and simply postulate a deutero-Isaiah who actually wrote 45:1 and 46:11 after the events they claim to predict. Or perhaps it was just a fluke that Micah predicted that Jesus would be born in Bethlehem. Or perhaps he was not born in Bethlehem at all and the New Testament writers simply recorded a myth of the early church, seeking to conform the Jesus they once knew to the Old Testament ideas of a Messiah.

Fruits

In a dialogue such as Pinnock and Brown's, there can be no question of the evangelical's drawing the liberal over to his own position, because the evangelical is already in principle in the liberal's position, albeit in a less consistent form of it. They share the basic presupposition of human autonomy from God, whatever "God" is. From this assumption flows irresistibly the entire liberalizing agenda of the last two hundred years.

As a result, liberals can safely continue to view Christian apologetics as just an irritation from the unenlightened fundamentalist past and can regard Clark Pinnock as a partially enlightened evangelical who is at last coming to agree that historic orthodoxy cannot survive the acids of modernity. Brown presents this case with meticulous clarity, while Pinnock's former certainties fall away on every page of *Theological Crossfire* as he gazes, fascinated, into the Heraclitean flux of process theology.

Idolatry Again

By the term "finite god" I mean a god who is limited by states of affairs that he does not control and who therefore must always adjust to fresh developments within the flow of being around him. Isaiah refers to these imaginary finite gods as idols. If there happens to be any spiritual reality behind the idea, the apostle Paul identified it as a "demon" (see 1 Cor 10:14-22). Paul knew how to be explicitly negative when the doctrinal stakes were high enough and demanded that his followers copy his emphasis and learn to distinguish things that differ. Hence two thousand years of Christian apologetics.

Finite godism is just another variety of pagan idolatry, while a "Christian" finite godism is just a form of syncretism, the fruit of intellectual worldliness, of abasement before the spirit of modernity as it reappears in successive ages. Neither syncretism nor modernity can be redeemed by a "dialogue" in which the God of the Bible is tacitly excluded as a condition for proceeding with the discussion. Philosophically, such a discussion is only an immanentist duet so long as the challenge of the presuppositions of the Christian worldview over against the presuppositions of apostate autonomism are not faced.

As for modernity, it is being abandoned right, left and center by its most committed adherents. One former liberal, the theologian Thomas Oden, gave up what he characterized as his craven pursuit of the latest idea and even joined the Evangelical Theological Society. He is now engaged in using his considerable God-given gifts in writing historically oriented expositions of classical theology in an effort to pull liberals back to a serious reconsideration of what classical Christianity actually was. And some of them are listening.

There is even a debate now unfolding on the liberal scene about how postmodernity itself is disintegrating and why. The hope that the postmodern movement would point the way to an intelligible future went sour in the 1980s, when the postmodernists followed the deconstructionists into the deconstruction of deconstructionism. Modernity turned out to be a kaleidoscope that turns itself at random, its flickering patterns showing little consistency and offering even less security.

It is not clear why Pinnock finds this black hole so fascinating. It is clear, however, why Pinnock's theological *theoria,* despite his disclaimers, is looking more and more like process thought. To refuse to question the freewill theory is to be pulled by default toward the fateful choice of whatever new forms of the rationalistic Stoics and the irrationalist Epicureans that modernity can generate, or into some compromise between them. In the meantime it remains true that apostate autonomism finally offers only three choices to its victims: pantheism, polytheism or a perpetual oscillation between the two while a "mediating position" is being sought. All three, of course, can take many forms and still be dressed up in the language of evangelical orthodoxy (or Hinduism or Mormonism for that matter).

The Openness of God

A new collection of essays—*The Openness of God* (Downers Grove, Ill.: InterVarsity Press, 1994) written by Clark Pinnock et al.—appeared after this book was almost finished, and I am currently preparing a larger critique of the freewill theism it represents. Pinnock's main contribution is the third essay on systematic theology, in which on several occasions he tries to distinguish his freewill theism from process theology (pp. 107, 118, 125, among others). I will make only three points now and refer the reader to the forthcoming critique, God willing.

First, the entire structure of freewill theism is based on reconstructing evangelical theology to conform to the presupposition of the autonomy of the human consciousness. This unproven presupposition is the heart of the noetic effects of the Fall, and should it happen to be false, the main foundation of the position evaporates.

Second, the broad attempt to modify what Reformed theology calls the incommunicable attributes of God represents a radical departure from orthodox theology closely parallel to Socinianism. As far as I know, the freewill theists have not begun to deconstruct the Trinity or the Incarnation yet, but they are already trying to empty hell (see Clark Pinnock's *A Wideness in God's Mercy* [Grand Rapids, Mich.: Zondervan, 1992]). The Incarnation and such concomitant doctrines as Christ's impeccability cannot logically survive the autonomist view of humanness, as the Socinians demonstrated in the 1600s.

Third, no one escapes the internal dynamic of his or her own presuppositions, the autonomists least of all. If they want to be illogical, they can certainly escape the more bizarre conclusions that should ensue, but it is more likely that they will follow the liberalizing path of the late 1800s. There is nothing static about evangelicalism, and there never has been; even fundamentalism has its own internal dynamic, as the shifts of the 1970s revealed.

The internal dynamic of Western philosophy since Socrates has shown that the four classical fields of ontology, epistemology, ethics and teleology are intimately interconnected—the choices made in one field limit the choices that can be made in the others. This means for the Christian that the Logos underlies the rationality of all reality, and that the Spirit of Truth testifies to all people of the ultimate coherence of the mind of God. The contemplation of this coherence is the intellectual element in the beatific vision. The Hindus have remembered what the secularization of philosophy in the West has forgotten, that philosophy is primarily the handmaid of worship, not just of theology. And all worship is either of the God of the Bible or of an idol. Evangelicalism must recover again the central message of the last epistles of Paul about the absolute necessity of sound doctrine: no doctrine, no truth; no truth, no faith; no faith, no life. All praxis is necessarily the practice of either true or false doctrine. There can be no neutrality in a created universe, for if God exists at all, he has already interpreted exhaustively from eternity all being, including his own.

Conclusions: A Virus Identified

We have examined the influence of the freewill theory on evangelical thought in several areas. I have sought to show from a survey of history, then directly from Scripture, then through a critique of freewillism's fruits in theology and apologetics, that this theory is really a disastrous combination of Christian and non-Christian assumptions about God and human nature, a tension held together by an unstable humanistic syncretism. This only encourages Christians to repeat the age-old dilemma of playing off the unity of logic against the discontinuity of chance, while covering up their self-contradictions by an appeal to paradox and mystery.

The presupposition of human autonomy, when protected from criticism, behaves much like a computer virus. It progressively deforms the content of any part of the biblical worldview that it infects. Christians have often conformed themselves to the course of this world by compromising with the dogma of Strato of Lampsacus that the universe is able to make itself intelligible to itself through the power of the autonomous human intellect quite apart from any prior revelation from God. Once this step is taken, to the degree that consistency is sought and maintained, *the Christian's worldview will tend to destabilize in the direction of a more consistent humanism.* Only the progressive reinterpretation of the Bible to increasingly evacuate it of its Reformed content and the preservation of numerous pockets of inconsistency can save even the appearance of theological orthodoxy. In particular, the assumption of human autonomy creates a continual pressure toward finite godism.

Modern evangelicals do not like to be reminded of the internal dynamic of their own thinking and may be tempted to think that I am envisioning some kind of domino theory or slippery slope of theological drift. But this has nothing to do with dominos; the internal dynamic is a matter of the necessary limitations of philosophy in a world created by the Logos that became flesh and dwelt among us, full of grace and truth, and himself wholly consistent.

This whole case could have been made through analysis of the syncretism of evangelical language with non-Christian psychological theories of personality in the current Christian counseling movement, and such a study is sorely needed. However, I have sought to demonstrate from the case of the Calvinist's debate with the Arminian what the issues are that animate its combatants. First philosophy, then theology and finally the theory of apologetics itself all demonstrate that apologetic method must be rooted in a fully coherent systematic theology. No one can escape taking sides in this debate, however hard they may try to straddle the fence of compromise while constructing yet another syncretism. The fence is itself an illusion, and history shows that syncretism is a characteristic besetting sin of the carnal mind. Repentance is the only real answer. According to the gospel, it is always the real answer for believer and unbeliever alike.

As far as the Bible itself is concerned, the challenge to the Christian who thinks of free will as a mark of evangelicalism is to start by demonstrating this fundamental presupposition from the text by exegesis. Since Augustine summarized the thought of the age of the Fathers in order to refute the Pelagians, this has proved impossible. Martin Luther in the 1500s, John Owen in the 1600s and John Gill in the 1700s all took the trouble to examine the texts for their own age to consider afresh. Pinnock's recent collections in defense of Arminianism require that Calvinists do it all over again for modern evangelicals. Part of the tragedy of what Mark Noll has called "the scandal of the evangelical mind" is the possibility that we may have already forgotten more than we ever knew.

I have chosen Pinnock as an illustration of how the syncretistic process repeats the drift away from orthodoxy in the life and writings of a deeply sincere and hardworking evangelical. He invited me to do so in *Grace Unlimited* (p. 18) and *A Wideness in God's Mercy* (pp. 15, 181). His highly public progress toward a shifting form of liberal evangelicalism has caused much puzzlement and misgiving among those of us who knew him formerly as a reliable defender of the faith. We quite reasonably fear for what he might give up next.

In the course of noting that some feminists may have abandoned "foundational symbolic language" in giving up the biblical image of God as "our Father," Pinnock correctly warns, "At issue is the authority of the Bible. . . . Many feminists . . . read it in overtly biased ways, and accord infallibility to their own experience instead. This places them firmly outside the mainstream Christian community" (*Theological Crossfire*, p. 77). If this be so, why would it not be equally true of someone who sought to modify not only the plan of salvation but also the orthodox conception of God's own nature in terms of a humanistic presupposition, and so in terms of a Greek dogma unfounded in biblical exegesis? Why does the shift of the freewill theists away from the uniform testimony of orthodox theology to God's omniscience and omnipotence not place these recent modernizers also "firmly outside the mainstream Christian community"?

Pinnock cannot hope to regain the intellectual offensive within the world of secular and liberal religious scholarship unless he is willing to face the damage done to the biblical vision by the notion of human autonomism. If ever there was an example of what servitude to an alien presupposition can do to an evangelical testimony, this would be it.

Every Thought Captive

The apostle Paul uses an expression in 2 Corinthians 10:5 that captures the methodological problem perfectly. He was speaking in the area of church ethics, but it applies equally well to the other three basic areas of epistemology, teleology and ontology. The believer cannot hope to please God or grow in holiness without "taking every thought captive to the obedience of Christ" (NASB). Only thus can we consistently challenge the intellectual strongholds erected by the fallen mind in its efforts to appropriate what of God's truth is convenient to its agenda, while suppressing whatever parts threaten its autonomy. Once it is acknowledged (in the form of a proposition!), a presupposition becomes a "thought" over which Christ necessarily claims lordship.

We have been warned by the apostle Paul that the world in its wisdom knows not God (1 Cor 1—2) and that fellowship with idols is "fellowship with demons" (1 Cor 10:20-21 NKJV). When Satan said to our first parents, "You will not surely die," he was providing a competitive *theoria,* an alternative beholding or worldview, for their consideration on an equal basis with God's revealed worldview. The ultimate reference point had shifted from God to the world. There had been a relocation of ultimacy. For the rest of the history of philosophy, under the influence of this demonic theoria, the human intellect would oscillate between the unity and the diversity of experience, never able to rise above the dilemma of James's "double-minded man, unstable in all he does" (Jas 1:8).

This double-minded man may be compared with the Prodigal Son. Having left his Father's land, he can be seen rowing his frail little self-made canoe out across the lowering darkness of the great sea of being-in-general. In the distance he can see the periodic flickering of the great lighthouse of propositional revelation, which his Father has built for travelers lost on the trackless ocean of mystery. In order to be sure of his direction, the miscreant must keep his eye on this lighthouse as he pulls further and further away from its rationality and solidity. Soon it will inevitably drop below the horizon, and the surrounding primeval darkness will be complete.

Further Reading

The interested reader should explore the relationship Clark Pinnock has developed with liberal thinking in *Tracking the Maze* (San Francisco: Harper, 1990), an analysis of modern liberal theology, and *Theological Crossfire* (Grand Rapids, Mich.: Zondervan, 1990), a dialogue written with Delwin Brown, a process theologian of the Iliff School of Theology in Denver, Colorado.

For an analysis of attempts to make sense of religion in general without first listening to God, see Gordon Clark's *Religion, Reason and Revelation* (Nutley, N.J.: Presbyterian & Reformed, 1969).

For a study of finite godism by an evangelical, read Robert Morey's *The Battle of the Gods* (Southbridge, Mass.: Crown, 1989). Morey examines the main issues involved in recent denials of the classically formulated attributes of God. Many of the contributors to collections edited by Clark Pinnock are referred to. Finite godism is, of course, a much larger field than the freewill theism that participates in it.

On the liberal habit of claiming that *t͑hôm* really reflects an ancient chaos concept, see the article by R. Laird Harris in the *Theological Wordbook of the Old Testament,* vol. 2, ed. R. Laird Harris et al. (Chicago: Moody, 1980), pp. 965-66. E. A. Speiser in his commentary *Genesis,* Anchor Bible (Garden City, N.Y.: Doubleday, 1964), simply renders *t͑hôm* as "seas" (p. 3). While Claus Westermann notes that "*t͑hôm* is a distant reminder of Tiamat" (*Creation* [Philadelphia: Fortress, 1974], p. 40), he is nevertheless eager to contrast the Genesis account with the Babylonian epics at many points. The lesson is that a bare etymological similarity tells us little or nothing about a specific later usage of a term by someone writing out of a wholly different worldview.

Glossary of Names and Terms

Each item in the glossary has been marked with an asterisk (*) at its first occurrence in the text.

Aquinas, Thomas (1224-1274). Influential Catholic theologian, expositor and apologist who tried to combine Aristotle with Christianity to create a Christian apologetics.

Aristotle (384-322 B.C.). Greek philosopher, student of Plato, empiricist and first formulator of the rules of logic. Taught that things are made of matter plus forms. Tried to prove existence of the Prime Mover, a kind of God. Denied creation, claimed matter is eternal, taught autonomy of the mind.

Arminianism. Protestant theology starting from the thought of Jacobus Arminius around 1580 in opposition to the Calvinism of the Dutch state church. Modifies the Reformation view of grace by compromising with the freewill theory.

Atonement, limited. Doctrine that God sent Christ to save only the elect. Also called particular redemption.

Augustine (A.D. 354-430). Great teaching bishop of Hippo in North Africa who represented and transmitted the most important patristic theology to influence the Middle Ages and the Reformation. The greatest Calvinist before Calvin.

Bondage of the Will. Luther's answer (1525) to Erasmus's *Diatribe,* a defense of the freewill theory.

Calvinism. The Reformation theology developed in the Augustinian tradition by John Calvin (1509-1564). Emphasizes sovereign grace and human responsibility before God, while denying the freewill theory.

Campbell, J. McLeod (1800-1872). Presbyterian pastor who gave up particular redemption and substitutionary atonement and was deposed.

Camus, Albert (1913-1960). French existentialist philosopher and novelist who was less consistent but more optimistic than Sartre.

Cassian, John (c. A.D. 400). Opponent of Augustine's theology whose theology foreshadowed Arminianism, often called "semi-Pelagianism."

Chain of being. Theory that all existence is a graded ladder of degrees of being, ranging from the good, spiritual and ineffable One at the top to a diverse evil chaos below. Everything is somewhere on this scale of entities, with human nature in the middle, part good, part evil.

Clark, Gordon H. (1902-1985). Calvinistic evangelical philosopher who emphasized the Christian's intellectual responsibility and challenged evangelicals to face the role of logic and presuppositions in developing a consistently Christian worldview.

Clement. Bishop of Rome about A.D. 90, author of the early *1 Clement,* but not of *2 Clement.*

Common grace. The view that God is genuinely merciful to nonelect sinners, generally preserving them from consistent sin and giving them life and good gifts they do not deserve.

Depravity, total. Doctrine that fallen human nature, including the will, is completely enslaved to sin and is unable to choose the good.

Determinism. The theory that all events in a finite world must be caused by previous states of affairs. That is, there are no uncaused events. Opposite of "indeterminism." Often confused with fatalism.

Diatribe on the Freedom of the Will. Title of Erasmus's defense in 1524 of free will, attacking Luther's views.

Diet of Worms. Council held at Worms in Germany in 1521, at which Luther was condemned.

Dooyeweerd, Herman (1894-1977). Professor of jurisprudence and international law at the Free University of Amsterdam. Produced an influential Christian philosophy along Calvinistic lines with his brother-in-law D. Th. Vollenhoven.

Dort, Synod of. Council held at Dort (Holland) in 1618-1619 to respond to Remonstrant objections to Calvinism. Produced the statement of the "five points" of Calvinism now included in the doctrinal formulations of most Reformed denominations.

Edwards, Jonathan (1703-1758). Congregationalist pastor and influential preacher during the Great Awakening in America. Greatest theological philosopher in the Americas of the 1700s and strong Calvinist apologist against the freewill theory.

Election. God's choice from eternity of which individuals will or will not be saved. Guaranteed to frighten the wicked and comfort the elect. Election is not only to heaven but also to a degree of holiness. Calvinists hold that it is not conditional on anything sinners might be foreseen to do, since they cannot believe of themselves.

Enlightenment. The secularizing intellectual movement away from the former Christian consensus that education should be based on the Christian revelation. Term coined to contrast with the supposed Dark Ages, when the universities were largely controlled by the church.

Epistemology. Theory of how we get and explain knowledge.

Erasmus of Rotterdam. Humanist scholar of the Northern Renaissance who published the Greek New Testament in 1516. Tried to reform the Catholic Church from within by education rather than by doctrinal change.

Ethics. Theory of how to justify the distinction between right and wrong behavior and of how to apply these principles to cases of conscience.

Euthyphro. One of Plato's dialogues in which Socrates inquires as to whether the good originates with the gods or is a property of being-itself, independent of the will or approval of a higher being.

Evangelicalism. General term for conservative, gospel-oriented Protestantism since about 1750. Includes Arminian, revivalist, millennialist, biblicist, fundamentalist, charismatic and conservative Calvinist traditions. Usually contrasted with formalism, nominalism, Catholicism, modernism or religious liberalism. Emphasizes personal evangelism, holiness and the reliability of the Bible.

Fatalism. Common but illogical pagan conclusion that because all things are caused (determinism), human choices have no meaning or are irrelevant to the outcome. Usually discourages moral action and excuses immoral action. Falsely equated with determinism and predestination.

Finney, Charles G. (1792-1875). Arminian revivalist of the later stages of the Awakening in America and early leader of the revivalist tradition of evangelism. Very concerned with education and social justice.

Flew, Antony G. N. (1923-). Modern English atheist philosopher of the empirical-analytic school.

Freewill theory. View that the human will is free to act independently of divine control or external causation. Arminians usually define it as the ability to choose good or evil equally. Hence "the liberty of indifference."

Freud, Sigmund (1856-1939). Main founder of modern psychiatric psychodynamic theory. An atheist and materialist, he taught that human authenticity requires increasing autonomy, coupled with adjustment to the conditions of life.

Gill, John (1697-1771). Calvinistic Baptist scholar, pastor and apologist in the days of Wesley. A precursor of Spurgeon, and the only man in church history to both preach and publish a full commentary on the entire Bible verse by verse.

Gottschalk (c. 805-869). An early medieval monk who tried to defend a more consistent form of Augustinianism against prevailing semi-Pelagian views. May be thought of loosely as a martyr for Calvinism before Calvin.

Grace. God's gratuitous kindness to sinners, who deserve only his condemnation. Calvinists hold it to be ultimately not resistible by the elect, since God makes them willing to trust and obey him.

Hierarchy. Literally, "rule by grades of priests," the levels of authority in the Catholic Church or any graded system of authorities.

Hitler, Adolf (1889-1945). Austrian-born dictator of Germany. The main human cause of World War II and prime mover behind the systematic slaughter of about six million Jews from 1938 to 1945. He liked painting, Alsatian dogs and talking his friends into a stupor late at night. Hard for non-Calvinists to explain easily. Proved quite conclusively that love is *not* all you need, and it *could* all happen again.

Hus, Jan (1373-1415). Bohemian pastor, follower of Wycliffe, who tried to call the Catholic Church back to the Bible. Was tried and burned at the stake at the Council of Constance.

Hyper-Calvinism. The illogical conclusion of some Calvinists that because God is sovereign and so will certainly save the elect, we are not responsible for our sin, for preaching the gospel, for inviting all sinners to come to Christ or for missionary endeavors. Some have also denied common grace, rejected missions and preached antinomianism.

Imago Dei. Latin for image of God, the essence of our humanness.

Indeterminism. Theory that at least some events do not have prior causes. Usually accompanies a dependence on chance to explain things.

Irrationalism. View that logic and reason have little value, since reality is ultimately contradictory, paradoxical or absurd. Denial of the possibility of truth. Really a form of skepticism.

Latitudinarianism. The mentality that insists theological opinions are unimportant and should not be required of a pastor or teacher in a state church. Extreme confidence in universal toleration as a solution to religious divisions. Lack of confidence in creeds or other doctrinal formulations.

Laud, William (1573-1645). Arminian archbishop of Canterbury appointed by King Charles I. High-church opponent of the Puritans; accused of trying to Romanize Anglicanism; executed for treason.

Lewis, C. S. (1898-1963). Evangelical Arminian Anglo-Catholic professor of medieval literature at Cambridge whose Christian apologetics and novels attracted much admiration.

Lloyd-Jones, D. Martyn (1899-1981). Welsh physician who became pastor of Westminster Chapel, London. Greatest English preacher since Spurgeon, and the main promoter of the revival of Calvinism in the twentieth century.

Lorenz, Konrad (1903-1989). Austrian zoologist and authority on animal behavior.

Luther, Martin (1483-1546). Great Augustinian reformer who attempted to pull the German Catholic Church back to the Bible and so precipitated the Protestant break with Rome.

Marcus Aurelius (A.D. 121-180). Stoic philosopher who became Roman emperor in 161. Encouraged persecution of Christians; wrote his *Meditations* about the wise way of life in submission to fate while allowing people to be tortured to death in the arena.

Marx, Karl (1818-1883). Secularized German Jewish scholar, atheist-materialist interpreter of social history. Borrowed heavily from the Greeks and from G. W. F. Hegel. Never admitted his debt to Christian ideals of social justice.

One-and-many problem. Question of how to find principles of unity (such as logic) and of diversity (such as chance) in the world and how to bring them together once identified. The most enduring philosophic problem underlying Western thought.

Ontology. Theory of the structure of Being, or of whatever exists.

Owen, John (1616-1683). Congregationalist Puritan pastor and apologist for Calvinism and Christian holiness in Cromwell's England. His works were collected and reprinted in twenty-four volumes, most of which are still in print.

Pascal, Blaise (1623-1662). French mathematician and apologist for Jansenist Catholicism. Saw that Christ appeals only to those with a sense of the need for God.

Pelagius. Popularizer around A.D. 380 of views of grace and salvation denying original sin and emphasizing the role of free will. He was refuted by Augustine, and his views were declared a heresy at the Second Council of Orange in 529.

Perseverance of the saints. Doctrine that truly born-again believers cannot finally be lost. Being kept by God's power, they always persevere to the end, despite temporary setbacks.

Pinnock, Clark H. (1937-). Modern evangelical theologian now teaching at McMaster Divinity College, Hamilton, Ontario, who gave up Calvinism for Arminianism.

Plato (428-348 B.C.). Greek philosopher and the great student and systematizer of Socrates. Taught upper and lower realms of being, denied that God was the Creator of the world. Precursor of the Gnostics and formulator of all the big questions in Western thought, including the great chain of being.

Platt, Frederic. Arminian professor of Old Testament at Wesleyan College in Manchester, England, at the turn of the twentieth century. Wrote the candid article "Arminianism" for the first volume of James Hastings's *Encyclopaedia of Religion and Ethics* (1908).

Pragmatism. Theory that truth is a function of success in achieving survival or some other aim. Defines good as "what works for me." Even the laws of logic are seen as being merely societal conventions.

Predestination. Doctrine that God has preordained that all events will effect his own plan for them.

Presuppositionalism. Theory that all thought is controlled by presuppositions ultimately unprovable. Thus Christian apologists must not compromise with heathen philosophies but challenge the sinner to repent of fallen autonomist axioms. The only final "proof" of anything comes by showing that only on a Christian basis is any question intelligible.

Rationalism. Theory that the human mind can understand the world autonomously using reason to establish truth, apart from revelation.

Remonstrants. Dutch Arminians of 1610-1619 and thereafter who compiled the *Remonstrance,* a statement and defense of five doctrines contrary to the Calvinism of the state church. Condemned at Dort in 1619.

Rookmaaker, Hans (1922-1977). Professor of art history at the Free University of Amsterdam. Strongly influenced Francis Schaeffer toward illustrating modernity through philosophy's influence on art.

Russell, Lord Bertrand (1872-1970). Atheistic philosopher and moralist who taught at Cambridge and wrote much linguistic philosophy before giving up any hope of a rational epistemology. Taught that mathematics was just a subcategory of formal logic. Wanted to ban the bomb.

Sartre, Jean-Paul (1905-1980). French existentialist atheist. Claimed meaning is created by our autonomous choices. Defined humanity as "the project to be God." Wrote depressing novels and incoherent philosophy. He reveled in inconsistencies, seduced his students and used "absurdity" as an excuse for lecherous behavior.

Schaeffer, Francis A. (1912-1984). Presbyterian missionary to Europe and the intellectuals of the West. Most responsible for sparking revival of evangelical intellectual and social responsibility in the twentieth century.

Semi-Pelagianism. A compromise theology originating in the fifth century. Taught (contrary to Augustine) that God's grace is not necessary for the free will to begin to act rightly. Condemned as heretical at the Second Council of Orange in 529, it was an important precursor to Arminianism, which repeats many of its errors.

Shedd, William G. T. (1820-1894). The last Calvinist systematic theologian to teach at Union Seminary, New York. Good clear writer, expounding mainstream Calvinism.

Similitudes of Hermas. An early semiallegorical Christian writing (c. A.D. 90-150?) sometimes treated as Scripture in Egypt up to the fourth century.

Skepticism. Theory that little or no knowledge is certain, leading usually to a form of pragmatism.

Socrates (469-399 B.C.). Greek philosopher and teacher of Plato, the most seminal mind of Greek history. Taught the West how to ask embarrassing questions.

Sola Scriptura. Latin for "by Scripture alone," a watchword of the Protestant Reformation. Means practically that the Bible is the sufficient and infallible source of Christian revelation.

Spurgeon, Charles H. (1834-1892). Calvinistic Baptist pastor and the greatest preacher of the 1800s in England. Forced out of the Baptist Union for challenging it to adopt an evangelical doctrinal basis. Fought theological liberalism, Arminianism, baptismal regeneration and revivalist extravagance.

Systematic theology (dogmatics). The necessary fruit of the centuries-long effort by Spirit-taught believers to gather and organize the contents of the Bible into consistently interrelated topics.

Teleology. The theory that the world and our individual lives have a design and purpose; the "doctrine of ends."

Tertullian (c. A.D. 150-220). Carthaginian Roman lawyer who became a Christian about 180 and joined the Montanist sect. Famous early apologist for the faith who spoke out against syncretism of theology with non-Christian views.

Toplady, Augustus (1740-1778). Anglican pastor, vigorous preacher, friend of John Gill and defender of the Calvinism of the Anglican Church against the Arminianism of the Wesleyan movement. Best remembered for the hymn "Rock of Ages."

Van Til, Cornelius (1895-1987). Calvinist professor of apologetics at Westminster Seminary and promoter of the presuppositionalist method of apologetics; shares with Gordon Clark the reputation of being the greatest apologetic intellect of the twentieth century. Highly critical of evangelical syncretism.

Wesley, Charles (1707-1788). Brother of John Wesley and most famous hymnwriter of the Methodist era. Strongly opposed to Calvinism.

Wesley, John (1703-1791). Anglican gospel preacher and leader in the Great Awakening in England and America. Founder of the Methodist Church. Encouraged Arminianism among non-Conformists.

Westminster Confession. Calvinistic doctrinal standard developed by the Presbyterian faction of the Anglican Church in 1646. Became the doctrinal standard of the Scottish Presbyterians.

Whitby, Daniel (1638-1726). Anglican apologist for Arminianism, answered by John Gill.

Whitefield, George. (1714-1770). Anglican Calvinist gospel preacher who began itinerant open-air preaching, starting the revival that led to the rise of Methodism. May have been the greatest preacher of all time.

Worldview. Our basic assumptions about reality, usually unquestioned; our fundamental outlook on life.

Wycliffe, John (1329-1384). Reformist and Augustinian lecturer at Oxford. One of the earliest Reformers to call the Catholic Church back to doctrinal purity. Attacked practical and doctrinal corruption. Inspired Jan Hus and the Lollards.

Zwingli, Ulrich (1484-1531). Swiss Reformer in Zurich who started to reform his church around 1509, even before Luther did.

Select Bibliography of Sources

Barna, George. *What Americans Believe.* Ventura, Calif.: Regal, 1991.

Bavinck, Herman. *The Doctrine of God.* Grand Rapids, Mich.: Baker, 1877.

Bebbington, D. W. *Evangelicalism in Modern Britain.* London: Unwin Hyman, 1989.

Berkouwer, G. C. *Man: The Image of God.* Grand Rapids, Mich.: Eerdmans, 1962.

_____ . *Sin.* Grand Rapids, Mich.: Eerdmans, 1971.

Bickersteth, Edward H. *The Trinity.* Grand Rapids, Mich.: Kregel, 1957.

Blamires, Harry. *The Christian Mind.* New York: Seabury, 1963.

Boettner, Loraine. *The Reformed Doctrine of Predestination.* Philadelphia: Presbyterian & Reformed, 1966.

Brown, Donald E. *Hierarchy, History and Human Nature.* Tucson: University of Arizona Press, 1988.

Buswell, J. Oliver. *A Systematic Theology of the Christian Religion.* Grand Rapids, Mich.: Zondervan, 1962.

Calvin, John. *Concerning the Eternal Predestination of God.* London: James Clark, 1961.

Campbell, McLeod John. *The Nature of the Atonement.* London: Macmillan, 1878.

Carson, D. A. *Divine Sovereignty and Human Responsibility.* Atlanta: John Knox, 1981.

Charnock, Stephen. *The Existence and Attributes of God.* Grand Rapids, Mich.: Baker, 1979.

Clark, Gordon H. *The Biblical Doctrine of Man.* Jefferson, Md.: Trinity Foundation, 1984.

_____ . *Biblical Predestination.* Nutley, N.J.: Presbyterian & Reformed, 1969.

_____ . *Religion, Reason, and Revelation.* Nutley, N.J.: Presbyterian & Reformed, 1969.

_____ . *Thales to Dewey.* Boston: Houghton Mifflin, 1957.

de Mello, Anthony. *Sadhana, a Way to God.* New York: Doubleday, 1984.

Denney, James. *Studies in Theology*. London: Hodder, 1910.

Dooyeweerd, Herman. *Roots of Western Culture*. Toronto: Wedge, 1979.

————— . *The Secularization of Science*. Memphis: Christian Studies Center, 1954.

Edwards, Jonathan. *The End for Which God Created the World*. Vol. 1 of *Works*. Edinburgh: Banner of Truth Trust, 1974.

————— . *The Freedom of the Will*. New Haven, Conn.: Yale University Press, 1957.

————— . *Original Sin*. New Haven, Conn.: Yale University Press, 1957.

Engelsma, David. *Hyper-Calvinism and the Call of the Gospel*. Grand Rapids, Mich.: Kregel, 1980.

Erickson, Millard. *Christian Theology*. Grand Rapids, Mich.: Baker, 1985.

Flew, Antony. *God and Philosophy*. New York: Harcourt Brace, 1966.

————— . *God, Freedom and Immortality*. New York: Prometheus, 1984.

Flew, Antony, and Alisdair MacIntyre. *New Essays in Philosophical Theology*. London: SCM Press, 1955.

Frame, John M. *The Doctrine of the Knowledge of God*. Phillipsburg, N.J.: Presbyterian & Reformed, 1987.

Gay, Peter. *The Enlightenment: An Interpretation*. New York: Alfred A. Knopf. Vol. 1. *The Rise of Modern Paganism*, 1966. Vol. 2, *The Science of Freedom*, 1969.

Geehan, E. R. *Jerusalem and Athens*. Phillipsburg, N.J.: Presbyterian & Reformed, 1971.

Geisler, Norman L., ed. *Inerrancy*. Grand Rapids, Mich.: Zondervan, 1980.

Gill, John. *The Cause of God and Truth*. London: W. H. Collingridge, 1855.

Good, Kenneth H. *God's Gracious Purpose As Seen in John's Gospel*. Grand Rapids, Mich.: Baker, 1979.

Hastings, James A., ed. *Encyclopaedia of Religion and Ethics*. 13 vols. Edinburgh: T & T Clark, 1908-1926.

Henry, Carl F. H. *God, Revelation and Authority*. 6 vols. Waco, Tex.: Word, 1983.

Hick, John. *Evil and the God of Love*. London: Macmillan, 1966.

Hodge, Charles. *Systematic Theology*. London: James Clarke, 1960.

Hooykaas, Reijer. *Religion and the Rise of Modern Science*. Grand Rapids, Mich.: Eerdmans, 1972.

Horton, Michael S. *Beyond Culture Wars*. Chicago: Moody Press, 1994.

Hunter, James Davison. *American Evangelicalism*. New Brunswick, N.J.: Rutgers, 1983.

————— . *Evangelicalism: The Coming Generation*. Chicago: University of Chicago Press, 1987.

Huxley, Aldous. *The Perennial Philosophy*. New York: Harper, 1945.

Jaki, Stanley. *The Origin of Science, and the Science of Its Origin*. South Bend, Ind.: Regnery, 1979.

————. *Science and Creation: From Eternal Cycles to an Oscillating Universe.* Edinburgh: Scottish Academic Press, 1974.

Jordan, Winthrop D. *White over Black.* Baltimore: Penguin, 1968.

Laidlaw, John. *The Biblical Doctrine of Man.* Edinburgh: T & T Clark, 1895.

Langston, Douglas C. *God's Willing Knowledge.* University Park, Penn.: Pennsylvania State Press, 1986.

Lewis, C. S. *The Abolition of Man.* London: Macmillan, 1947.

Lewis, Gordon R., and Bruce A. Demarest. *Integrative Theology.* 3 vols. Grand Rapids, Mich.: Zondervan, 1994.

Lovejoy, Arthur O. *The Great Chain of Being.* Cambridge, Mass.: Harvard University Press, 1948.

May, Gerhard. *Creation Ex Nihilo.* Edinburgh: T & T Clark, 1994.

McCabe, L. D. *Divine Nescience of Future Contingencies a Necessity.* New York: Phillips and Hunt, 1882.

McConkie, Bruce R. *Mormon Doctrine.* Salt Lake City: Bookcraft, 1966.

McGrath, Alister E. *Evangelicalism and the Future of Christianity.* Downers Grove, Ill.: InterVarsity Press, 1993.

Morey, Robert A. *Battle of the Gods.* Southbridge, Mass.: Crown, 1989.

Murray, Iain H. *The Forgotten Spurgeon.* Edinburgh: Banner of Truth Trust, 1978.

————. *Revival and Revivalism.* Edinburgh: Banner of Truth Trust, 1994.

Nash, Ronald. *The Concept of God.* Grand Rapids, Mich.: Zondervan, 1983.

Nettles, Thomas J. *By His Grace and for His Glory.* Grand Rapids, Mich.: Baker, 1986.

Noll, Mark. *The Scandal of the Evangelical Mind.* Grand Rapids, Mich.: Eerdmans, 1994.

Orr, James. *The Progress of Dogma.* London: Hodder, 1901.

Owen, John. *The Death of Death in the Death of Christ.* Introduction by J. I. Packer London: Banner of Truth Trust, 1959.

————. *A Display of Arminianism.* London: Banner of Truth Trust, 1967.

————. *The Saints' Perseverance Explained and Confirmed.* London: Banner of Truth Trust, 1966.

————. *Vindiciae Evangelicae: The Mystery of the Gospel Vindicated and Socinianism Examined.* Edinburgh: Banner of Truth Trust, 1976.

Pinnock, Clark H. *Biblical Revelation.* Chicago: Moody Press, 1971.

————. *A Defense of Biblical Infallibility.* Nutley, N.J.: Presbyterian & Reformed, 1977.

————. *Reason Enough.* Downers Grove, Ill.: InterVarsity Press, 1980.

————. *The Scripture Principle.* San Francisco: Harper and Row, 1984.

————. *Tracking the Maze.* San Francisco: Harper, 1990.

————. *A Wideness in God's Mercy.* Grand Rapids, Mich.: Zondervan, 1992.

Pinnock, Clark H., ed. *The Grace of God, the Will of Man.* Grand Rapids, Mich.: Zondervan, 1989.

————. *Grace Unlimited.* Minneapolis: Bethany House, 1975.

Pinnock, Clark H., and Delwin Brown. *Theological Crossfire.* Grand Rapids, Mich.: Zondervan, 1990.

Pinnock, Clark H., and David Wells, eds. *Toward a Theology for the Future.* Carol Stream, Ill.: Creation House, 1971.

Piper, John. *The Justification of God.* Grand Rapids, Mich.: Baker, 1983.

Plato. *Dialogues.* Trans. Benjamin Jowett. New York: Random House, 1937.

Rupp, E. Gordon, and Philip S. Watson. *Luther and Erasmus: Free Will and Salvation.* Philadelphia: Westminster Press, 1969.

Schaeffer, Francis A. *Escape from Reason.* Downers Grove, Ill.: InterVarsity Press, 1968.

————. *How Should We Then Live?* Old Tappan, N.J.: Revell, 1976.

Shedd, W. G. *Systematic Theology.* 3 vols. Chicago: Moody Press, 1970.

Sire, James W. *The Universe Next Door.* Downers Grove, Ill.: InterVarsity Press, 1976.

Steele, David, and Curtis Thomas. *The Five Points of Calvinism: Defined, Defended, Documented.* Phillipsburg, N.J.: Presbyterian & Reformed, 1963.

Tillyard, E. M. W. *The Elizabethan World Picture.* New York: Random House, 1969.

Toplady, Augustus. *Works.* London: J. Cornish, 1861. (Contains "Proof of the Doctrinal Calvinism of the Church of England" and "The Scheme of Christian and Philosophical Necessity Asserted.")

Turretin, Francis. *Institutes of Elenctic Theology.* 3 vols. Phillipsburg, N.J.: Presbyterian & Reformed, 1992.

Van Til, Cornelius. *Christian Theistic Ethics.* Ripon, Calif.: Den Dulk, 1971.

————. *A Christian Theory of Knowledge.* Grand Rapids, Mich.: Baker, 1969.

————. *The Doctrine of Scripture.* Ripon, Calif.: Den Dulk, 1967.

————. *Paul at Athens.* Privately printed by Lewis J. Grotenhuis, n.d.

————. *A Survey of Christian Epistemology.* Ripon, Calif.: Den Dulk, 1967.

Walsh, Brian J., and J. Richard Middleton. *The Transforming Vision.* Downers Grove, Ill.: InterVarsity Press, 1984.

Warfield, B. B. *The Inspiration and Authority of the Bible.* Philadelphia: Presbyterian & Reformed, 1948.

Wells, David. *No Place for Truth.* Grand Rapids, Mich.: Eerdmans, 1993.

Westminster Divines. *Confession of Faith.* London, 1646. Reprint Glasgow: Free Presbyterian, 1976.

Zanchius, Jerome. *Absolute Predestination.* Grand Rapids, Mich.: Sovereign Grace Publishers, 1971.

Index of Names and Topics